IMAGES
of America

PLAINFIELD

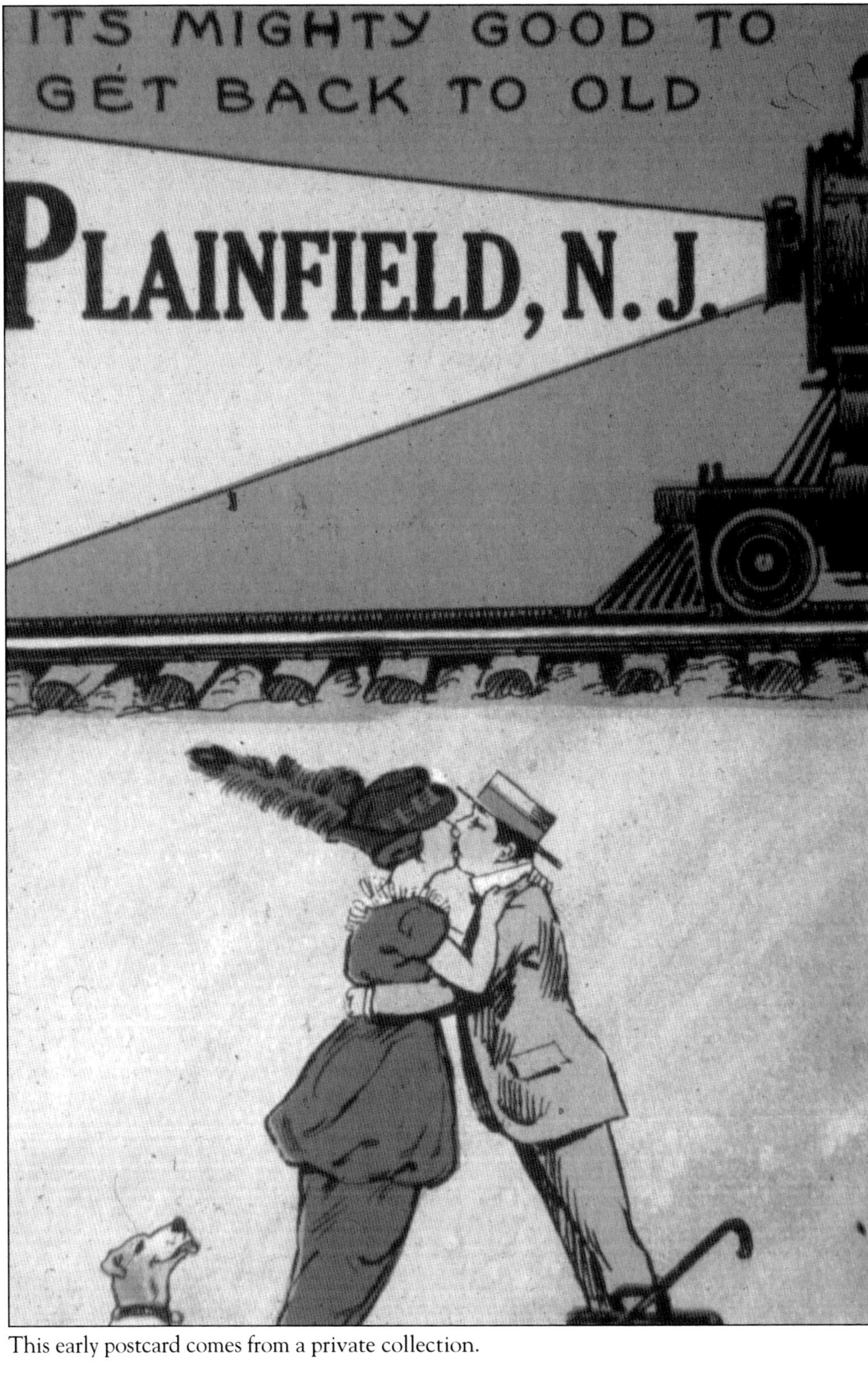

This early postcard comes from a private collection.

IMAGES
of America

PLAINFIELD

John A. Grady and Dorothe M. Pollard

ARCADIA
PUBLISHING

ISBN 978-0-7385-0925-9

Published by Arcadia Publishing
Charleston, South Carolina

Printed in the United States of America

Library of Congress Catalog Card Number: 2001091403

For all general information contact Arcadia Publishing at:
Telephone 843-853-2070
Fax 843-853-0044
E-mail sales@arcadiapublishing.com
For customer service and orders:
Toll-Free 1-888-313-2665

Visit us on the Internet at www.arcadiapublishing.com

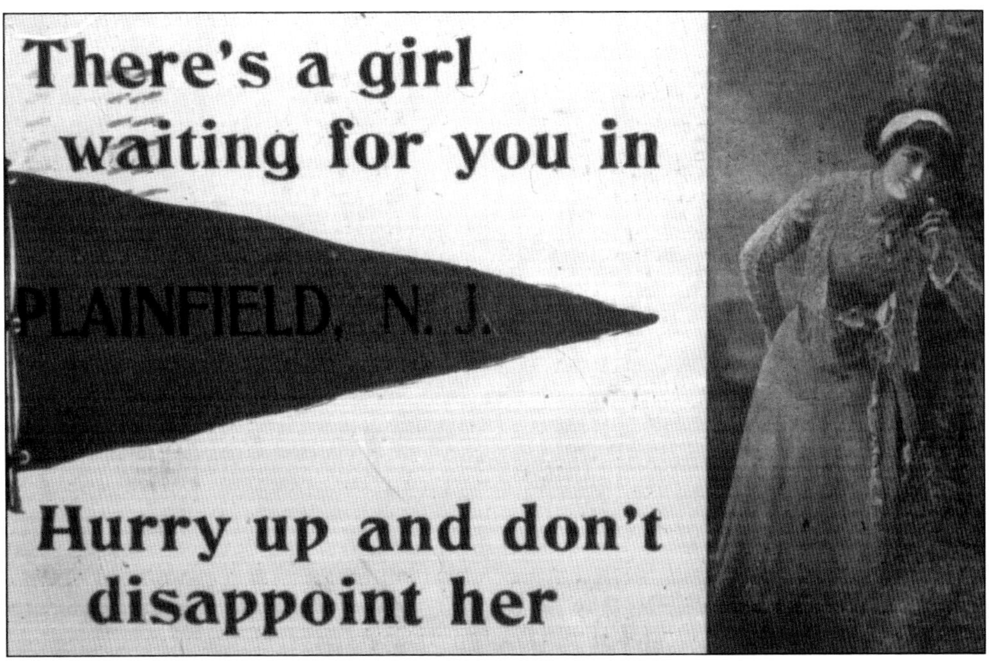

CONTENTS

ACKNOWLEDGMENTS

Our sincere gratitude goes to Judith A. Bailey of Centreville, Virginia; Frank H. Blatz Jr.; E. Gary Cleveland; Drake House Museum; ERA Suburb Realty; Edward Enners; Fanwood Memorial Library; Christine Fahrenholz of the Hillside Cemetery Association; William Garrett; John Hoffman; King's Daughters Day School; Linnea Layton of Acton, Massachusetts; Lt. David Locke of the Plainfield Fire Department; many photographers (professional and amateur, known and unknown) who took the wonderful pictures; Molly Marsh; Jean Mattson and JoAnn Ball of the Plainfield Historical Society; Mary Mazepa and William Tuthill of the South Plainfield Historical Society; Dr. Guido and Louise Mino; Muhlenberg Regional Medical Center; Paul O'Keefe; Albert Pittis; Bruce Ryno; Julie Shortridge; Carolyn Siegelman; Kathleen Smythe of the Wardlaw-Hartridge School; Robert Stone; Michael Wroble; and the UnitedTrust Bank.

INTRODUCTION

The city of Plainfield is a microcosm of the world in which it was conceived and developed. As such, its story is like that of every other community in the United States. It is about a place and the people who lived here. This is a story of what they did, what they thought, what they accomplished, and what they bequeathed to generations yet to come.

The story of Plainfield is unlike any other community in the United States for the very same reasons—and that makes all the difference.

More than three centuries of a city's existence is too broad a subject to be encompassed within the pages of this book. It is material for many volumes. Look on this book as a glimpse of life from 1684 until the early 20th century through the eyes of those who lived it. We hope others will pick up the story line and delve deeper into the sources to discover why Plainfield has always claimed a spot in the hearts of its residents, as it has in ours.

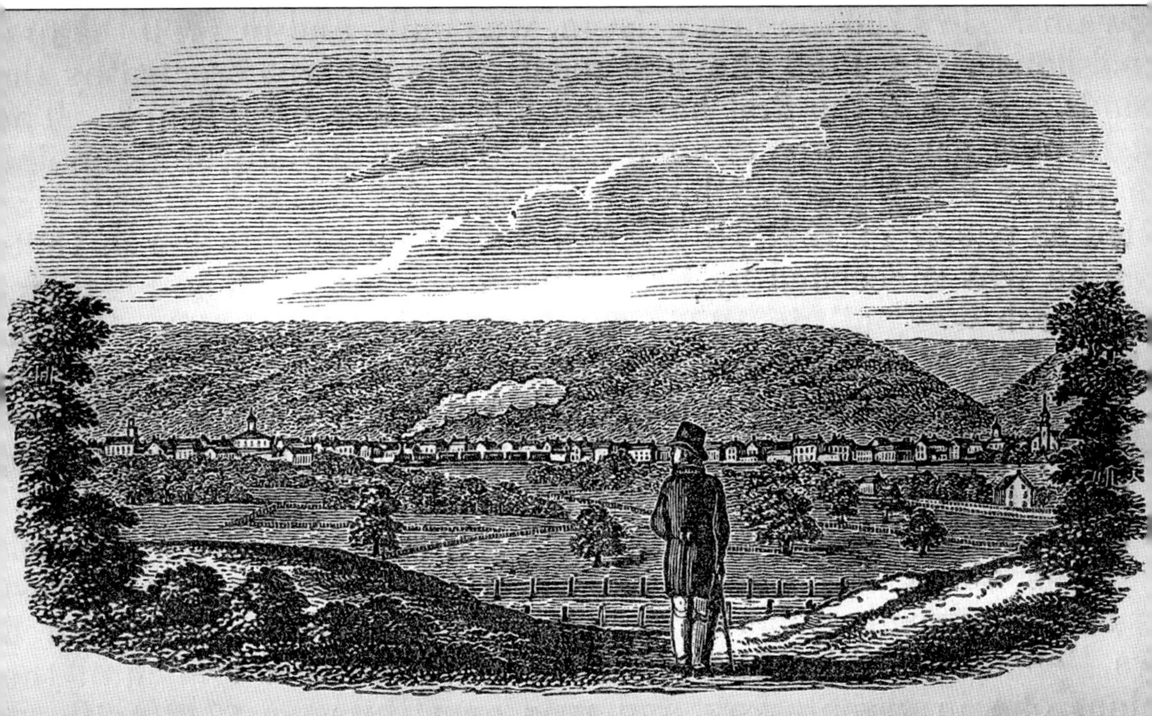

Plainfield, from Randolph or Chestnut Hill.

One

We Are Gathered Here

Imagination is a poor substitute for the actual words of the first Europeans who settled in Plainfield. From the hand of Thomas Gordon at the Cedar Brook of East New Jersey to George Ellison, advocate, in Edinburgh, Scotland, February 16, 1685, we learn:

"Upon the 18th day of November, I and my servants came to the woods and eight days later my wife and children came also. I put up a wigwam in 24 hours, which served us until we put up a better house; which I made 24 feet long and 15 feet wide, containing a hall and kitchen both in one, and a chamber and study, which I put up pretty well with vertical logs on the sides and shingles on the roof . . . I am settled here in a very pleasant place, upon the side of a plain almost free of woods and near the waterside . . ."—Part of a series of 17th-century letters from *History of Plainfield and North Plainfield*; F.T. Smiley; the Courier-News Company, Plainfield, N.J.; 1901.

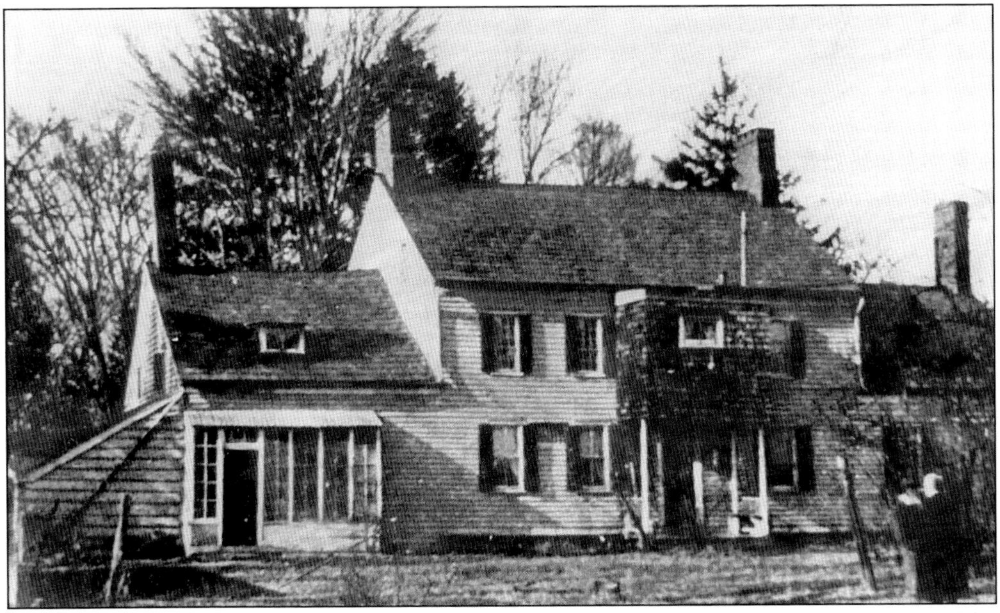

Seen here is the original front elevation of Cedar Brook Farm. The frame building raised by William Webster in 1717, after his purchase of the Gordon plantation, is on the left. The main block of the farmhouse was completed by Webster's son, John, before his death in 1800. The awkward bump over the front door contained Plainfield's first indoor bathroom.

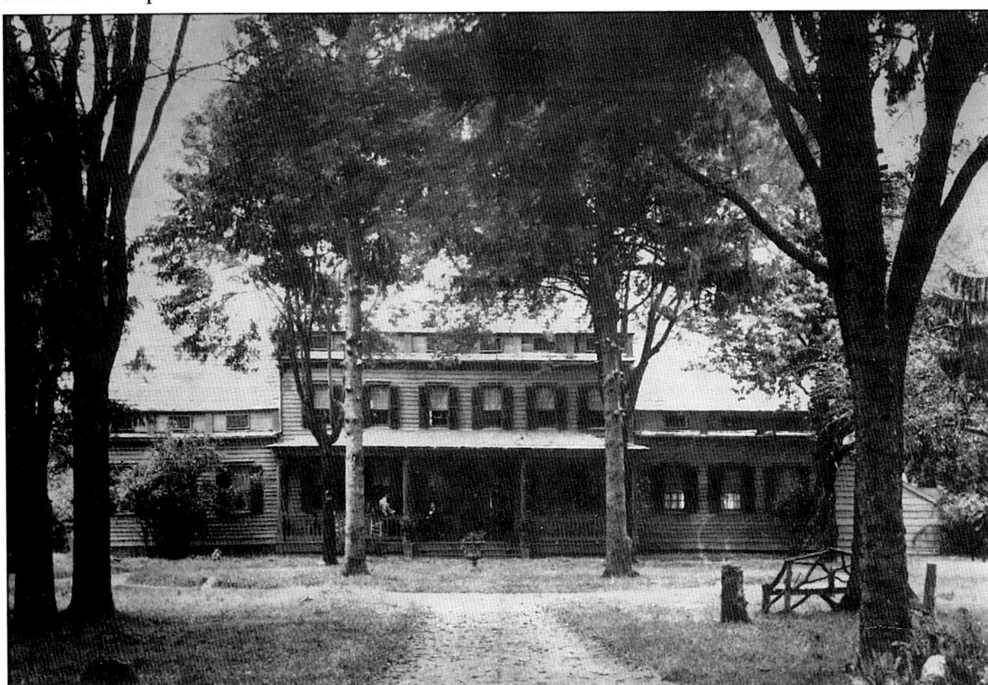

Shown here is the rear of Cedar Brook Farm, which became the front entrance in the 19th century. The 1717 farmhouse is on the right, and the ballroom addition of Sen. James E. Martine is on the left. This view of the facade is framed by still-existing stone pillars, on Watchung Avenue.

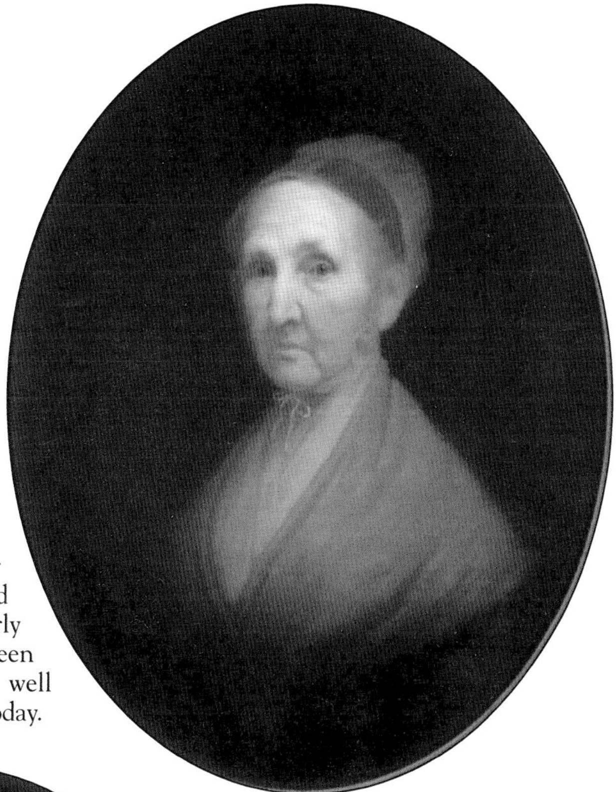

The Vails and Websters shared more than an interest in the local mills. Beginning with the marriage of Anna Webster and Nathan Vail on June 24, 1801, the families joined in wedlock many times over the years. The Green Brook marked the boundary of farmlands in early days, just as it marks the line between Plainfield and North Plainfield, as well as Union and Somerset Counties today.

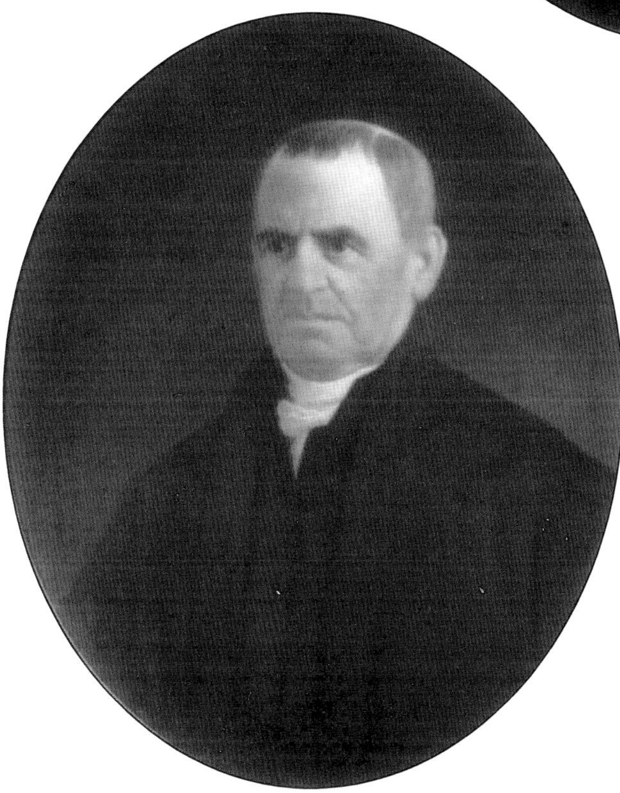

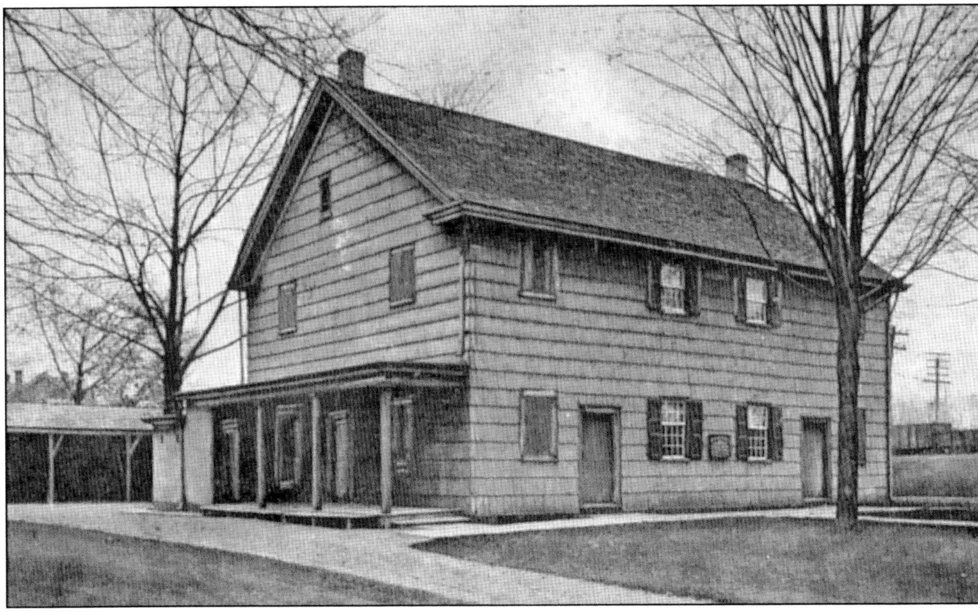

John Laing purchased the 1685 Barclay grant just south of Thomas Gordon's homestead in 1692. Retaining the name Plainfield Plantation from Barclay's day, the Laings hosted First day meetings for neighboring farmers until John Laing willed land for a meetinghouse on Woodland Avenue in 1731. The first mention of Plainfield as a locality appears in the record for Elizabeth Laing, "born at Plainfield ye 11th day of ye 10th month, 1707."

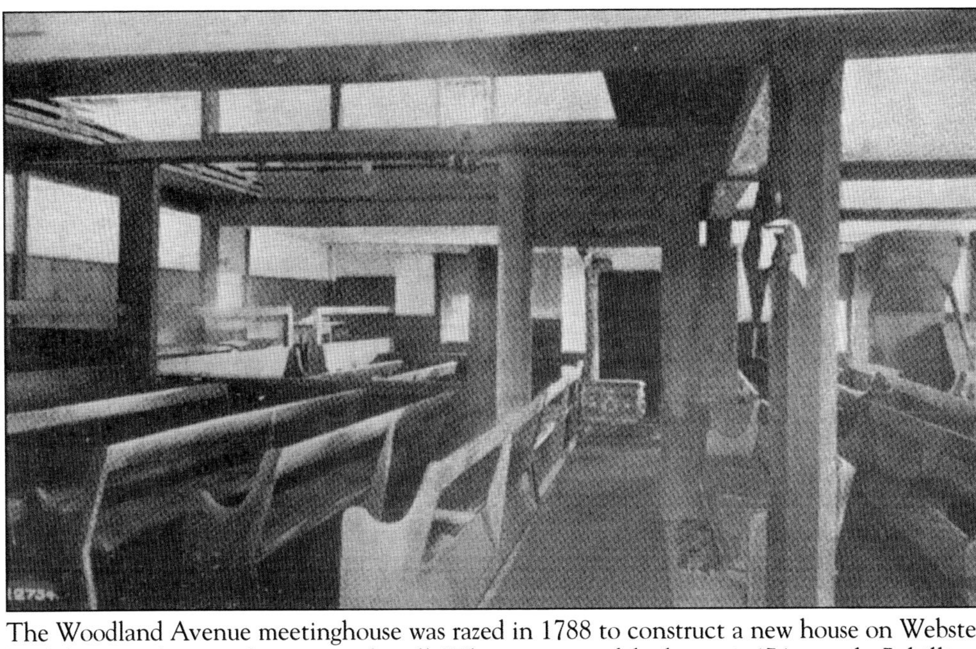

The Woodland Avenue meetinghouse was razed in 1788 to construct a new house on Webster land that was closer to the crossroads mill. "The expenses of the house is 474 pounds, 7 shillings and 10 pence, exclusive of what stuff was got from the old Meeting House." The building still stands on Watchung Avenue, formerly Peace Street, and lent its name to the village when the post office was established on April 1, 1800.

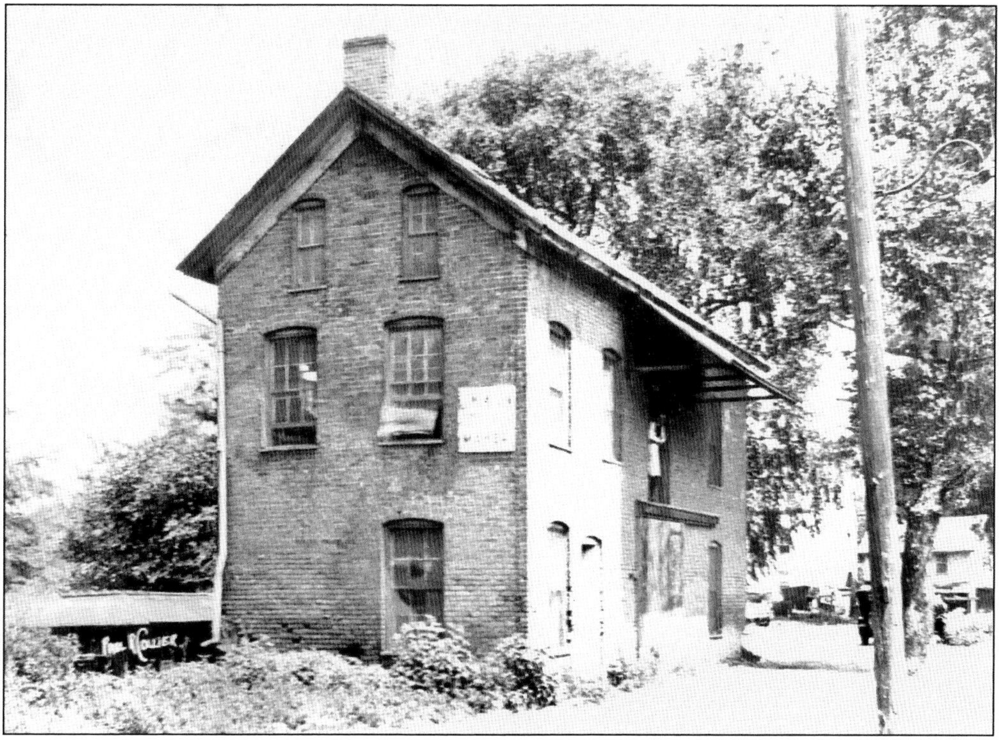

John Vail's mill on the Green Brook, c. 1735 to 1750, was in Webster family hands by 1760. It was moved farther downstream to Mountain Road (Somerset Street) in 1782. Purchased by Phineas French in 1839, it operated as the City Mills until 1900. The complex contained a flour mill, gristmill, sawmill, cider mill, and distillery. The building was razed in 1927.

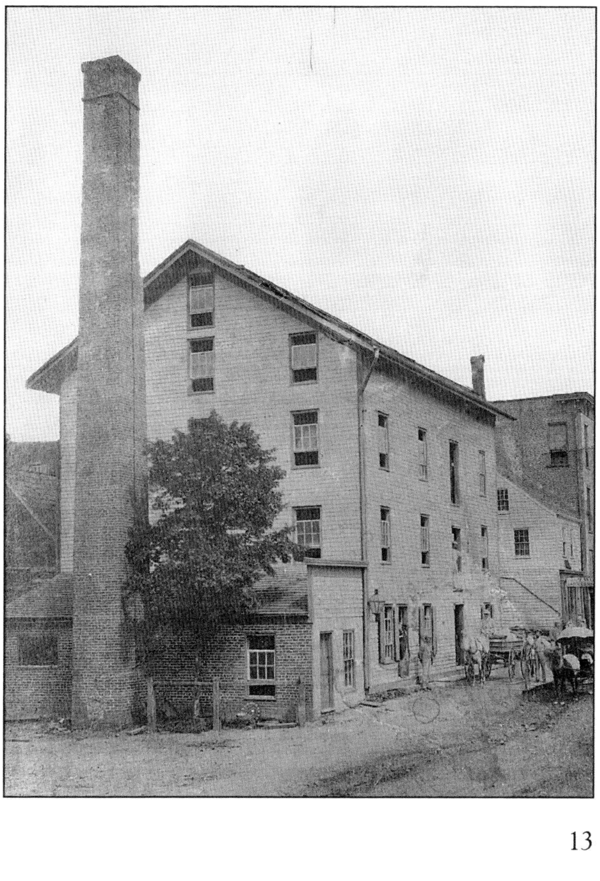

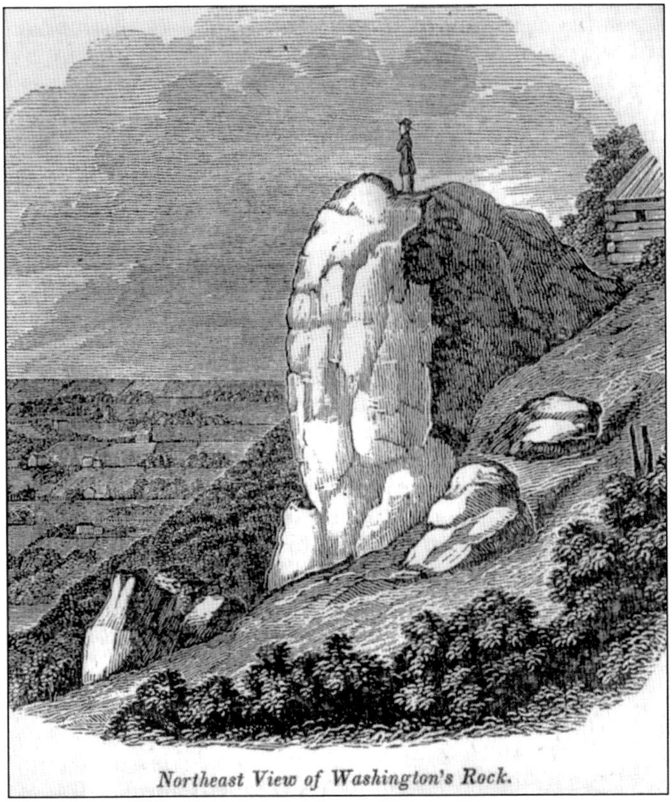

Northeast View of Washington's Rock.

Edward FitzRandolph was visiting the Jonah Vail farm in Green Brook when Gen. George Washington, encamped at Middlebrook, paused in his search for a lookout point on the first ridge of the Watchungs. "I know the best point on the mountain for that purpose," FitzRandolph replied, and he promptly accompanied the military leader to the spot. This vintage engraving clearly shows the scene as they viewed it that day.

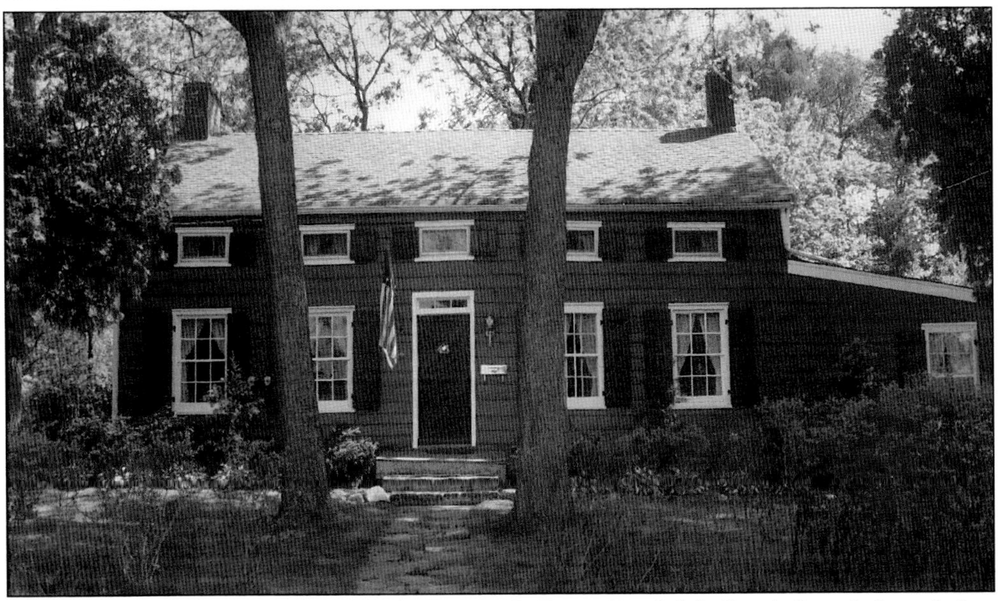

Seen here is the FitzRandolph farmhouse *c.* 1717, on Randolph Road. It is believed that Edward FitzRandolph lived in the farmhouse during his fateful visit to Washington's Rock. FitzRandolph was born in Plainfield and was wed in Plainfield to Mary Webster of Cedar Brook Farm. The couple had nine children in this homestead. A carpenter, FitzRandolph helped raise the new meetinghouse on Peace Street.

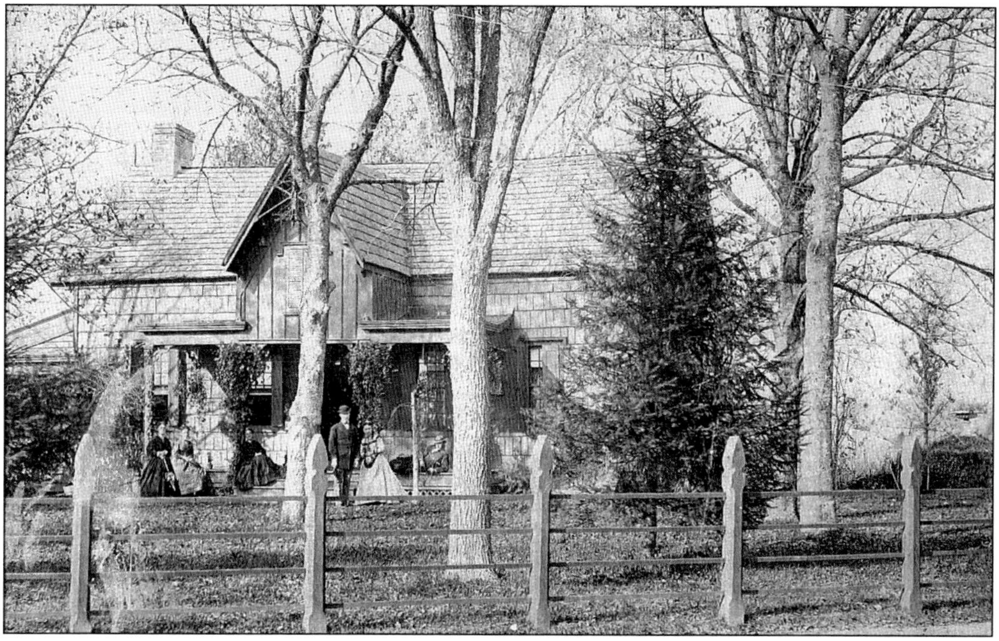

This is the earliest known photograph of the Drake House, which was George Washington's headquarters during the Battle for the Short Hills, on June 25, 1777. The house was built in 1746 by Isaac Drake for his son, Nathaniel. This *c.* 1870 view shows the first alterations to the humble four-room farmhouse by the Harbergers, who bought it as a summer place in 1864. The more grandiose embellishments we recognize today were soon to follow.

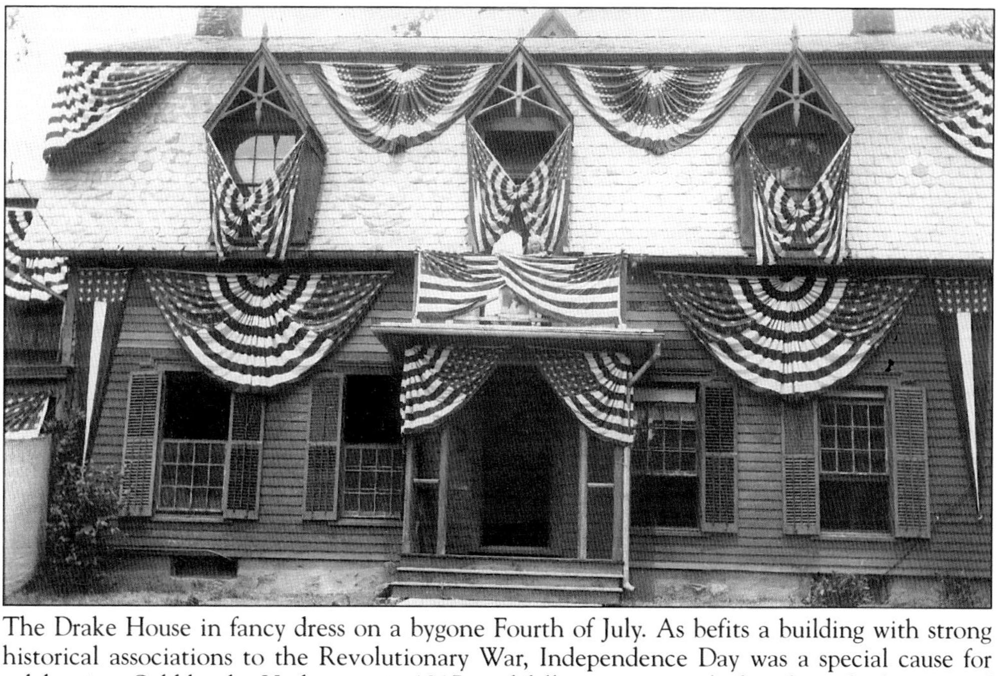

The Drake House in fancy dress on a bygone Fourth of July. As befits a building with strong historical associations to the Revolutionary War, Independence Day was a special cause for celebration. Sold by the Harbergers in 1917, and following a period of neglect, the homestead was deeded to the city of Plainfield in 1920. It was then placed under the management of the historical society.

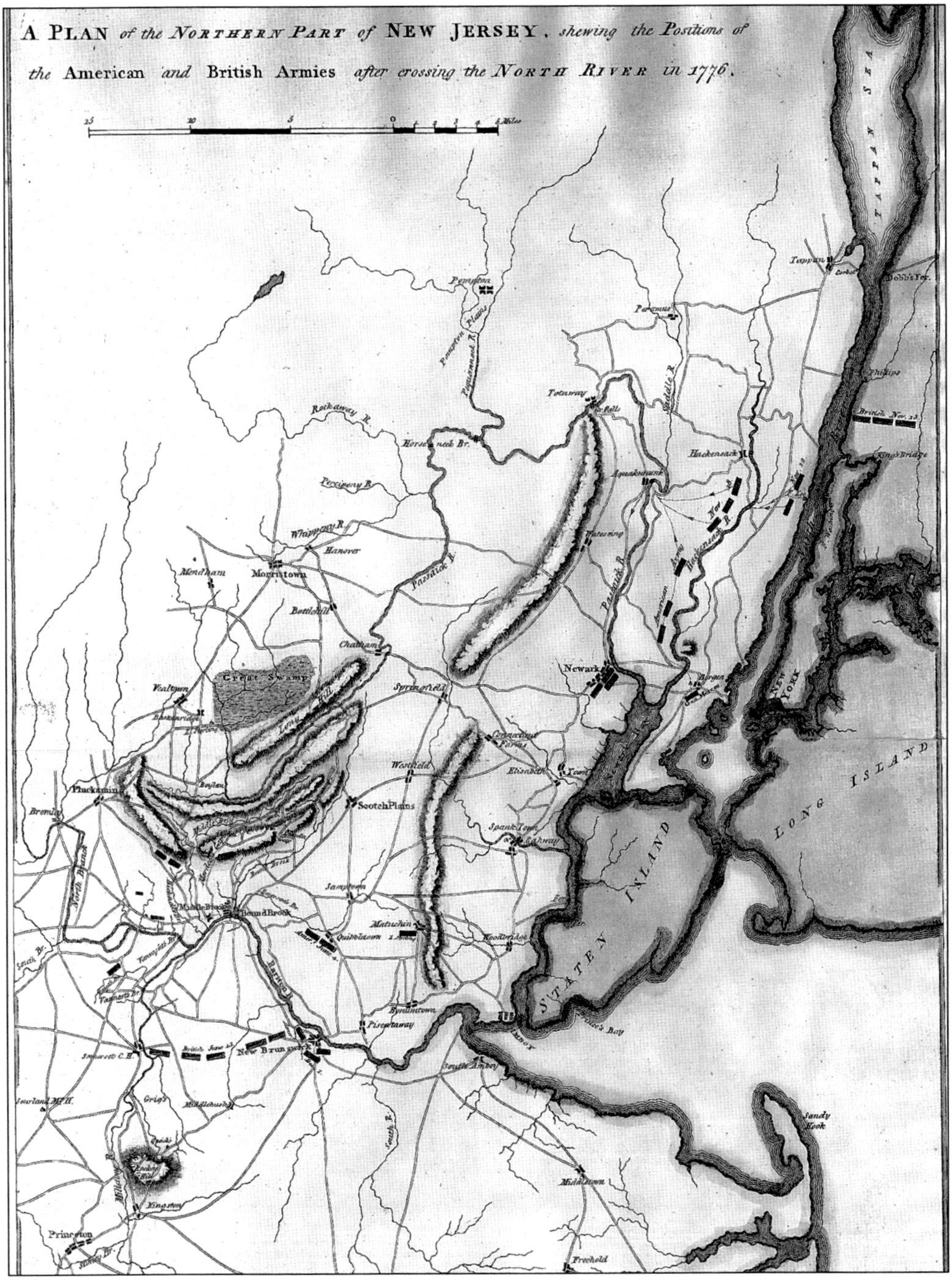

An 1807 map from John Marshall's *The Life of George Washington* locates the positions of American and British armies in 1776. It depicts the Watchung Mountains where Washington's Middlebrook encampment was entrenched. On the plain below the Watchungs, Scotch Plains and Samptown are identified. Between them, the scattered farms of Plainfield lay, open to the raids of British and Hessian troops. Here, Drake family members and their former slave, Caesar, strove to provision the militia at the Blue Hills Fort and Encampment, on Cornelius Vermeule's plantation, just across the Green Brook.

Two

THE OLD MILLSTREAM

The words of Emma Randolph to her friend and future husband, Walter Dunn, at Jarvis United States General Hospital in Baltimore, Maryland, bring the Civil War close to us. She writes from Plainfield on July 24, 1864, to her very "Dear" Walt:

"Yes Uncle Dan and Aunt Mary remain on the farm. Ems moving up to Plainfield and taking [up] dressmaking. She with cousin Julia live up in the house just the other side of Laing Hotel . . . Ollie has gone to Elisabeth City to pay the money down that exempts him from this draft only. We were much surprised to hear he was drafted but he will never go he says no matter if he is drafted again. I hope and trust he will get along all right today for I would tremble for him should he be forced into the army. But I hope he will not be. I could give him up willingly did he volunteer but being drafted is diferent. I'll keep out of it."—Excerpted from *After Chancellorsville, Letters from the Heart*; Judith A. Bailey and Robert L. Cottom; Maryland Historical Society, Baltimore, Maryland; 1998.

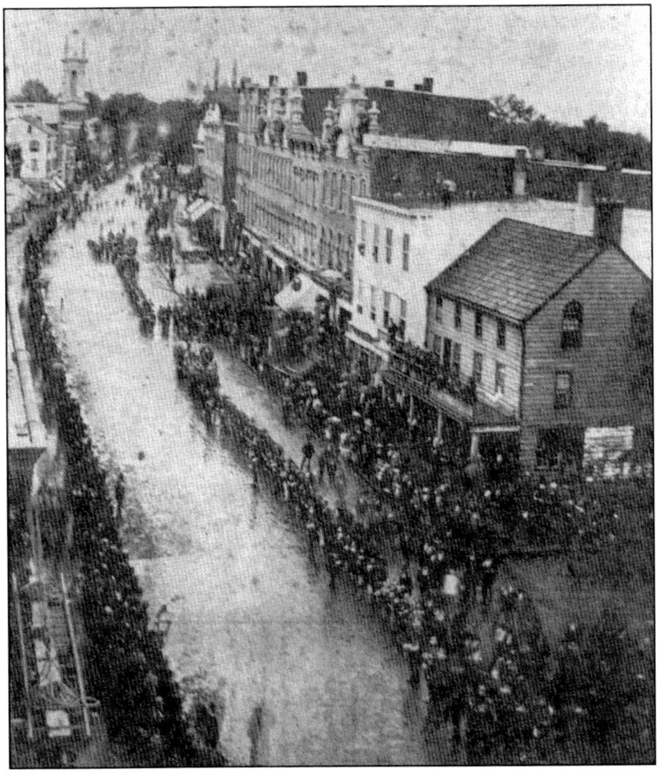

Civil War veterans became a part of every parade passing the corner of present-day Front and Somerset Streets. The Gloekler Building, on the right, marks the site of Nesbit's trading post and village pump of the 1750s, at the joining of Old York Road and "the road to the mountain." The building appears on Stillman's map of 1832, and survived until 1911.

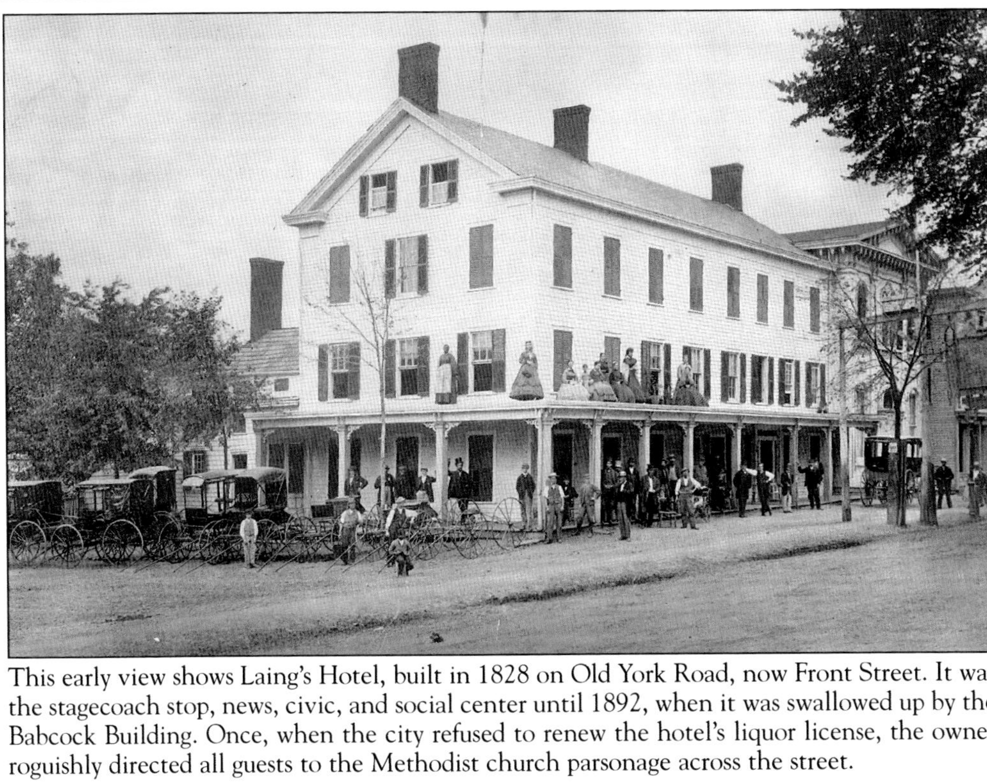

This early view shows Laing's Hotel, built in 1828 on Old York Road, now Front Street. It was the stagecoach stop, news, civic, and social center until 1892, when it was swallowed up by the Babcock Building. Once, when the city refused to renew the hotel's liquor license, the owner roguishly directed all guests to the Methodist church parsonage across the street.

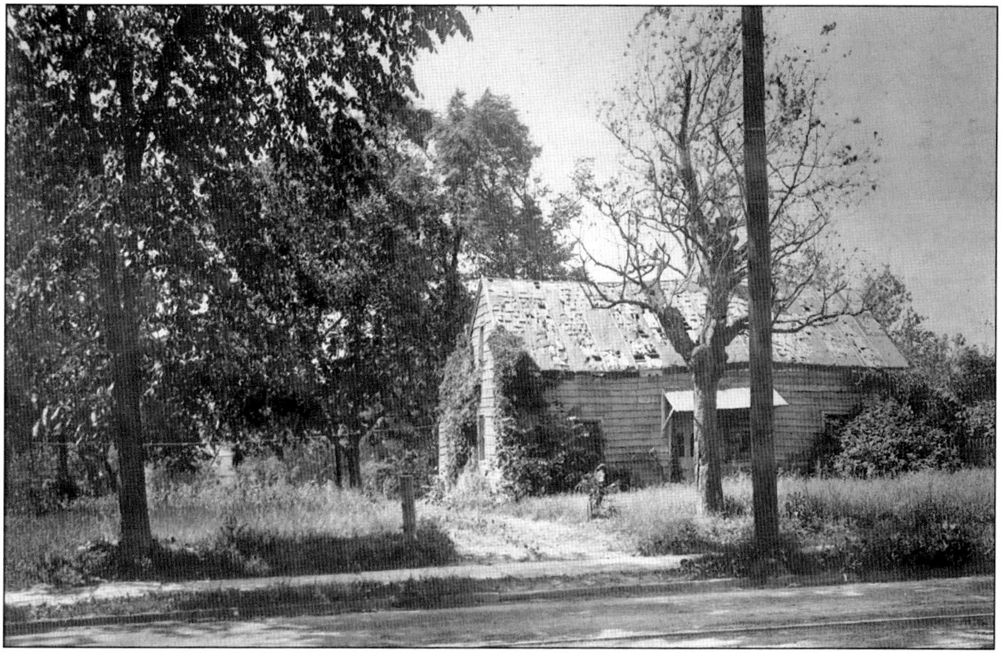

An early house on West Front Street recalls the days when hatters used the Green Brook to prepare fabrics for Plainfield's flourishing hat industry. On many days "the water would be almost the color of ink from the dye stuffs used." The industry, which was established by John Wilson in 1808, operated 15 shops and had more than 300 employees by 1835. It had dwindled to only three shops by 1860.

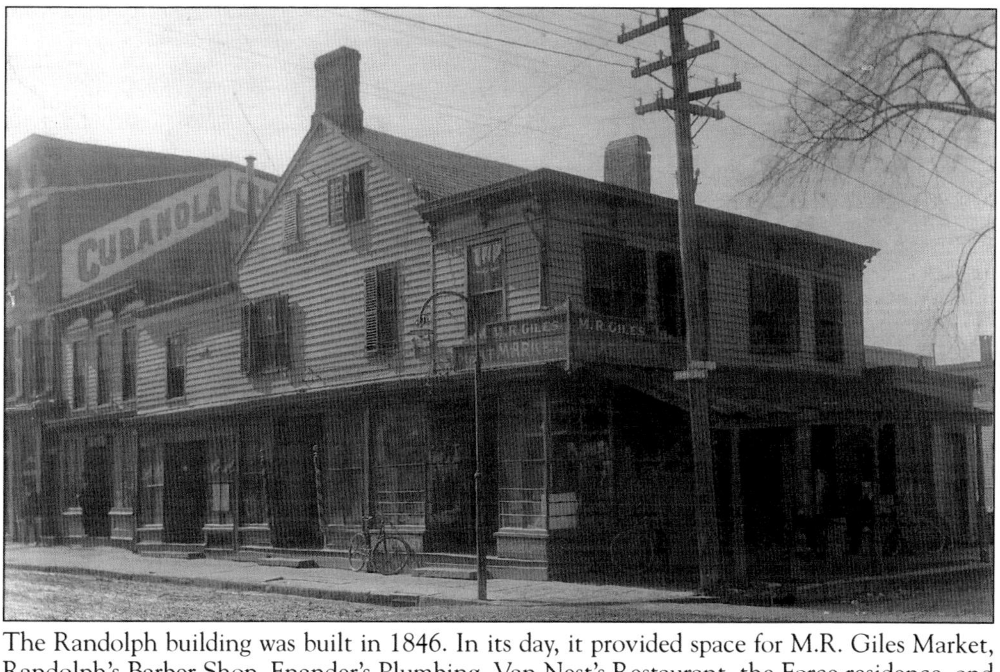

The Randolph building was built in 1846. In its day, it provided space for M.R. Giles Market, Randolph's Barber Shop, Enander's Plumbing, Van Nest's Restaurant, the Force residence, and C.M. Fine's Tobacco Shop. The first commercial structure to be built on Cherry Street, now Park Avenue, the building stood its ground until 1905.

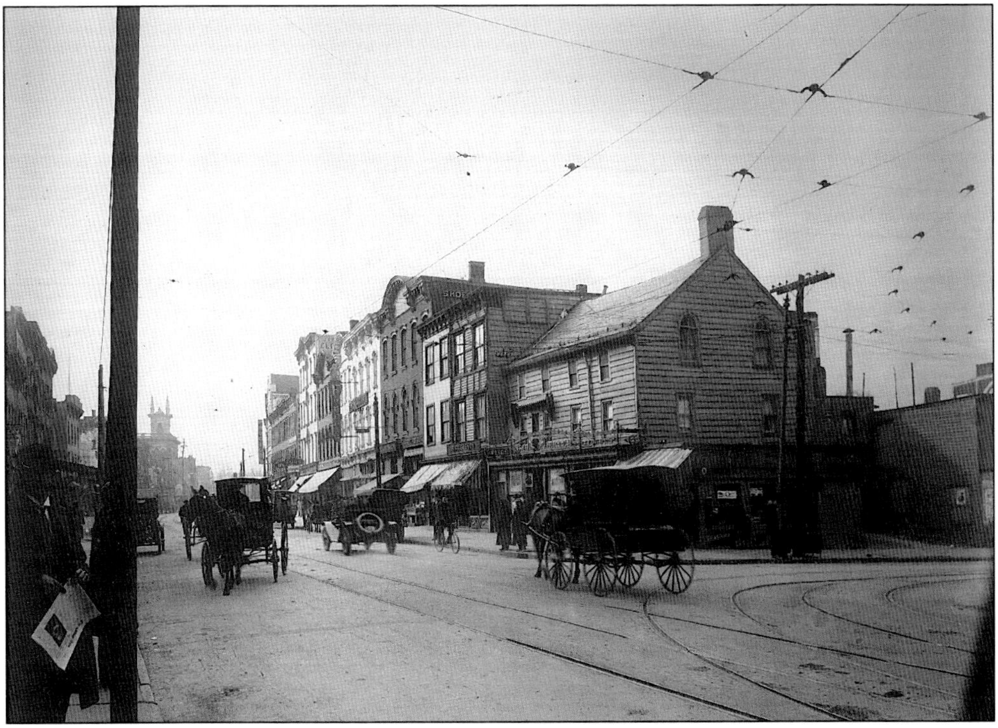

Gloekler's was typical of the buildings of its time. Sturdy and plain, downtown shops stood companionably shoulder-to-shoulder along streets that were dusty in summer and muddy in spring and fall. Concrete curbs and steps sometimes lifted entrances above the mire, until paved streets began to enter the picture in 1869.

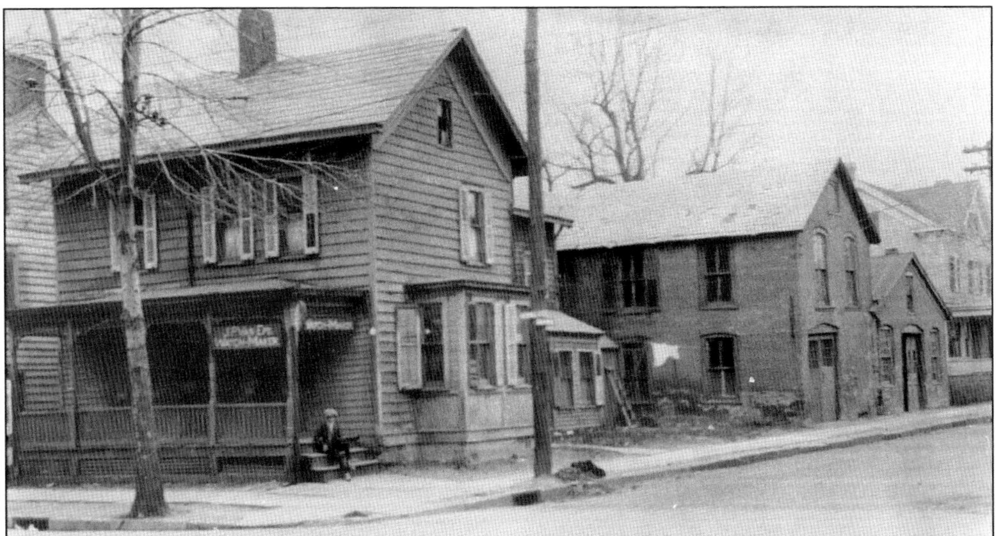

During the Civil War era, many simple shops lined the streets of Plainfield's commercial district. So it must have looked when local barber Thomas Smith appeared to cast the first vote polled in the city after passage of the 15th Amendment. Fellow African American Francis Wyckoff arrived soon after to tell the crowd he had paid taxes for 50 years for the privilege of voting in the 1870 township election.

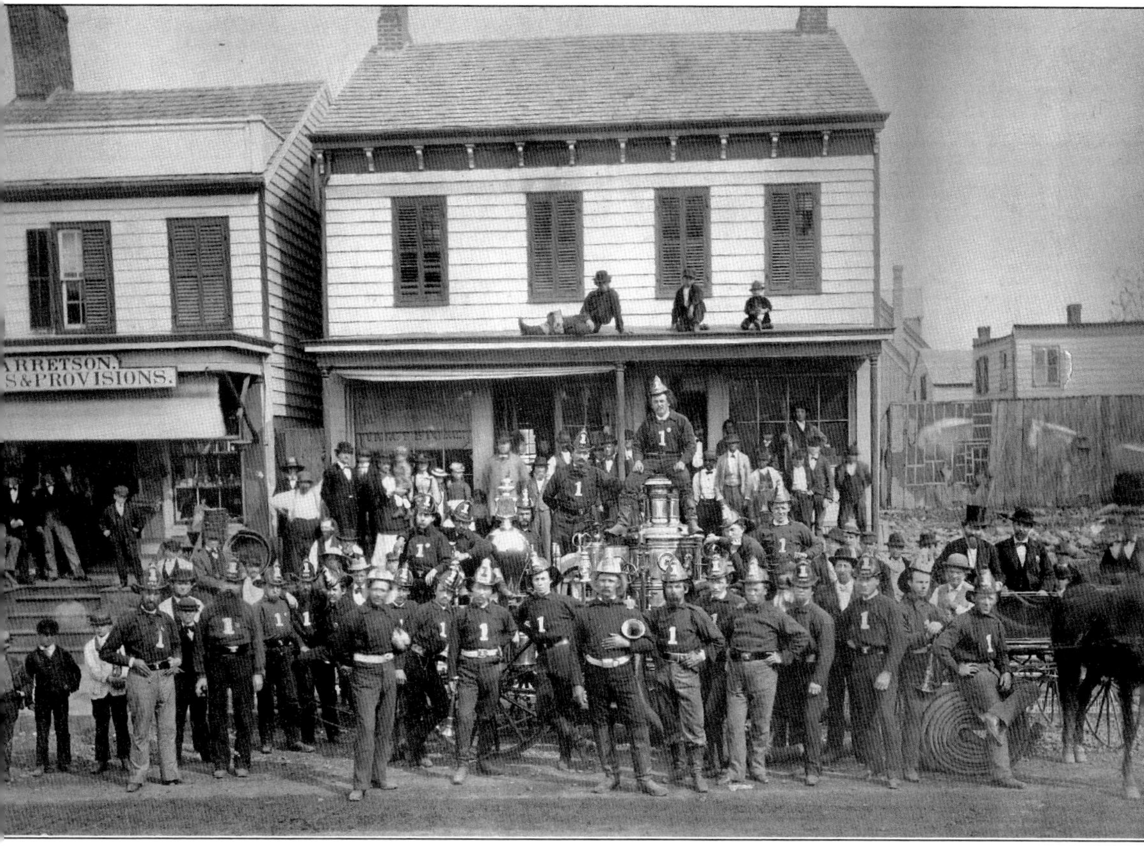

By 1865, at the close of the Civil War, the members of Gazelle Engine Company No. 1 still eligible for duty had faded to four. Returning veterans helped swell the membership to over 50. A steam fire engine was purchased in 1867 and was in service when a disastrous fire threatened the entire downtown district. Members of the company cluster around their new steamer, in this period photograph. Do not search for the face of Walter Dunn among the assembly. Sadly, the wounded veteran, his wife, Emma, and their infant daughter died before this picture was taken. All were, in their own way, casualties of war.

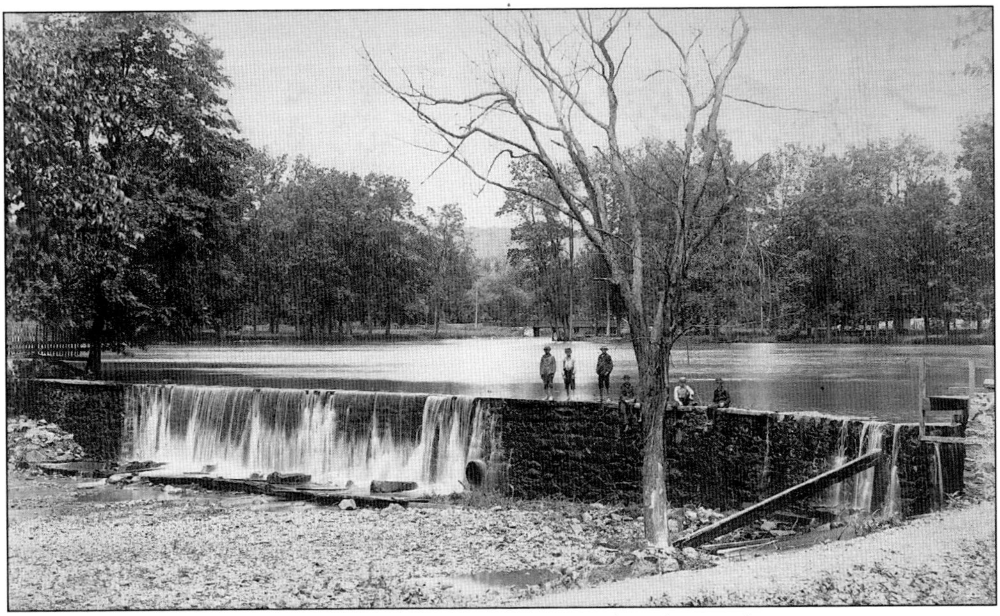

Tier's Pond was the scene of many outings. Daytime and nighttime boating parties, picnics, strawberry festivals, ice-cream parties, fireworks displays, swimming in the summer, and skating in the winter all centered around the old millpond.

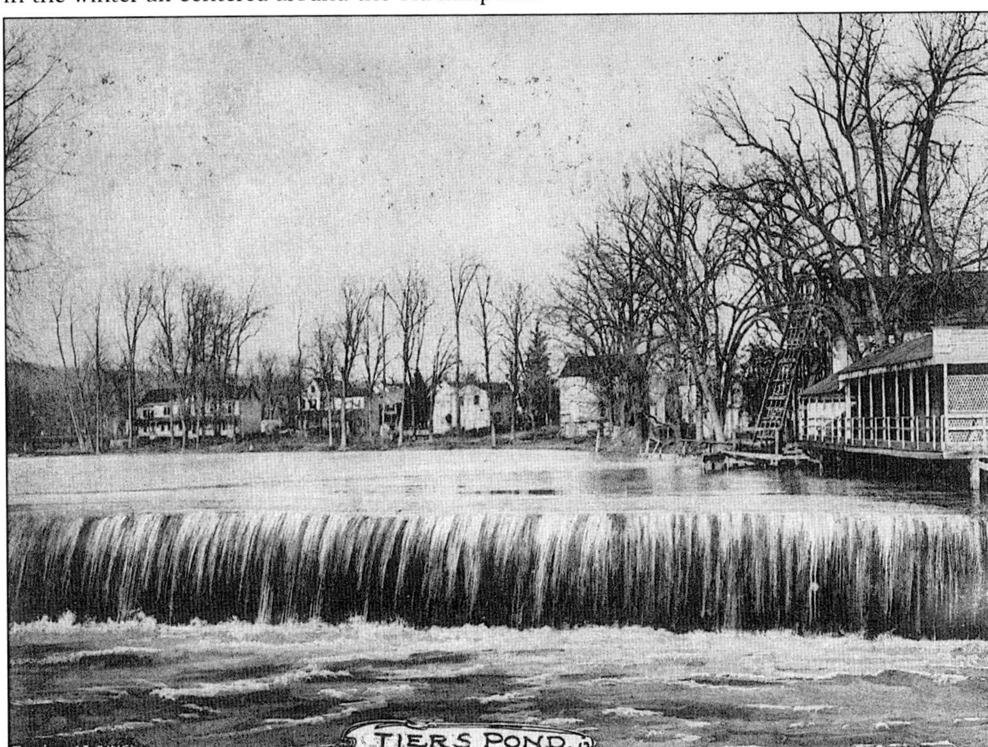

John Tier's ice-cream pavilion was also the center of controversy. Excommunicated by the Presbyterian Church for selling ice cream on Sundays, Tier gallantly refused to identify his best Sunday customers—two elders and a deacon of his church.

Three

In the Good Old Summertime

The excitement expressed in Virginia Jester's letter to her mother in Dover, Delaware, on December 3, 1891, is contagious as she describes the party given in her honor by her uncle Gen. William H. Sterling at his Plainfield home:

"I have so much to tell you about my fine times that I really don't know where to begin. I will, I think, start off with our theatre party of last night . . . The dinner was perfectly heavenly. I wore my new frock, Bertie wore bright red, Aunt Tilly her mulberry broadcloth and the men wore their dress suits and looked awfully handsome. The table was just lovely . . . Uncle Will bought bunches of sweet double violets to put by each plate, and two great bunches of roses for the middle of the table. We all put on our violets and Bertie carried the white roses and I the pink ones to the play . . . (The play was called 'Mr. Wilkinson's Widows' and kept the whole house in a perfect uproar.)"—Portion of a family letter shared by Linnea Layton of Acton, Massachusetts.

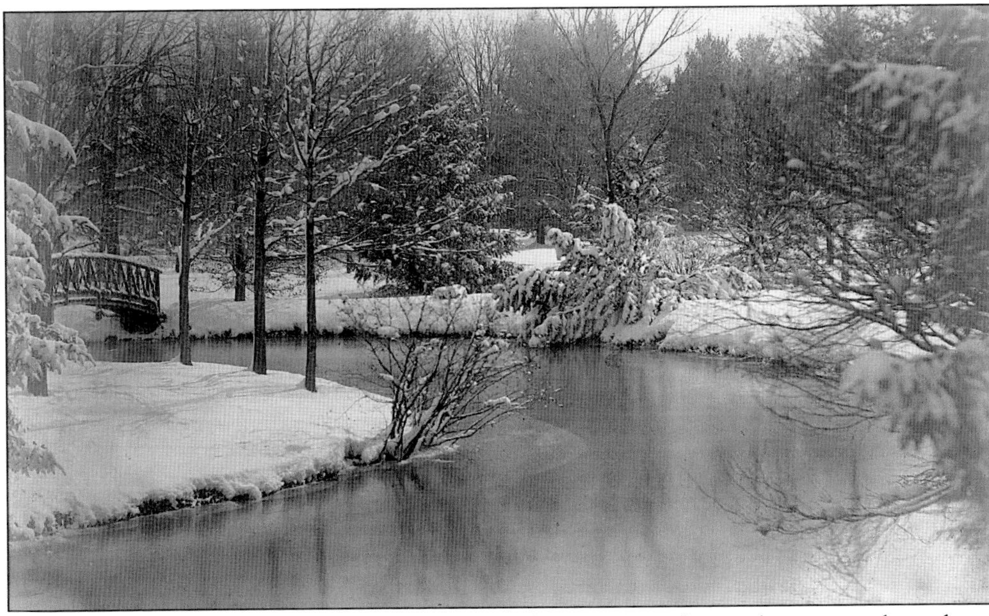

When Virginia Jester wrote her letter on December 3, 1891, the earth was snowbound and activities were naturally restricted. Summer was soon to come, and many more leisure pursuits would beckon when ice melted on the Green Brook.

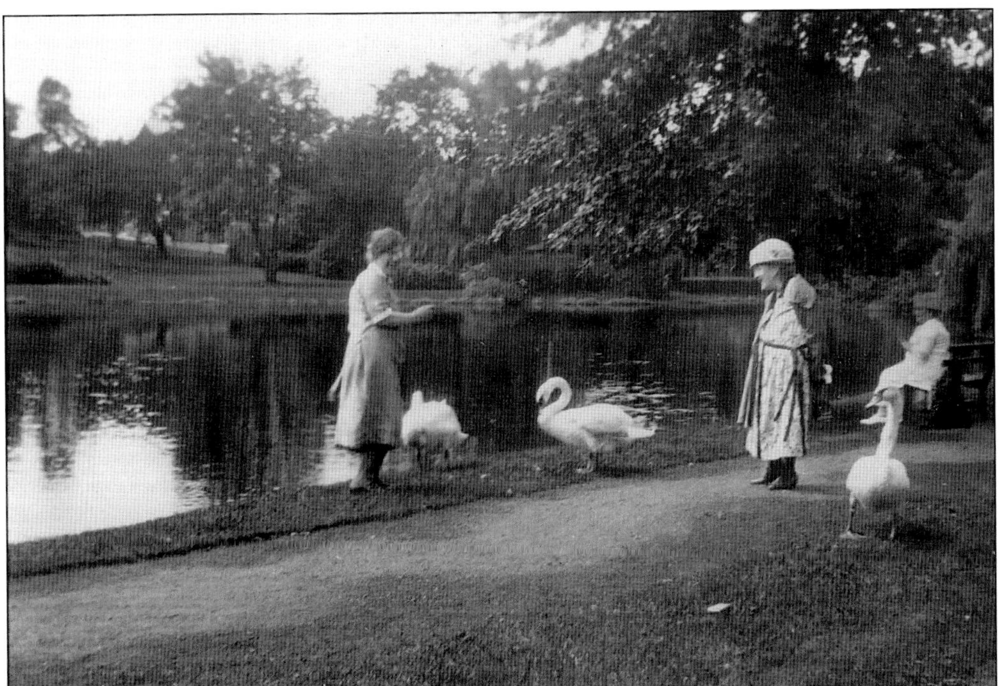

Summer days in 19th-century Plainfield were as graceful as a swan upon the waters of the Cedar Brook. Virginia's "Uncle General" suggested a great variety of outings in the summertime. His niece enjoyed them all.

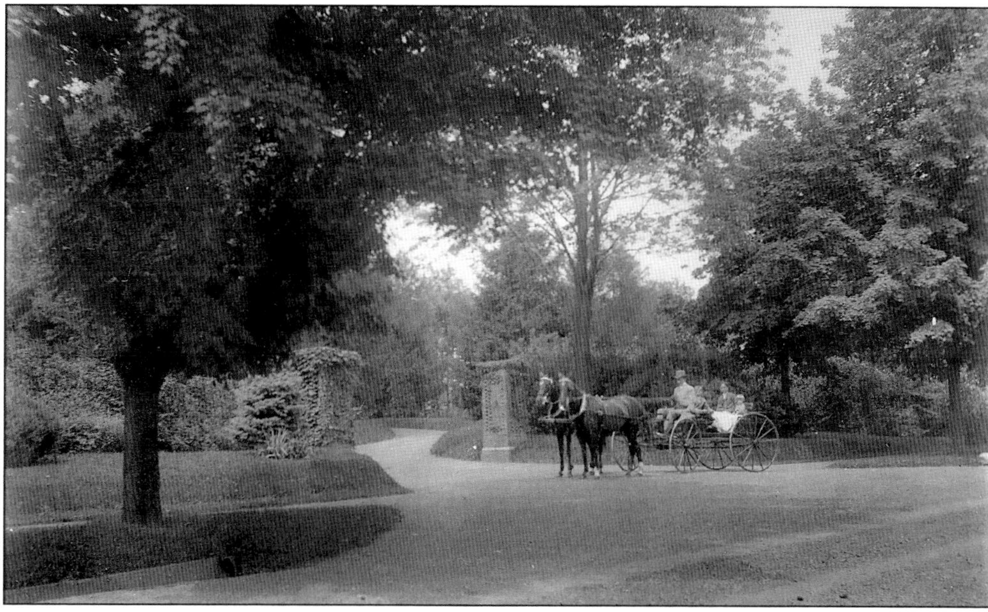

There have always been many ways to occupy leisure time in Plainfield. High in popularity were carriage rides down tree-embowered residential streets, up into the hills, and through the surrounding countryside. Rural delights were never far from the center of town.

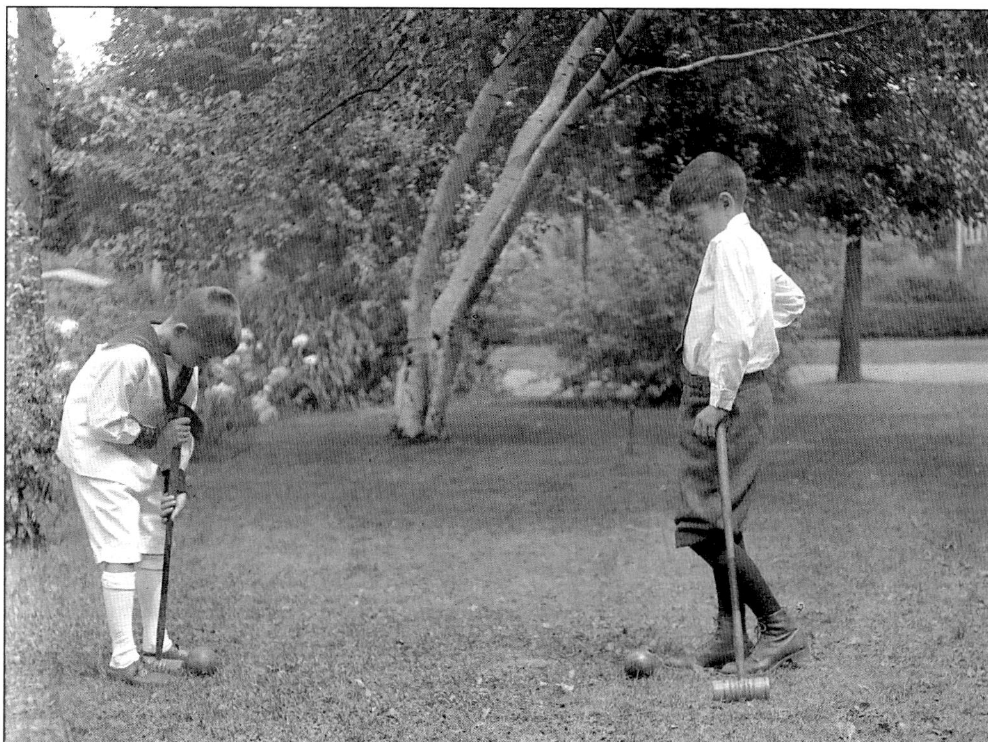

A game of croquet with family or friends on a summer afternoon offered simple pleasures: the scent of nearby gardens, laughter, playful skirmishes, and a glass of lemonade at game's end. Shown are the Gilman brothers on their Lenox Avenue lawn.

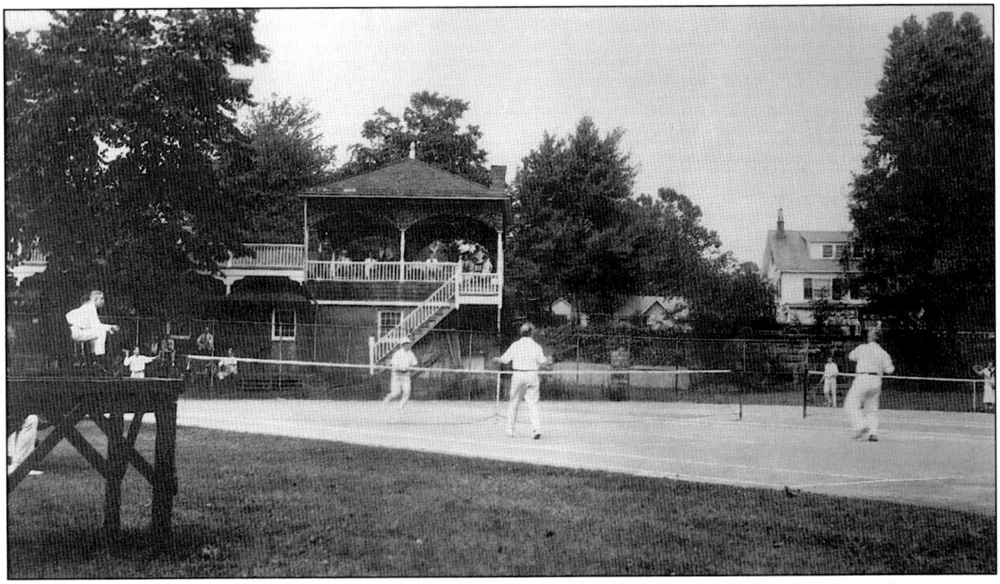

Tennis at the Park Club provided a hearty workout. Whether at a private club, a public court, or in one's own backyard, tennis was a perennial favorite. Badminton ran a close second as a less strenuous but equally competitive game.

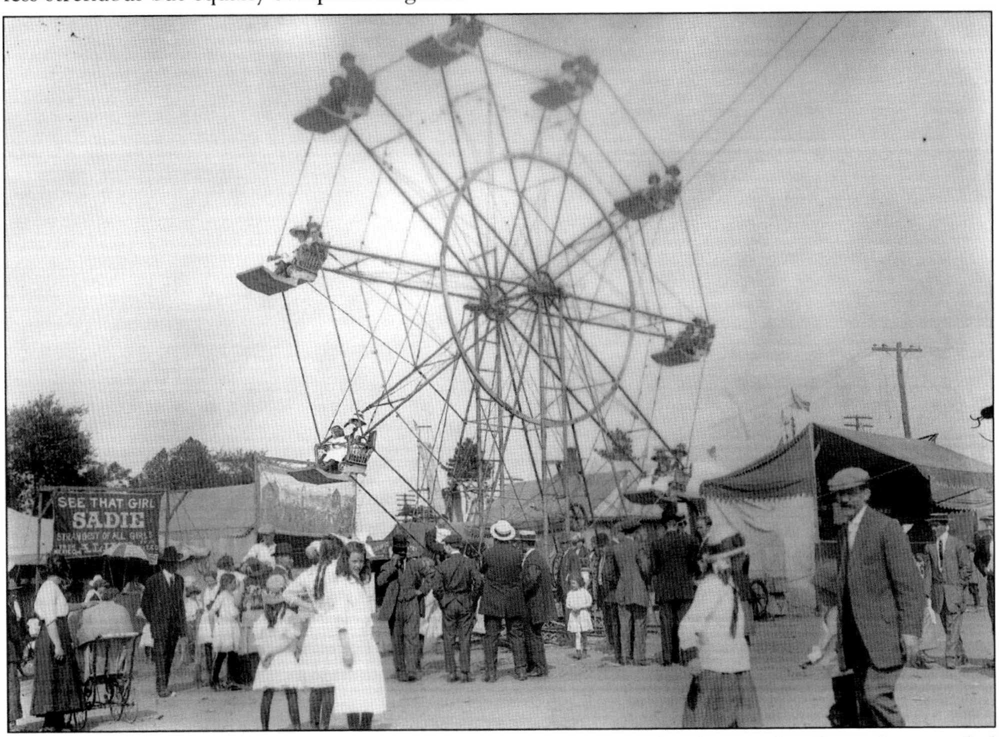

A May 1905 carnival raised more than $5,000 for the hospital. Thousands of people attended the week-long event, which covered 10 acres of ground and provided many attractions and amusements. In addition to the great aerial artist Ouda, there was a laughing gallery, a merry-go-round, an educated horse and, most thrilling of all, an imitation electrocution in the electric chair.

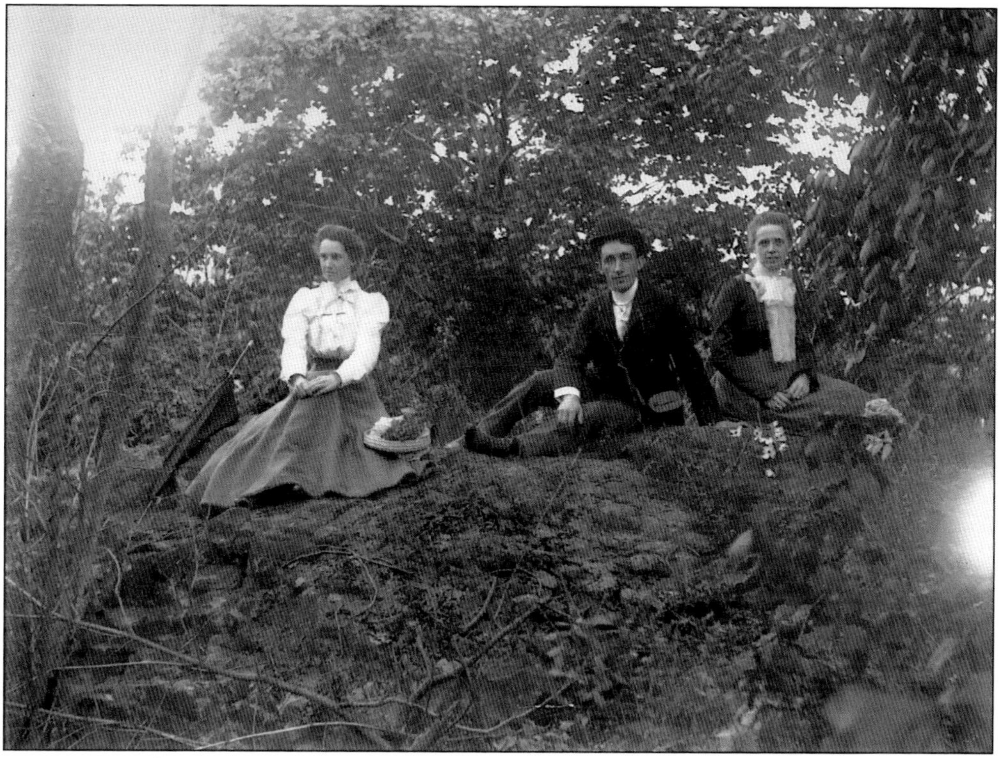

Picnics were always under way. The charms of Vail's Grove, on West Front Street, Wooden's Grove, on Somerset Street, and Stelle's Grove, on Plainfield Avenue, were not to be denied. Chicken, strawberry shortcake, and root beer were the foods of choice. They still are.

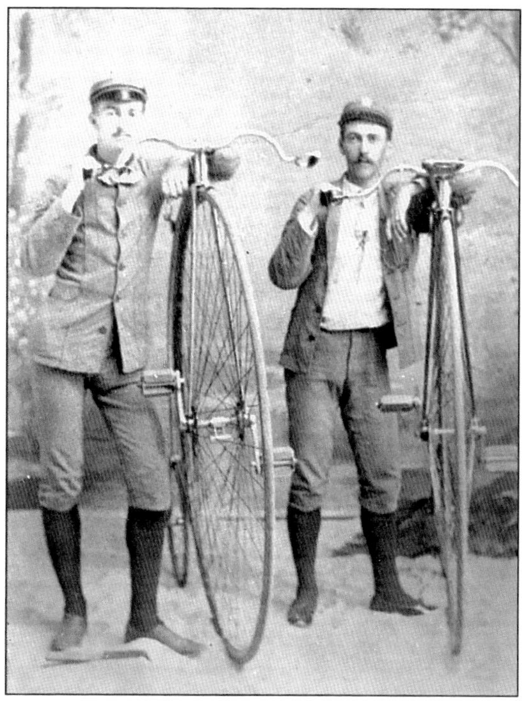

Bicycling was high-style recreation for the masses. Many people also spent the day at the races sponsored by the Crescent Wheelman's Association. The track was specially constructed and was considered the most up-to-date one in the country. Shown are insurance broker Robert Murray, left, and architect A.L.C. Marsh––both active cyclists.

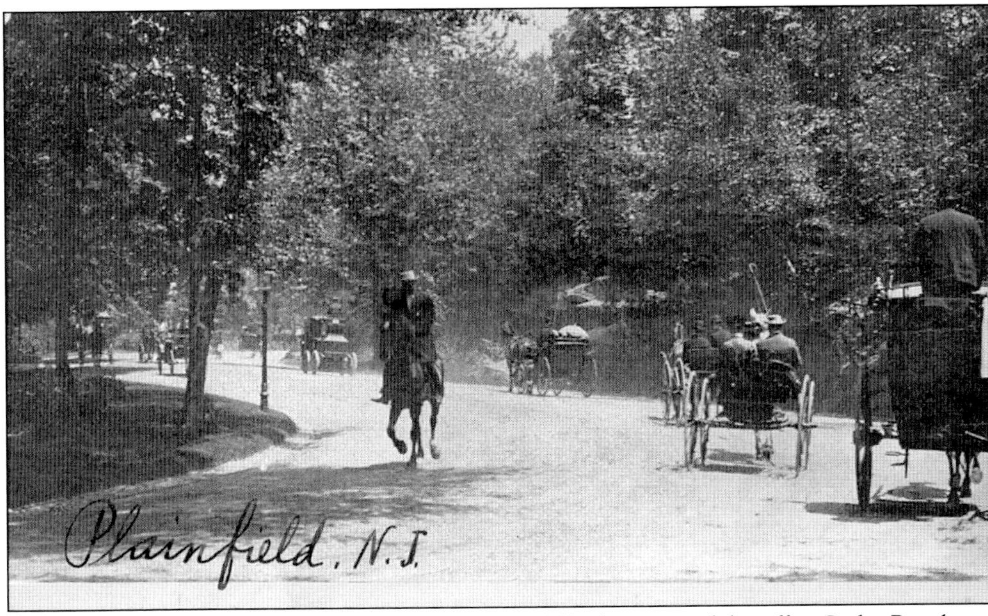

Parks were for public pleasure, and the public took full advantage of the offer. Cedar Brook was prime ground for Sunday carriage rides and canters on a favorite mare. The edge of the lake invited quieter pursuits, such as casual strolls, intimate conversations, and impromptu wading. Young boys with fishing poles, the very essence of summer, were often on the scene.

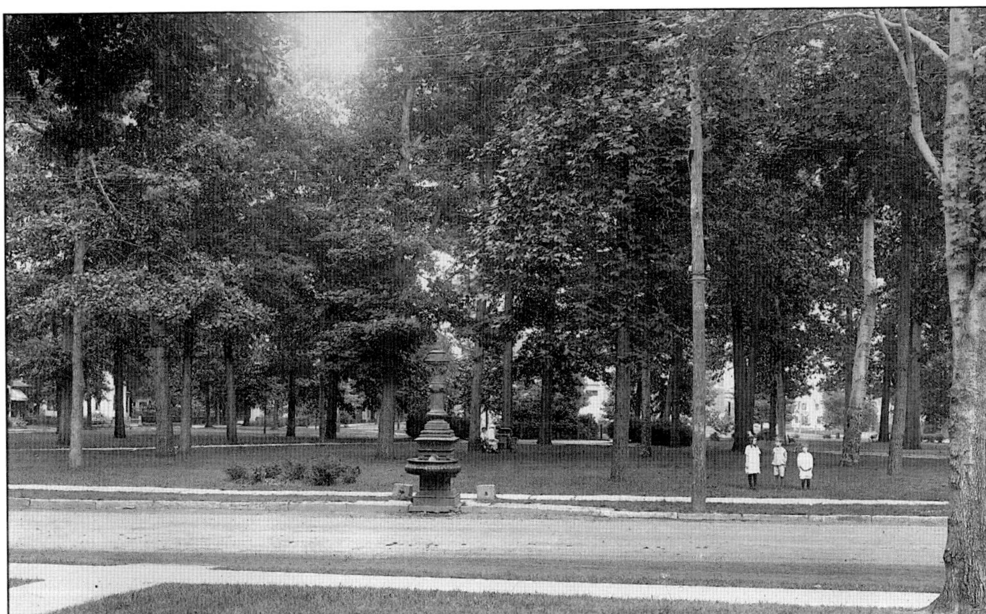

The old oaks of Library Park have been witness to much activity, many gatherings, and have even been the focus of legal action. Addressing townsfolk in the park on May 12, 1912, former president Theodore Roosevelt tried, but received little support in his acrimonious battle, to run against Pres. William Howard Taft. In other action, a private home was built on the southwest corner of the park by a man believing he had a legal title. In a well-publicized case, the citizen lost and had his home moved across the street.

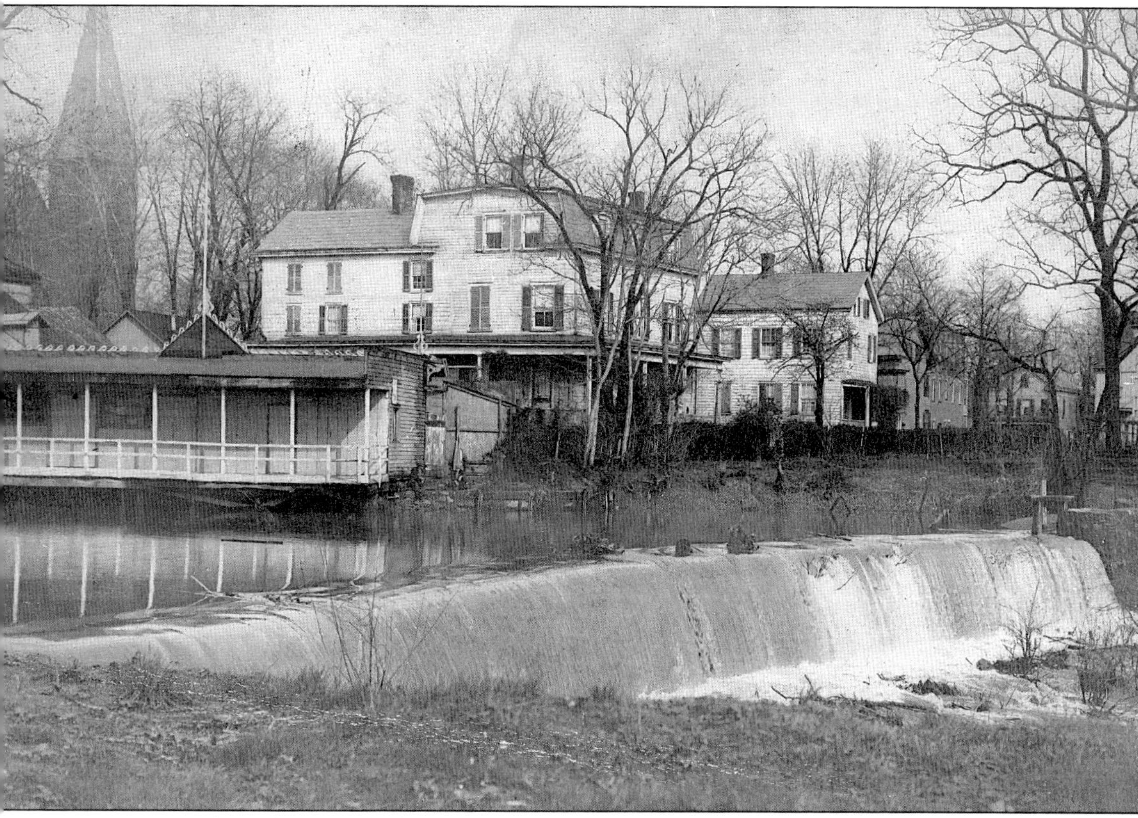

Since pioneer days, the "two little rivers watering the plain" have never lost their power to enchant. Park recreational activities still center around both the Green and Cedar brooks. Green Brook, the larger and swifter of the two, became more fully developed. Early-20th-century postcards give us a last and loving look at Tier's Pond and its ice-cream pavilion. Memories linger on.

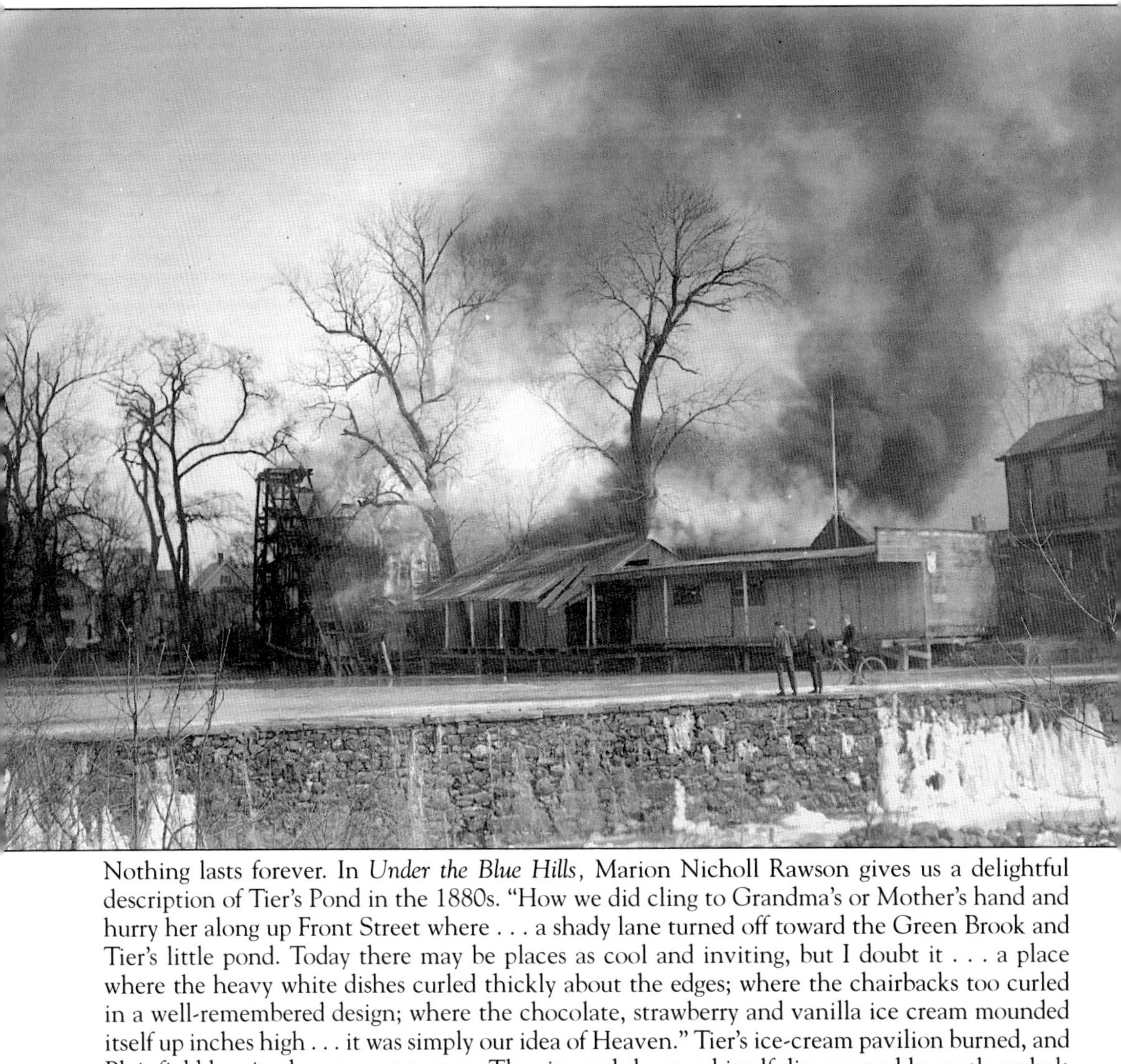

Nothing lasts forever. In *Under the Blue Hills*, Marion Nicholl Rawson gives us a delightful description of Tier's Pond in the 1880s. "How we did cling to Grandma's or Mother's hand and hurry her along up Front Street where . . . a shady lane turned off toward the Green Brook and Tier's little pond. Today there may be places as cool and inviting, but I doubt it . . . a place where the heavy white dishes curled thickly about the edges; where the chairbacks too curled in a well-remembered design; where the chocolate, strawberry and vanilla ice cream mounded itself up inches high . . . it was simply our idea of Heaven." Tier's ice-cream pavilion burned, and Plainfield lost its downtown treasure. The site and the pond itself disappeared beneath asphalt and macadam, a sacrifice to urban development.

Four

PORCHES, PEONIES, AND PONIES

Eliza Elvira Kenyon, principal of the Plainfield Seminary, has left written testimony of her desire to join the growing ranks of householders willing to accept guests during Plainfield's heyday as a summer resort. Her advertisement follows:

"Wanted—a few first class boarders for eight or ten weeks in the country. Persons who would hold the host responsible for the weather need not apply. Persons who have never seen a bat or a water bug or a fly or a mosquito need not apply. Persons who expect to get quarters in a large airy brick building with high ceilings and extensive well kept grounds at the same rate as in a low ceiling wooden building with no grounds need not apply. People who require that all servants work shall be laid aside and all conversation suppressed for their afternoon naps need not apply. Persons who suppose that the whole steak is tenderloin need not apply. Persons who wish their nurses and babies to sit in the parlor need not apply."—From *Reflections of Old Plainfield*; Edward W. Taylor; Plainfield, N.J.; 1976.

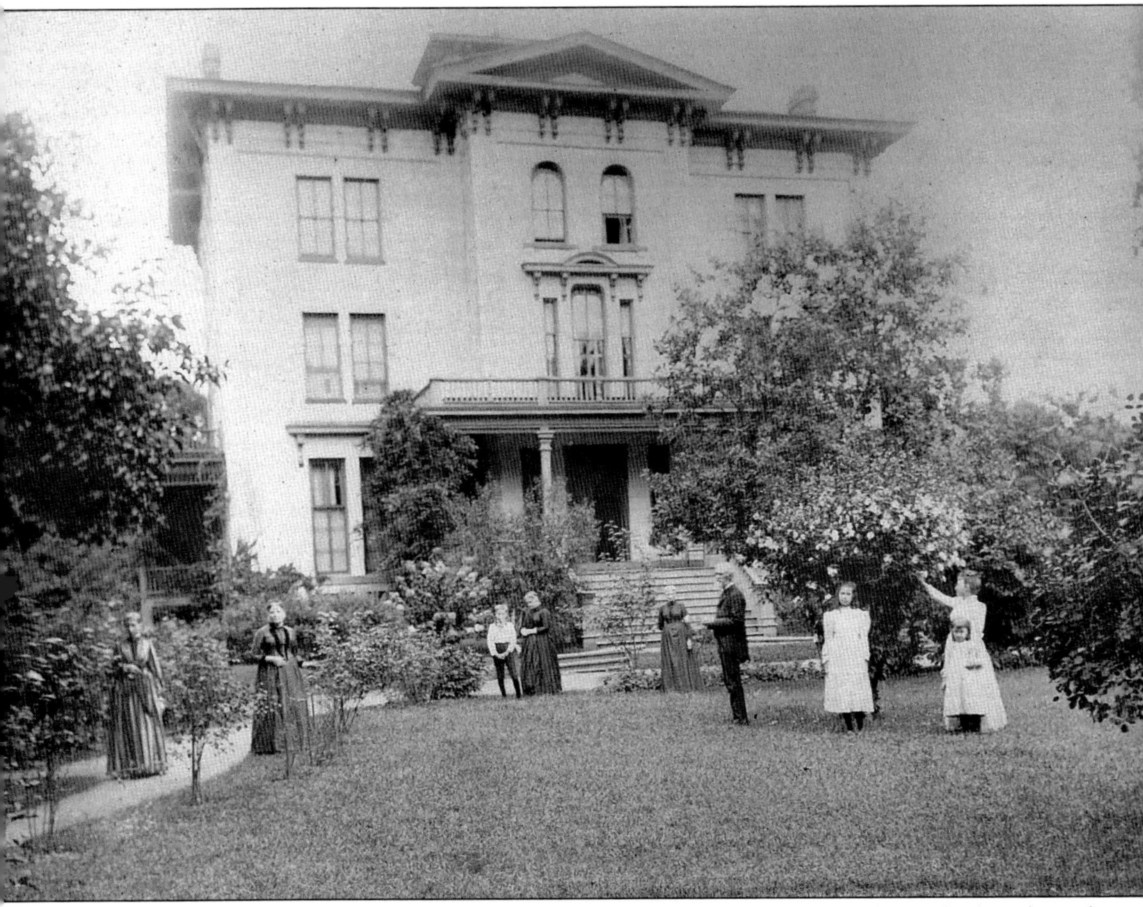

It sounds strait-laced, but Eliza Elvira Kenyon's tongue-in-cheek humor shines forth in her ad for summer boarders. Her school, the Plainfield Seminary, opened in 1867. Eliza Elvira Kenyon was an active civic leader, founding both the Monday Afternoon Club and the Auxiliary of Muhlenberg Hospital. A pupil at the school recalls that "Mr. Dawes in white tie and tails in mid-afternoon, presided weekly at Miss Kenyon's Seminary, where we were later instructed in the correct manner of walking, sitting, bending and waltzing to Strauss."

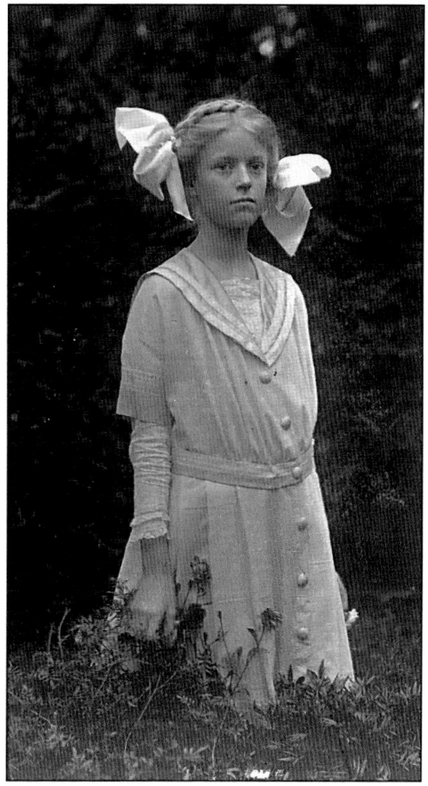

Margaret Kimball (right), and Dorothea Dix Lawrence (below), were best friends during their school days at the Plainfield Seminary. The classmates shared many interests and similarities in dress. Perhaps bows were popular with beaux in the 1915–1917 era.

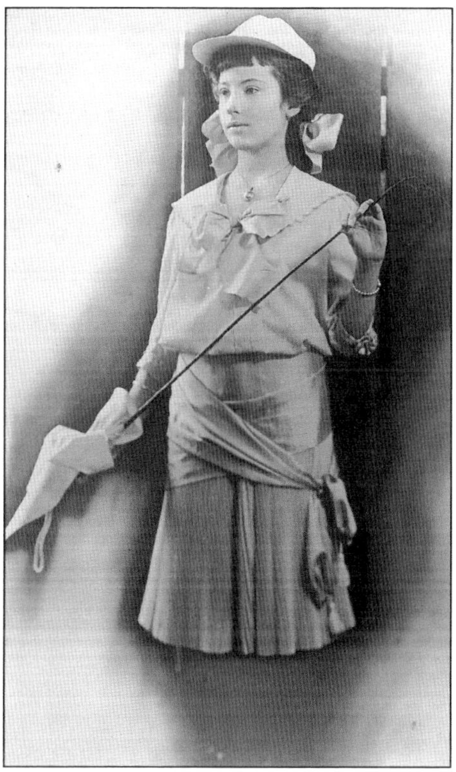

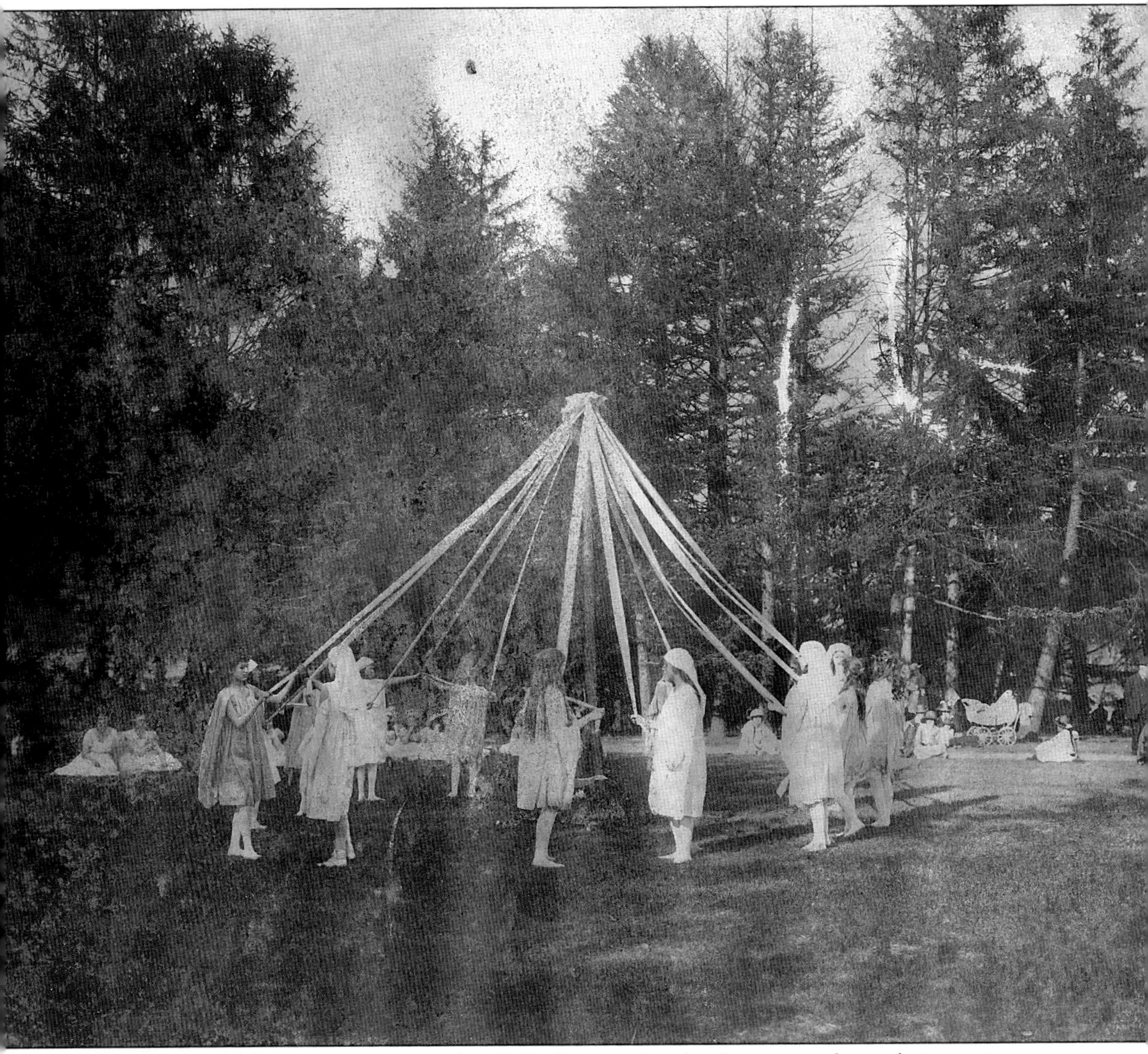

May Day celebrations in the early 1900s had evolved a long way from their ancient roots. Dancing around the maypole was an annual event at the Plainfield Seminary, symbolizing a welcome to spring and a rebirth of nature. Also, with the dances and games, May Day was fun. The long streamers extending from the maypole symbolized the rays of the sun.

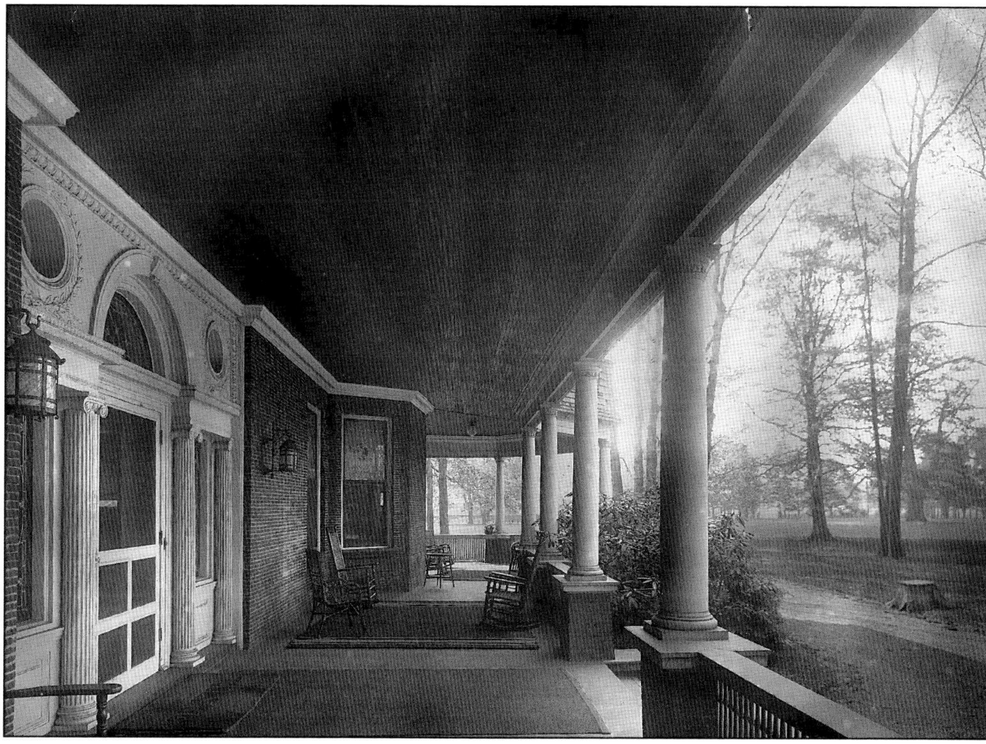

Porches were as fascinatingly diverse as the architecture of the homes they graced. Many were original to the house; others were added to impress the neighbors; some were remodeled to update a home's facade. One-upmanship was popular with every generation.

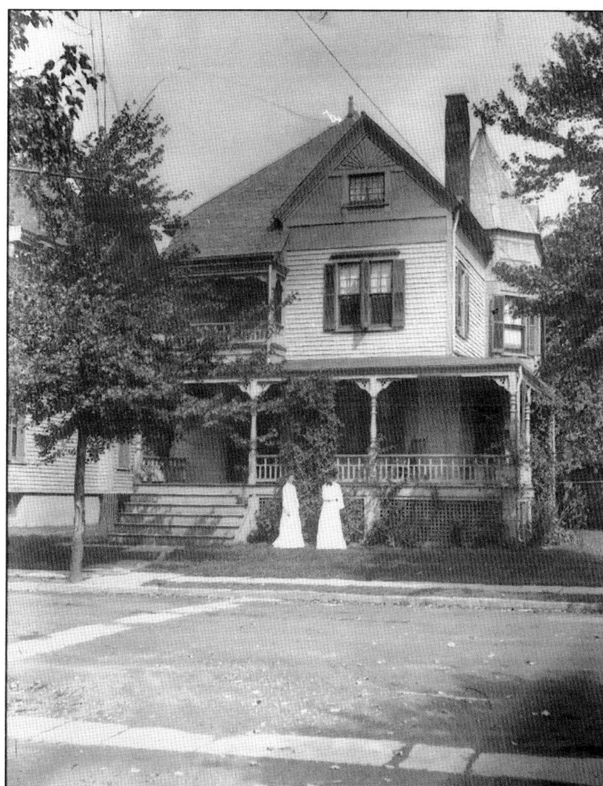

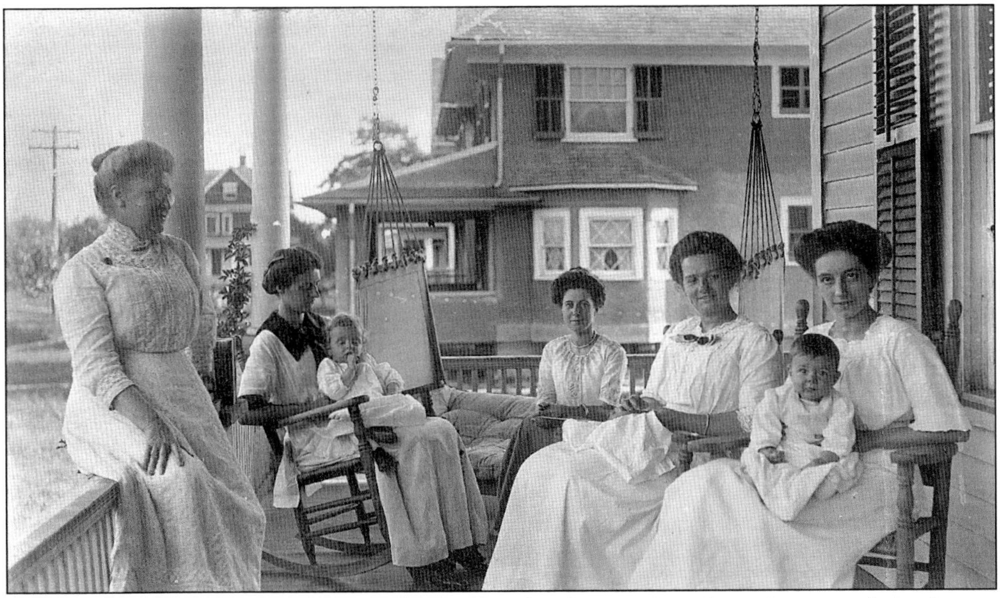

Unlike today, summer social life took place at the front rather than the rear of the house. Homeowners wanted to observe passersby—and be noticed by them. Porches were the proper place for wicker, rocking chairs, climbing roses and wisteria, afternoon tea, hammocks, naps, courting couples, and firefly watching on a summer night. Above, the women of Lenox Avenue gather on a fine day. Below, Edwin Lawrence catches up on his reading at his Stelle Avenue home.

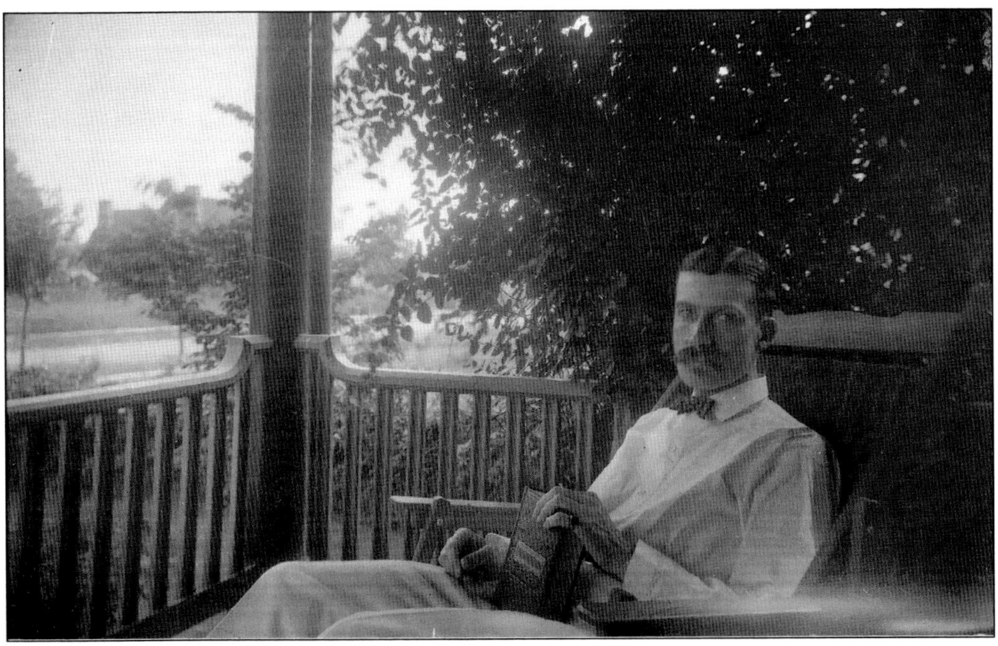

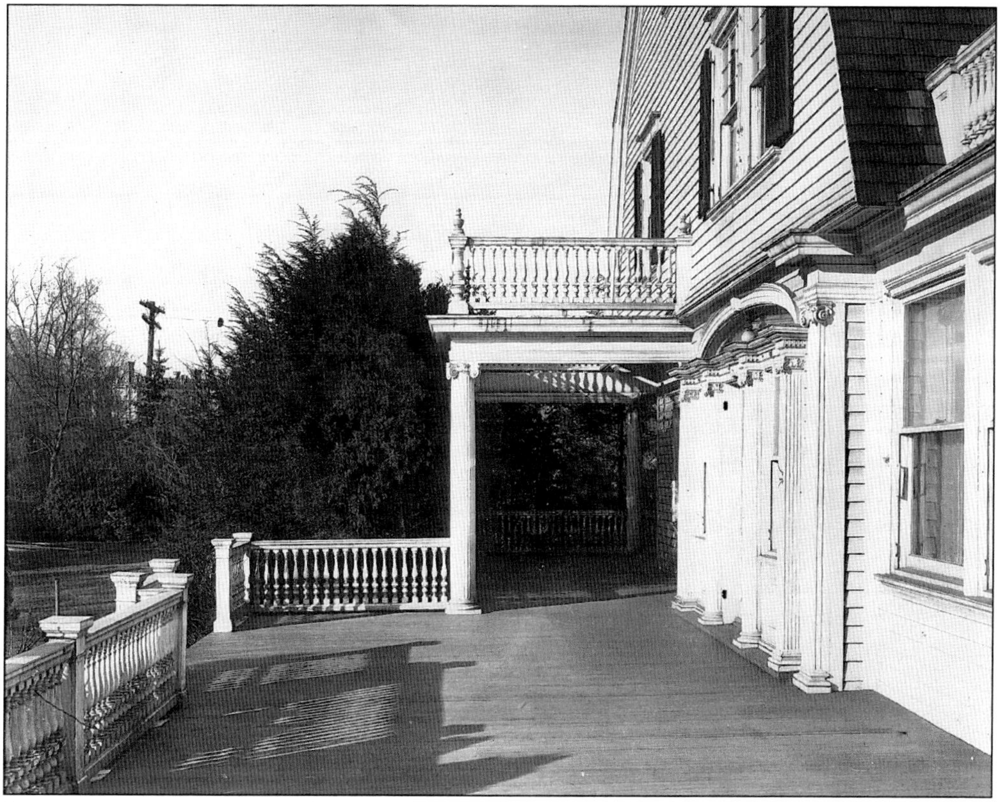

It is interesting to contrast the magnificent with the modest. A porch grandiose enough to stage a summer dance has its appeal for formal occasions, but nothing compares with the restful charm of the familiar.

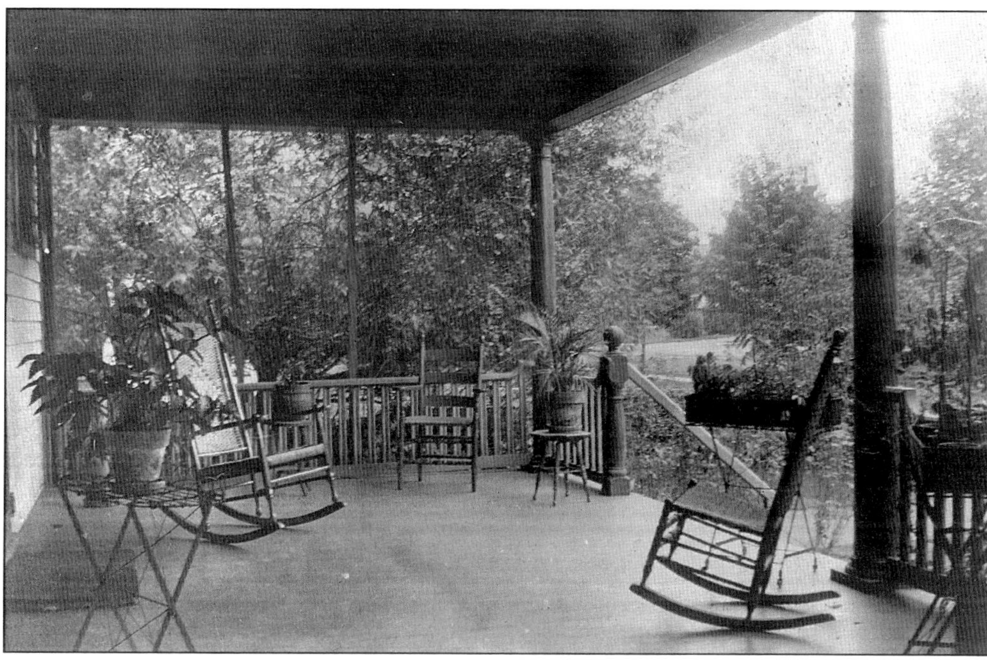

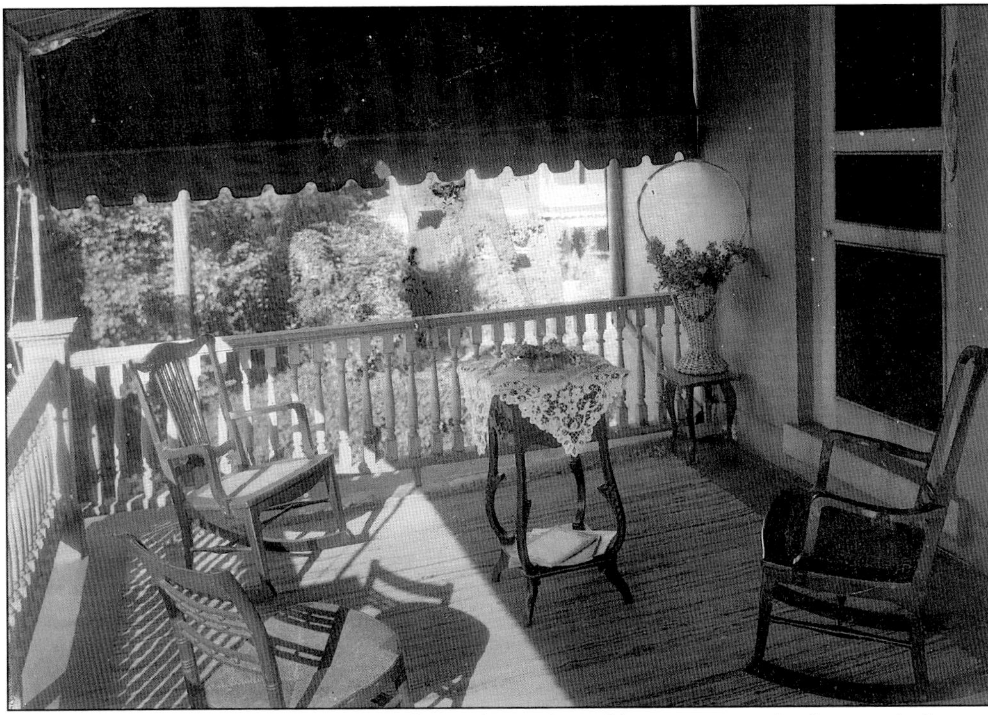

A preference for socializing on the porch may be explained by comparing the front with the rear of typical vintage buildings: comfort and shade at one end, austerity and outhouses at the other. Backyards served necessary purposes, along with space for vegetable patches, clotheslines, and a chicken or two.

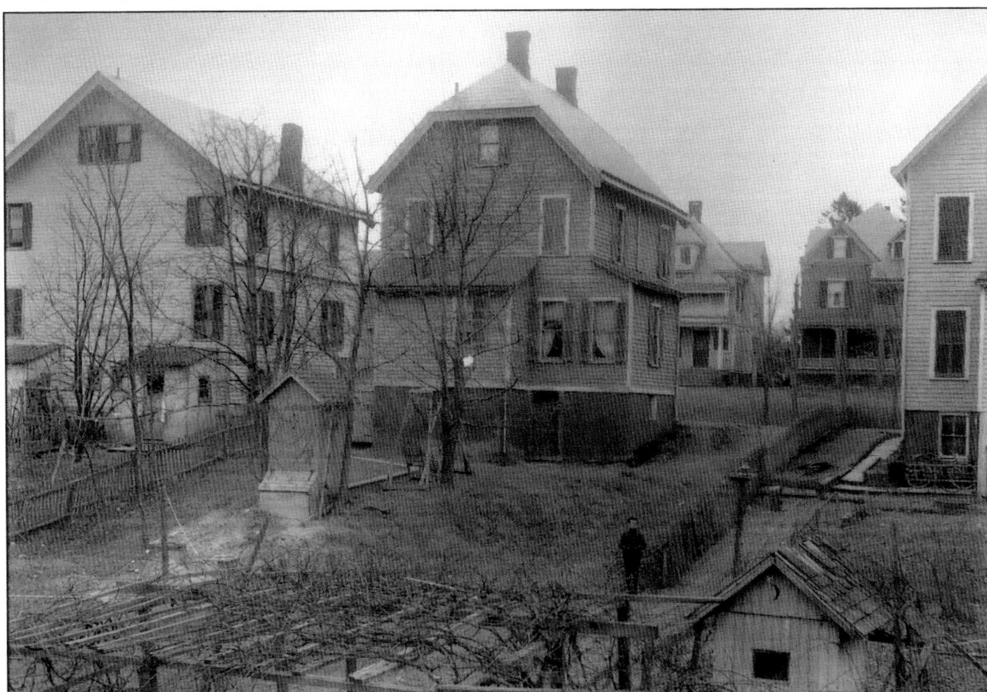

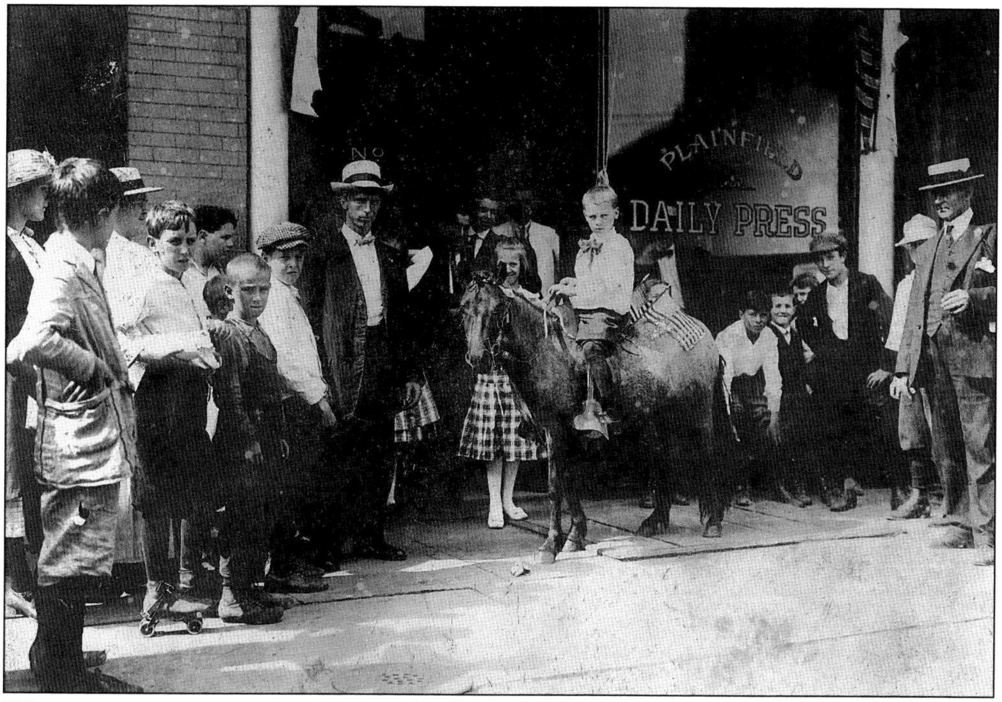

What youngster at some point in childhood has not yearned for a pony? Many 19th-century children were fortunate in that respect, for ponies and pony carts were often seen in residential areas.

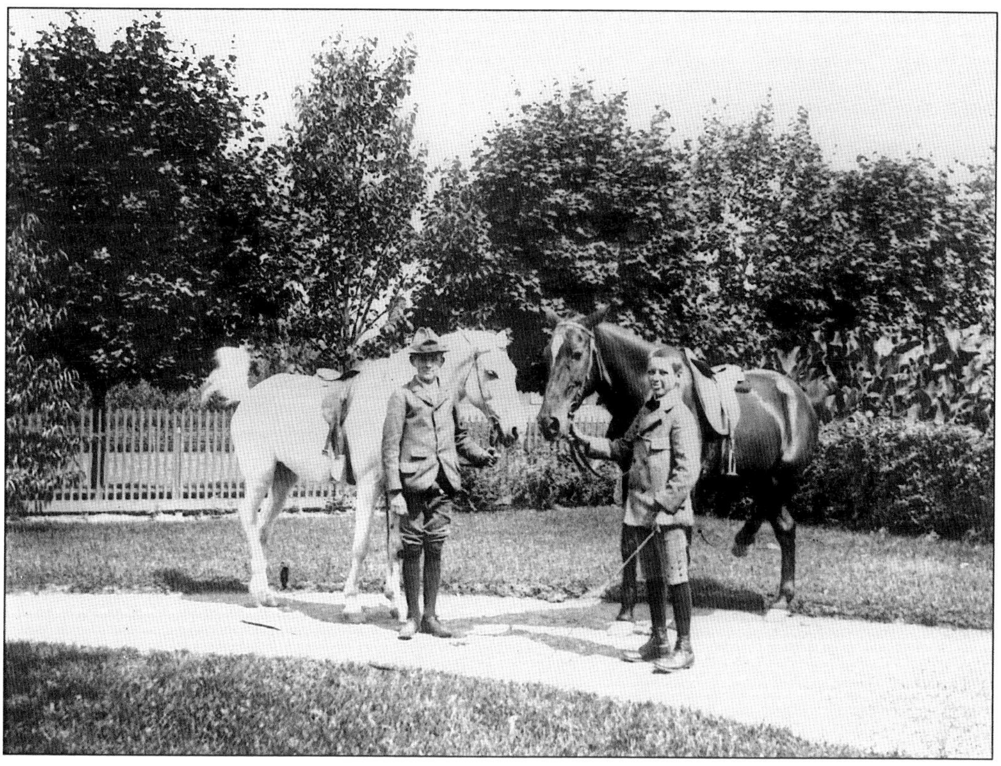

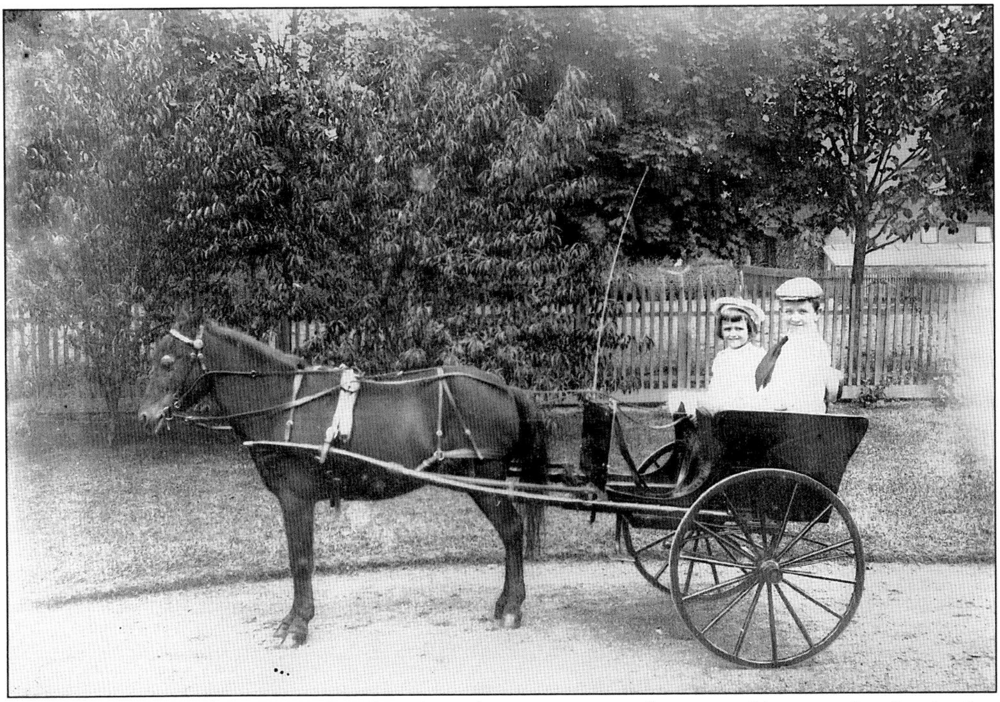

While ponies were the norm, other four-footed creatures were also pressed into service. Intriguing and attractive, this billy goat must have raised a few eyebrows—and a few jealousies—among neighborhood children.

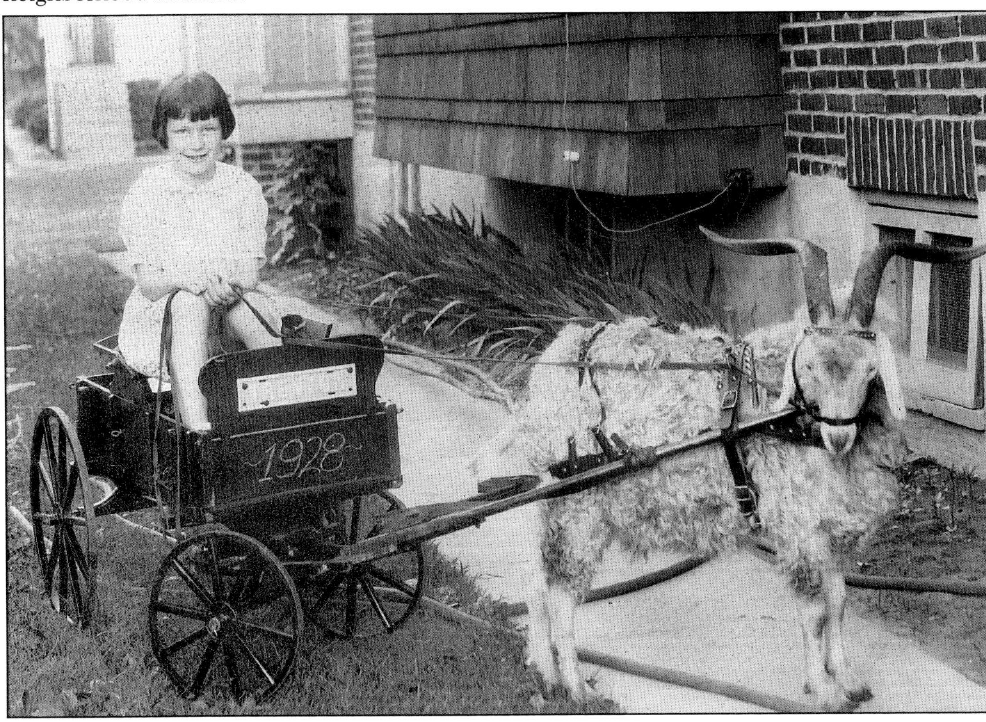

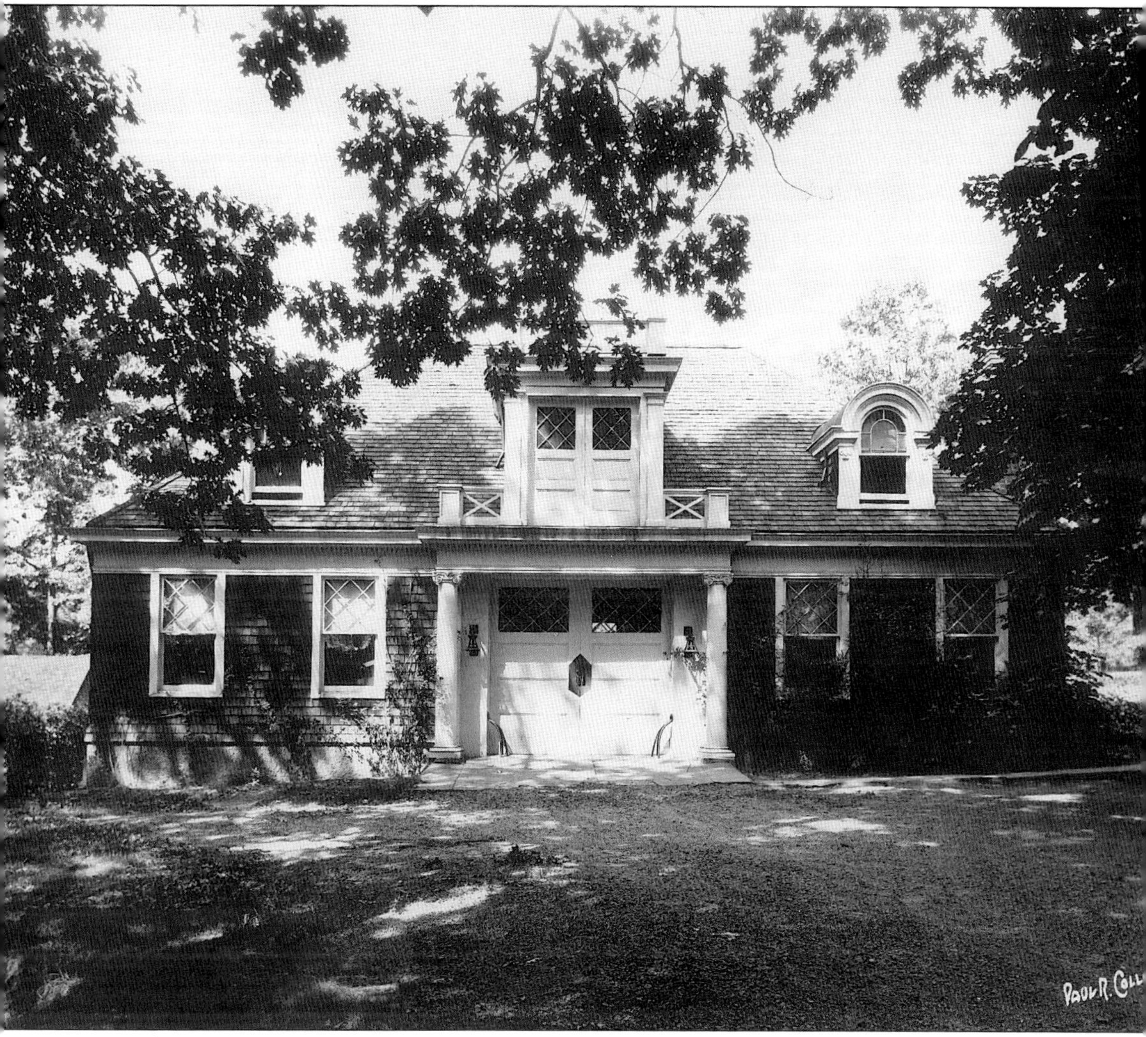

Carriage houses were prolific in Plainfield's wealthier residential areas. Here, the horses and ponies, their carriages and carts and, maybe, even the goat were housed. Families with less spacious grounds boarded their animals at livery stables in town. A great variety of these outbuildings still remain, remodeled for the homeowner rather than the livestock. This charming Colonial Revival carriage house was converted later in its life to a private residence. Facing Charlotte Road, it originally serviced a handsome home farther up the hill on Belvidere Avenue.

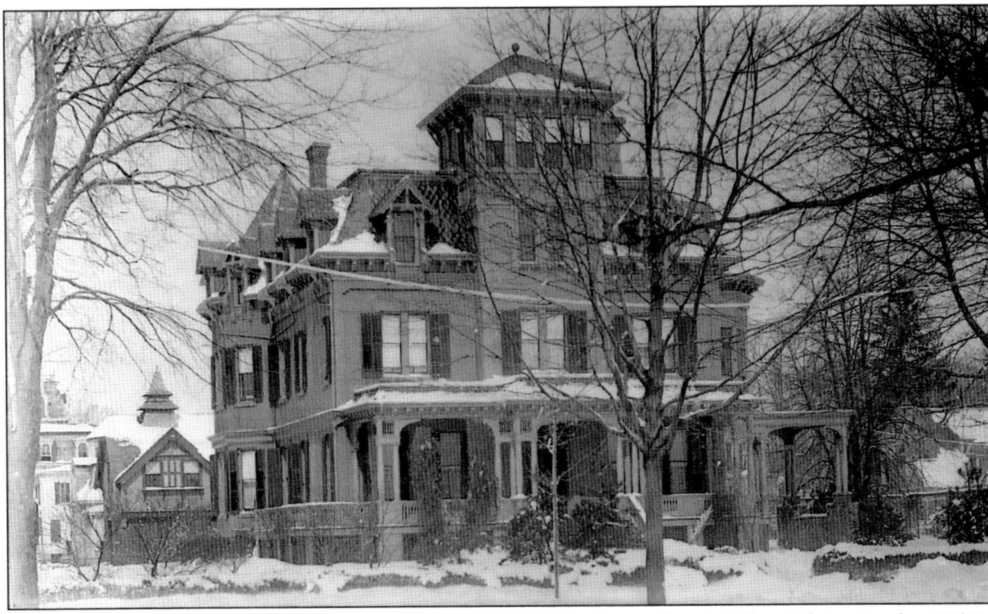

The Cranehurst carriage house on Field Avenue was converted to residential use in the 1930s. Retaining all of its horsey charm on the outside, the inside provides unique and comfortable living space.

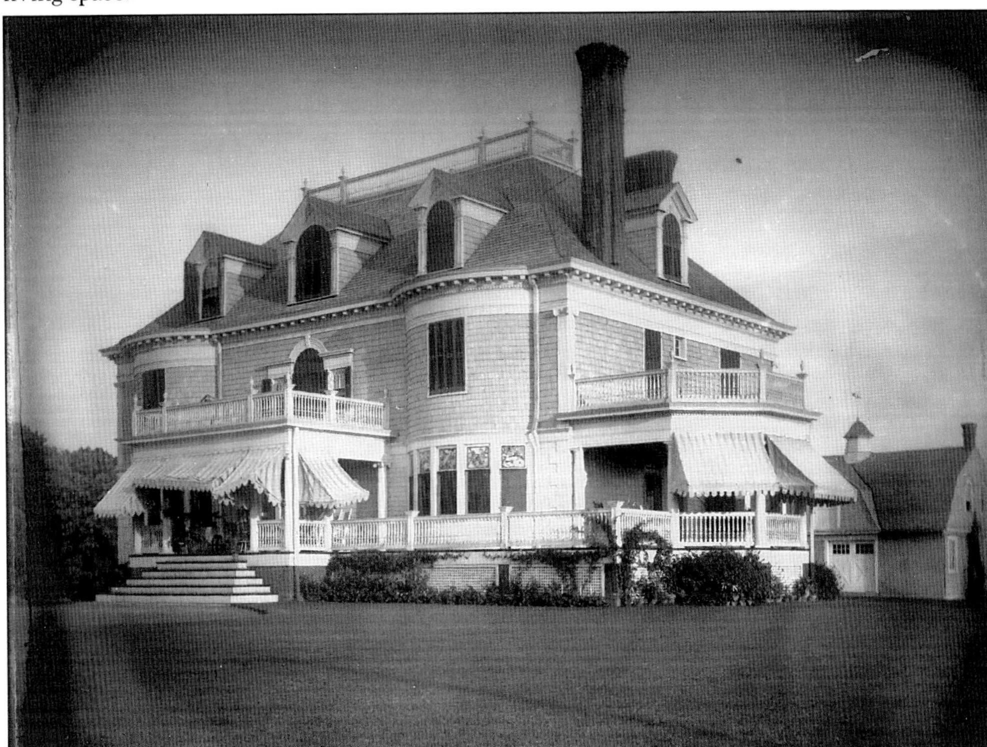

This Neo-Georgian mansion still stands, with minor modifications, on its original Stelle Avenue lot. Its companion carriage house was not so fortunate. The carriage house was destroyed by fire in the 1980s.

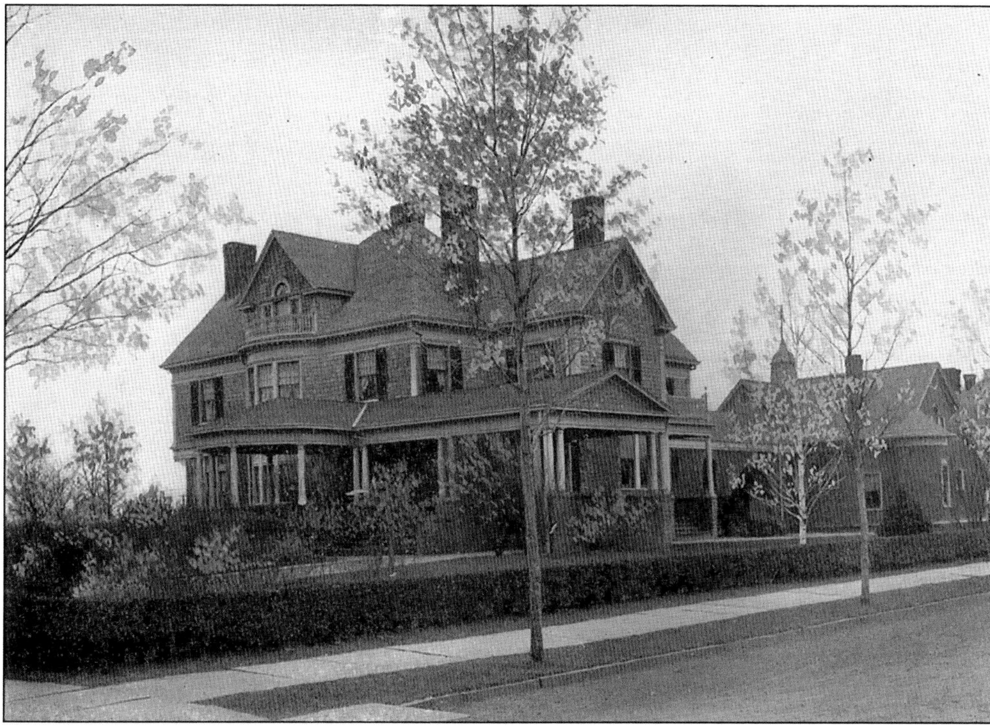

This 1883 carriage house was attached directly to the Charles F. Abbott home, on Central Avenue. It served a double purpose as gatehouse to the mansion's spacious grounds.

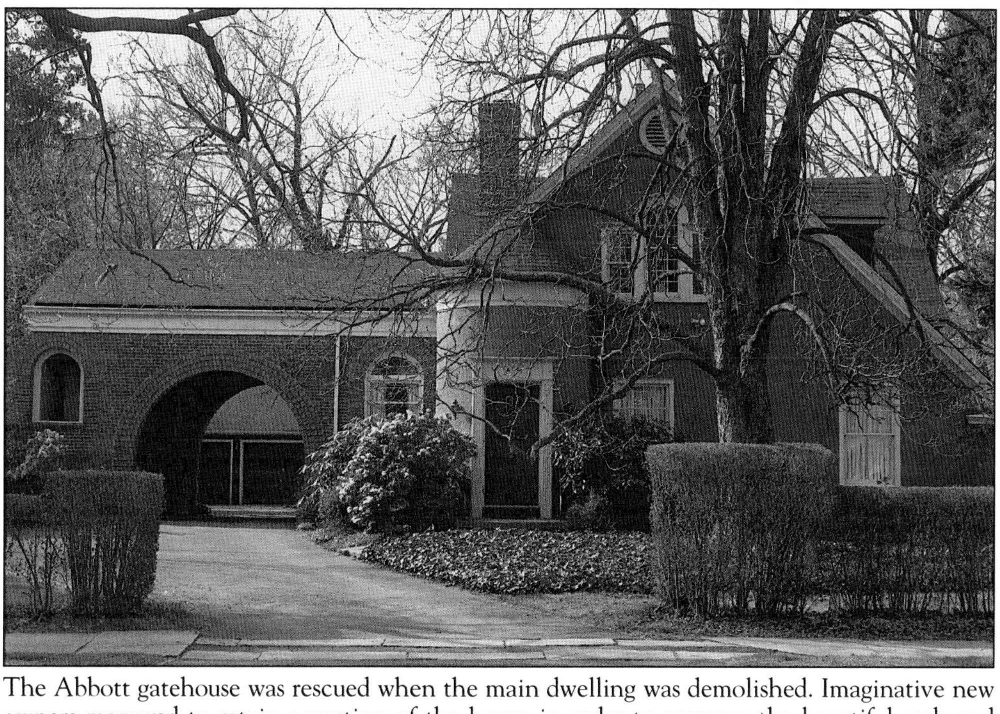

The Abbott gatehouse was rescued when the main dwelling was demolished. Imaginative new owners managed to retain a portion of the house in order to preserve the beautiful arch and curved windows that once connected the two buildings.

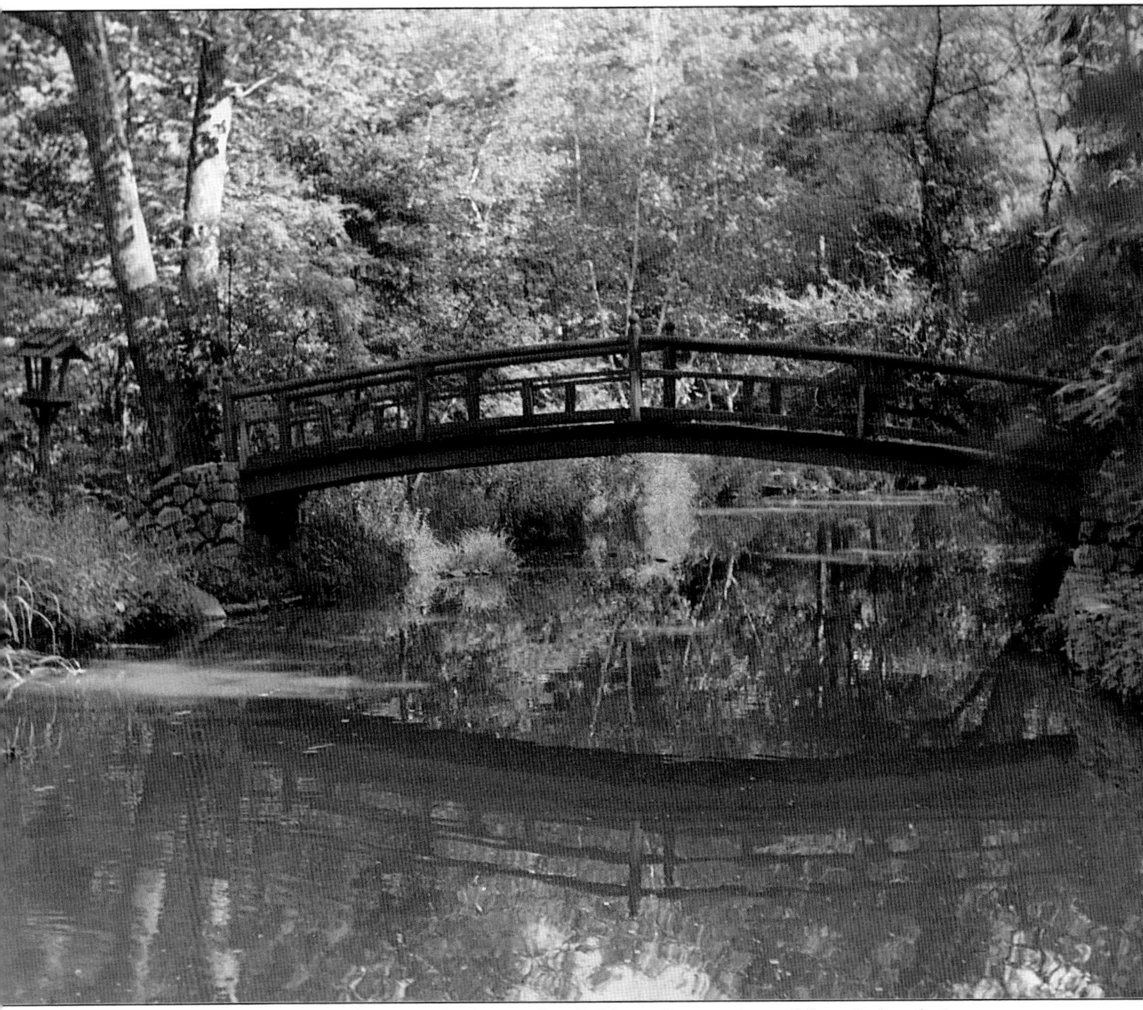

In 1907, Persian consul general Phiroz D. Saklatvala purchased his Leland Avenue estate, remodeling an old farmhouse and transforming the grounds. The spectacular result was Gulestan (Garden of Flowers), designed by renowned architect Takeo Shioto, who designed the New York Botanical Gardens. This bridge over the brook duplicates the Japanese imperial family's sacred bridge at Nikko, Japan. Today, a contemporary co-op complex is enhanced by the vision of its former owner.

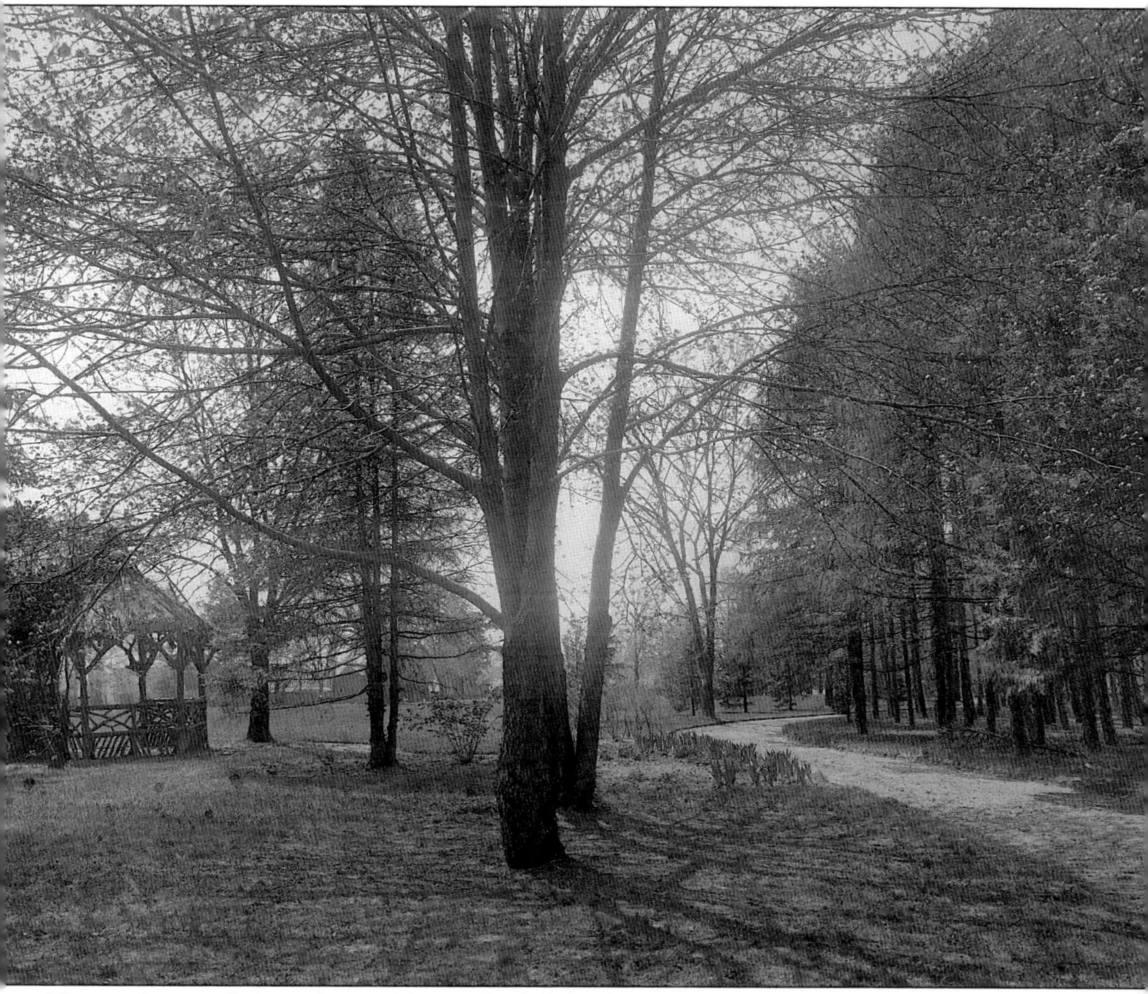

The gardens at Oakwood were like an English landscape painting. Expansive, natural, and serene, the woodland setting was much admired and imitated in its day. The rustic gazebo lends a human touch.

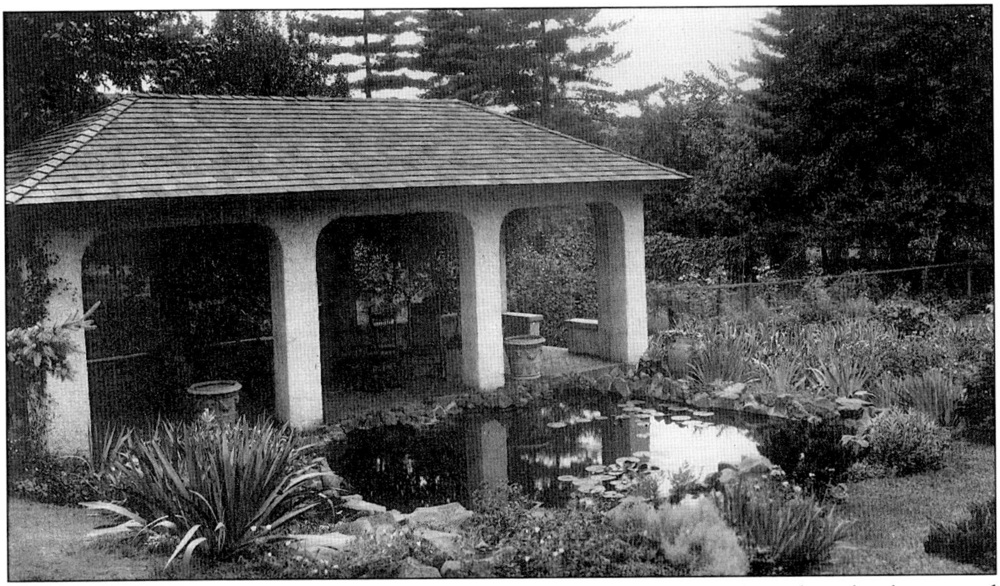

Garden structures introduce the hand of man to a natural setting. A formal garden house and fish pond on Hillside Avenue (above) and a pergola on Stelle Avenue (below) add notes of grace to a garden symphony.

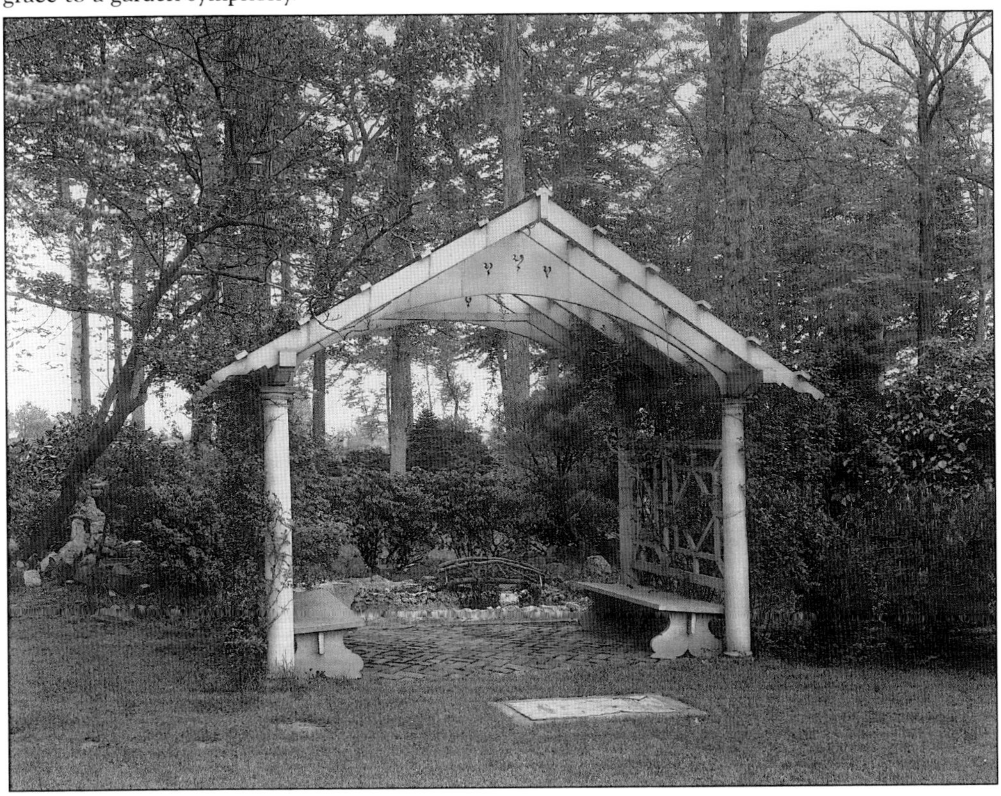

Five

DOWNTOWN DIVERSIONS

Four-footed transportation was giving way to horsepower of another kind when the following advertisement appeared in the *Plainfield Courier-News* edition of January 11, 1917:

"Mr. Louis Chevrolet invites you to come to the automobile show and see the American Six Made In Plainfield. In producing this new car Louis Chevrolet—whose name is another word for automobile leadership—has given to the world a car that is distinctly uncommon among cars of moderate price. It is uncommon in its individual lines and superior finish. It is uncommon in its ample proportions and generous dimensions. It is uncommon in its sound and substantial construction. It is uncommon in its driving ease and riding comfort. In all that goes to make an automobile worth owning American Six is a car of uncommon distinction. See it at the Palace—on the fourth floor. American Six $1285."—The Plainfield Courier-News Company, Plainfield, N.J.; 1917.

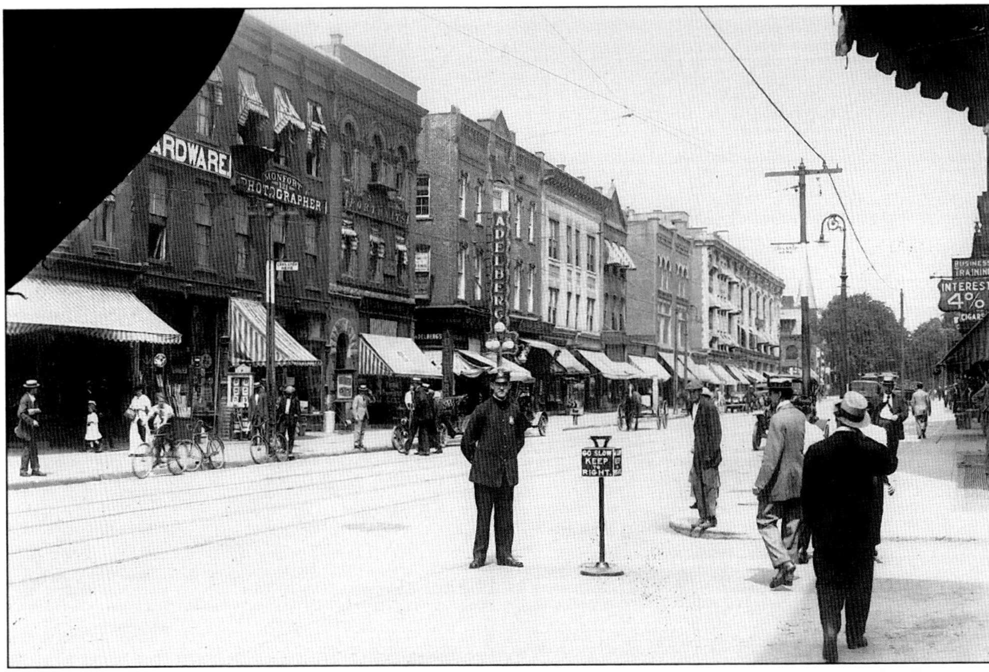

Solid brick and stucco buildings replaced their wooden predecessors along streets in the business district. Less vulnerable to fire, stone was the material of choice when Woolworth's, Van Arsdale's, Woodhull and Martin, Kresge's, the Outlet, the Paris, Masur and Son, Montfort's, Adelberg's, and DeMeza and Blimm were erected. Stone was not a viable alternative for the average small businessman.

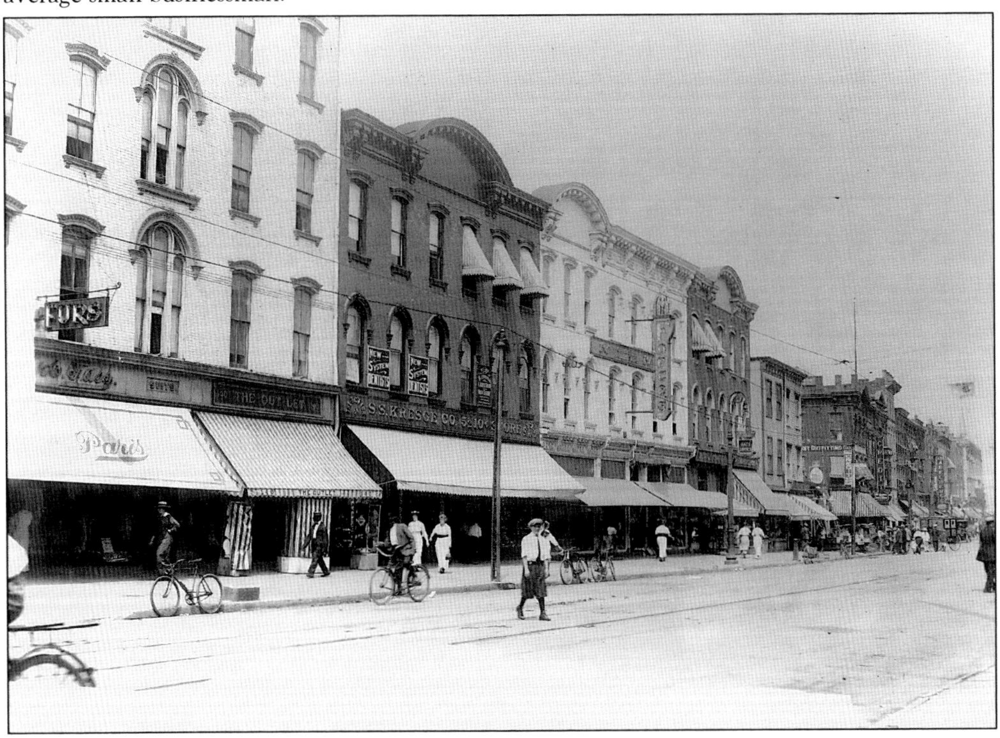

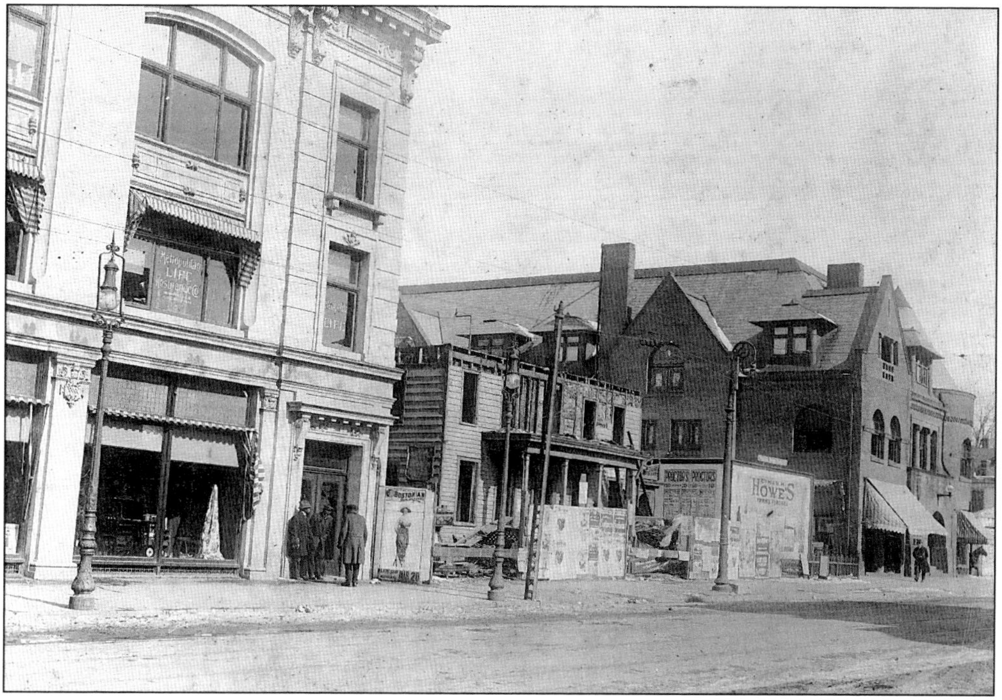

The changing face of downtown Plainfield is captured on film at the moment of transition. A modest East Front Street residence gives way to progress. Consumers' needs took precedence, as more and more shoppers from surrounding towns chose Plainfield as their prime market area.

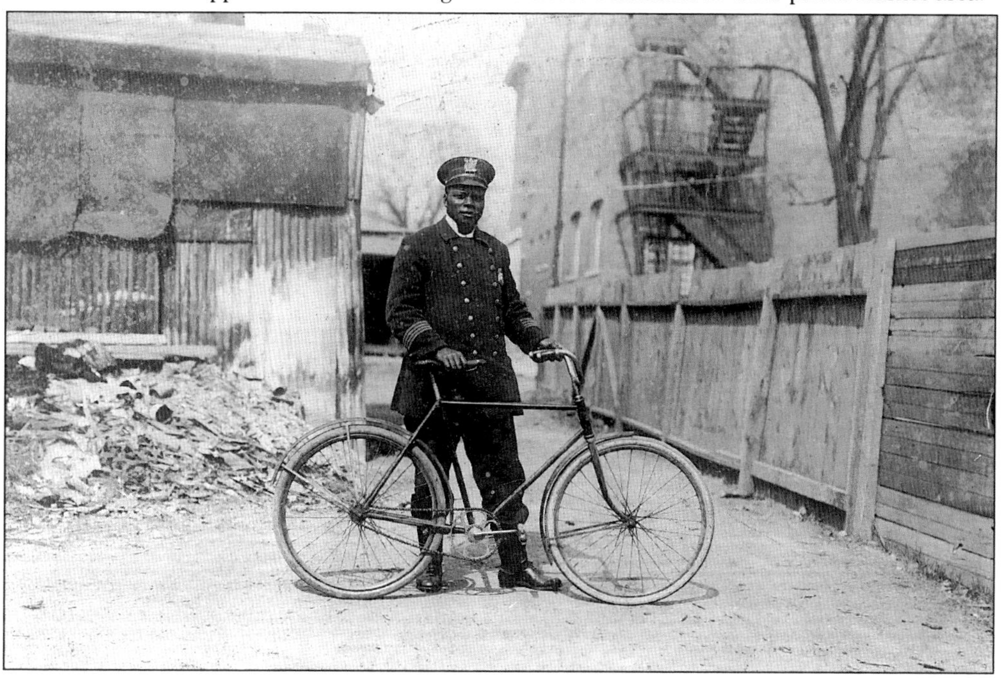

As businesses spread up and down the commercial district, the need for delivery services grew. A handsomely uniformed courier poses beside his wheels. Before the advent of the automobile, the term "wheels" was used exclusively for bicycles.

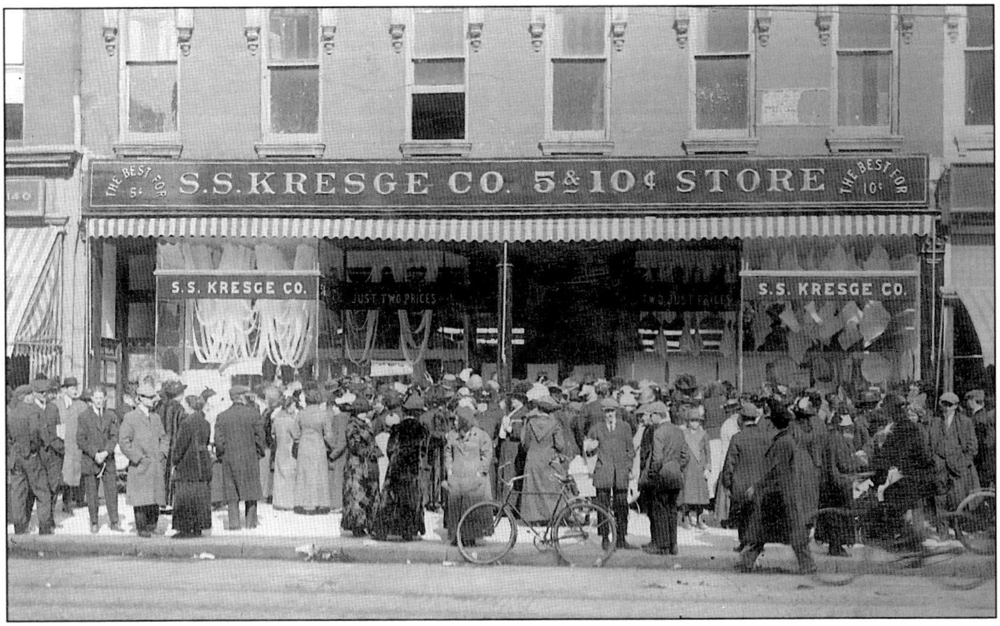

Kresge's opening day in 1917 really drew the crowds. Store openings or not, the city streets were routinely thronged with eager buyers from all over central New Jersey. Shopping in Plainfield was an all-day affair, replete with lunch and/or dinner. There were exceptions to the rule, however, as seen below.

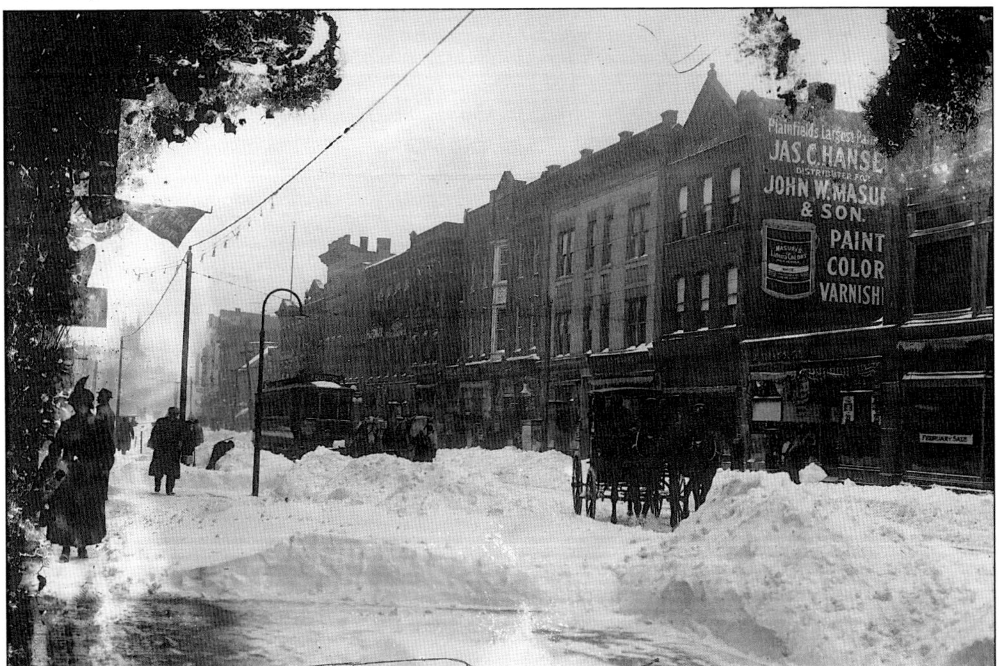

The legendary blizzard of March 12, 1888, hit hard in Plainfield, resulting in terrific winds and 15-foot-high snowdrifts. Commerce came to a virtual halt and, in the days that followed, consumers found that in the stores that were open, the price of eggs had skyrocketed from 10¢ to 19¢ a dozen, while butter had jumped to 20¢ a pound.

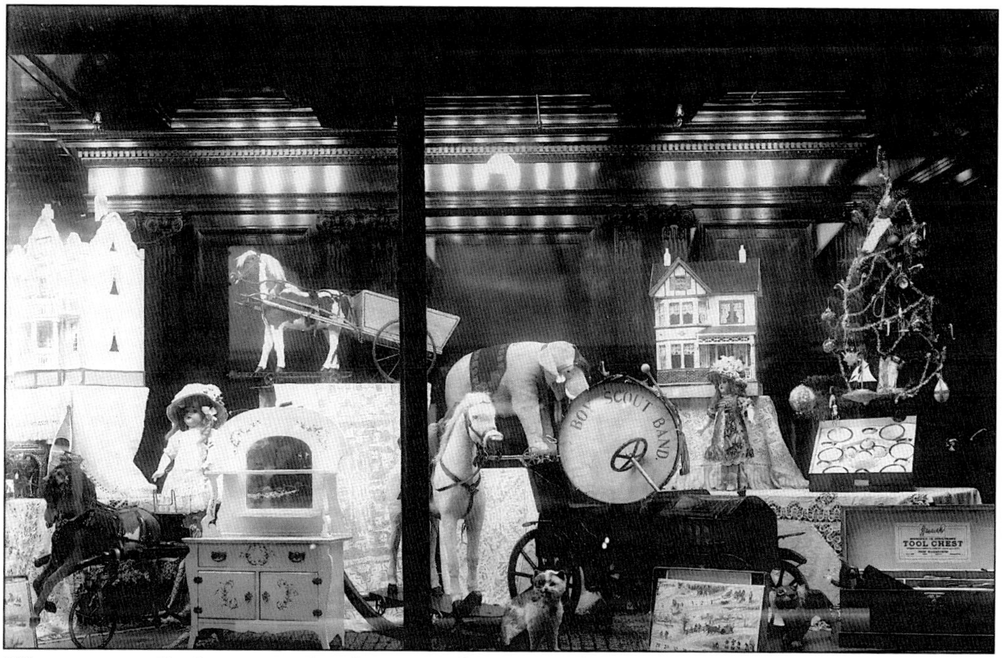

What were all these people shopping for? Everything imaginable. If it was available anywhere, you could find it in Plainfield. In the words of an early-20th-century shopper: "The Plainfield business houses afford every facility for purchasing all that caters to the needs of individual or family."

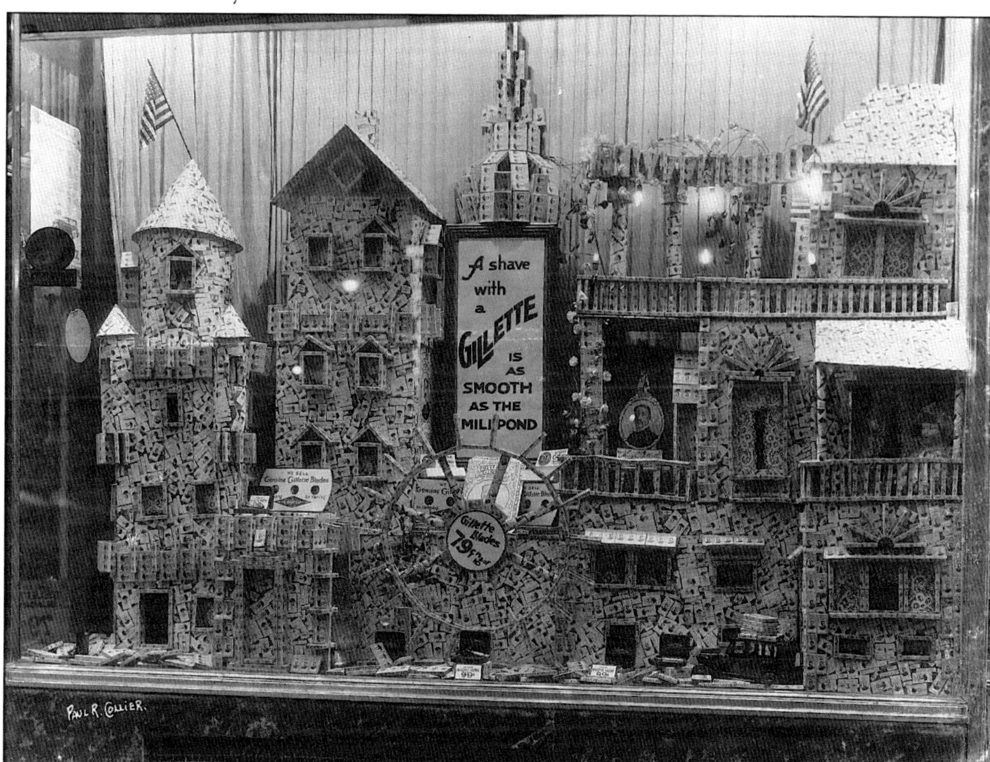

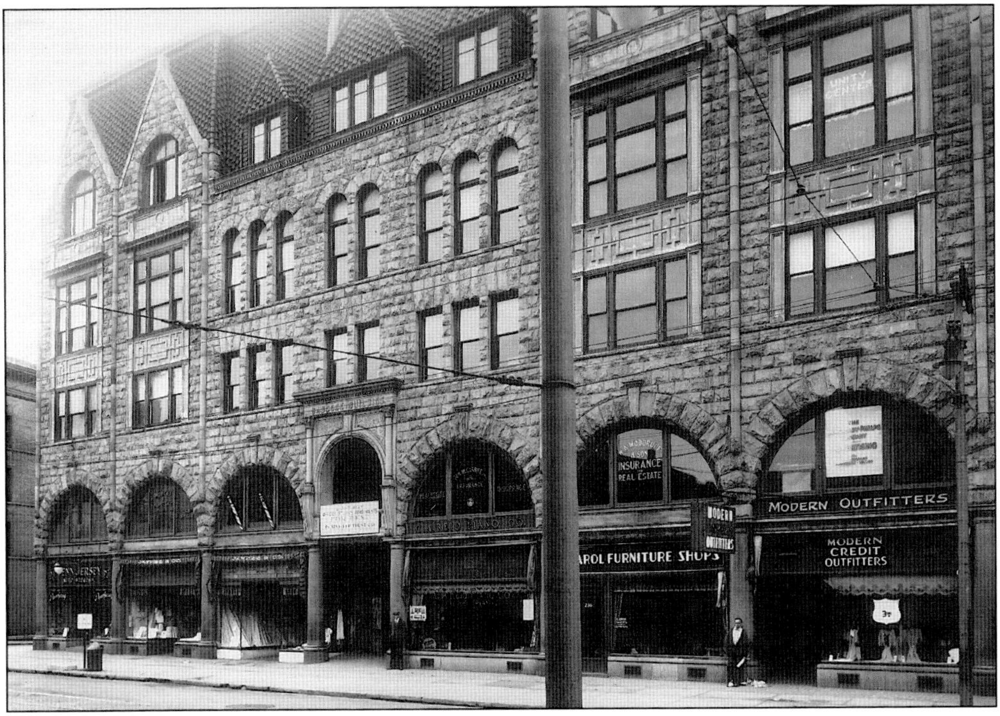

The ill-fated Babcock Building was certainly one of the architectural gems of downtown Plainfield. Then referred to as one of the "finest business houses in the state," it was heavily damaged by a fierce fire on March 6, 1902. Immediately rebuilt, it suffered two more fires before being demolished in the late 1960s.

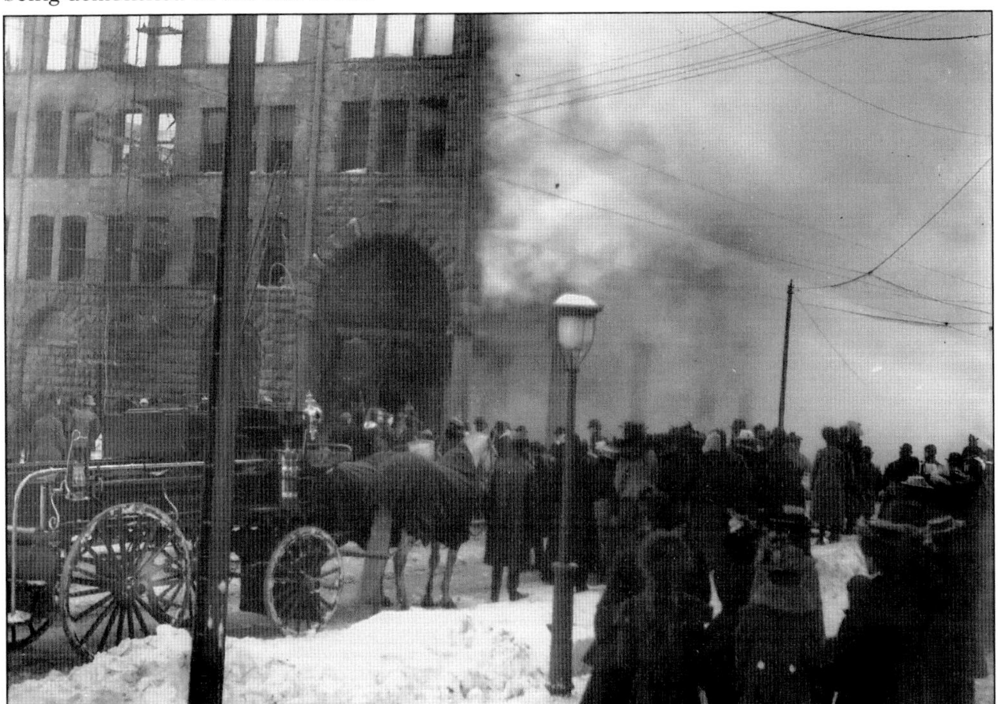

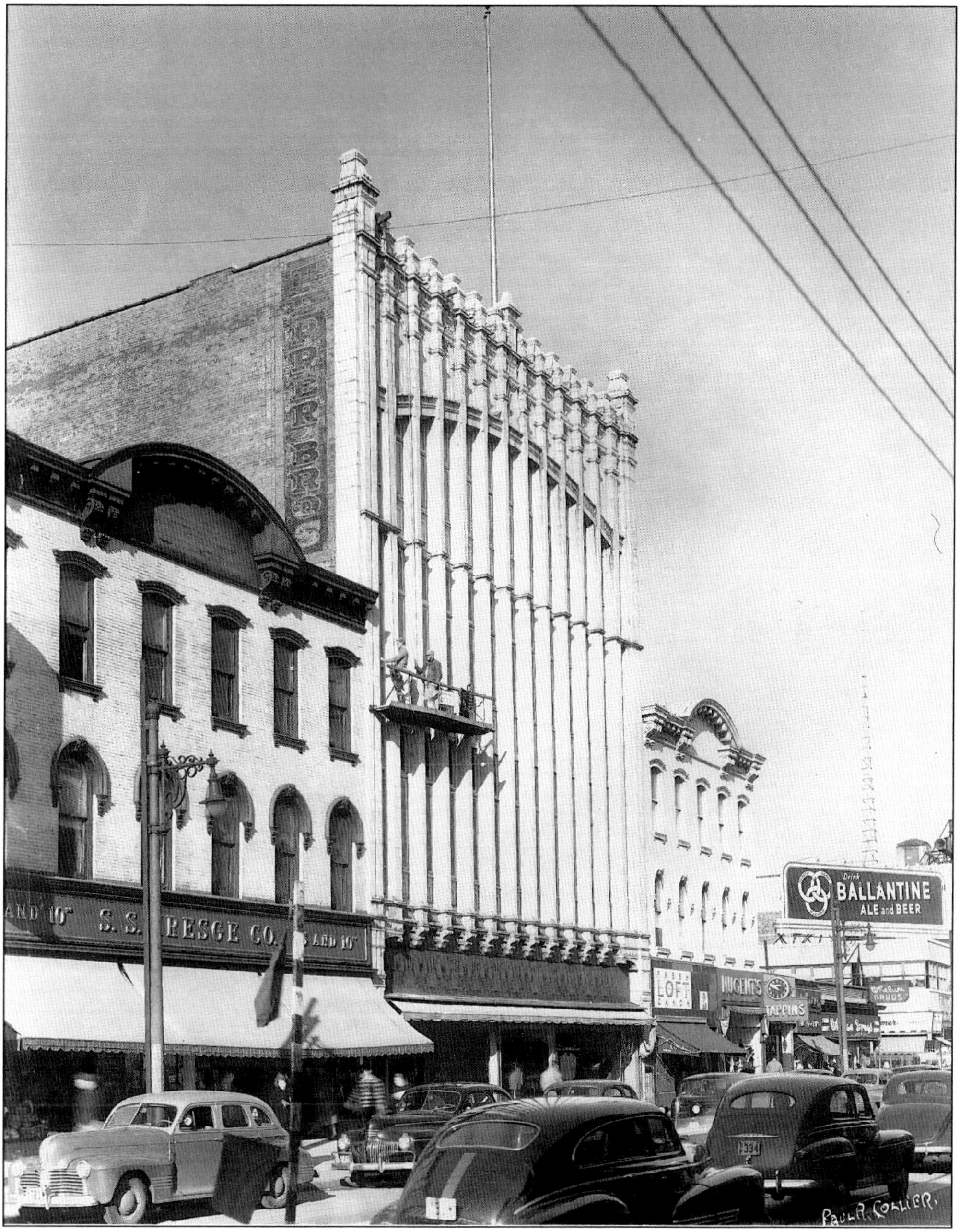

Established in 1907, Tepper Brothers was opening a smart new store on West Front Street by October 1919. Several thousand people from Plainfield and surrounding areas strolled through the new store to the strains of instrumental music. Later, the employees were treated to a celebratory dinner at the Queen City Hotel.

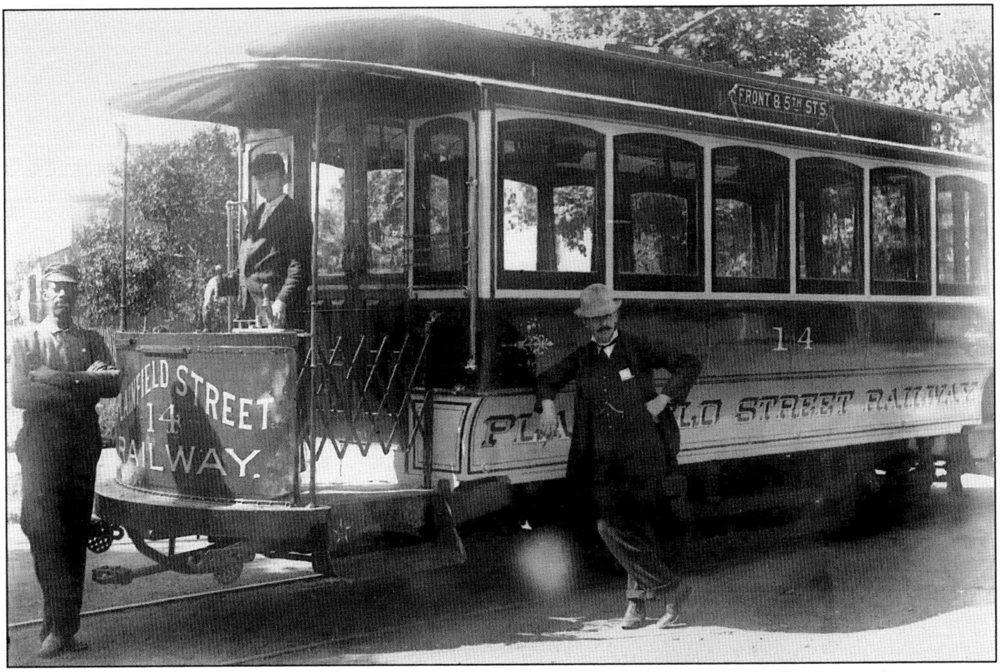

Trolley tracks were laid in 1892, adding greatly to the ease of downtown shopping. Buses were stirred into the metropolitan mix c. 1909. The clang of the trolleys and the blare of the buses were not an unpleasant combination. They signaled growth and prosperity in the business district. A choice of public transportation existed until 1935, when trolleys ceased to run.

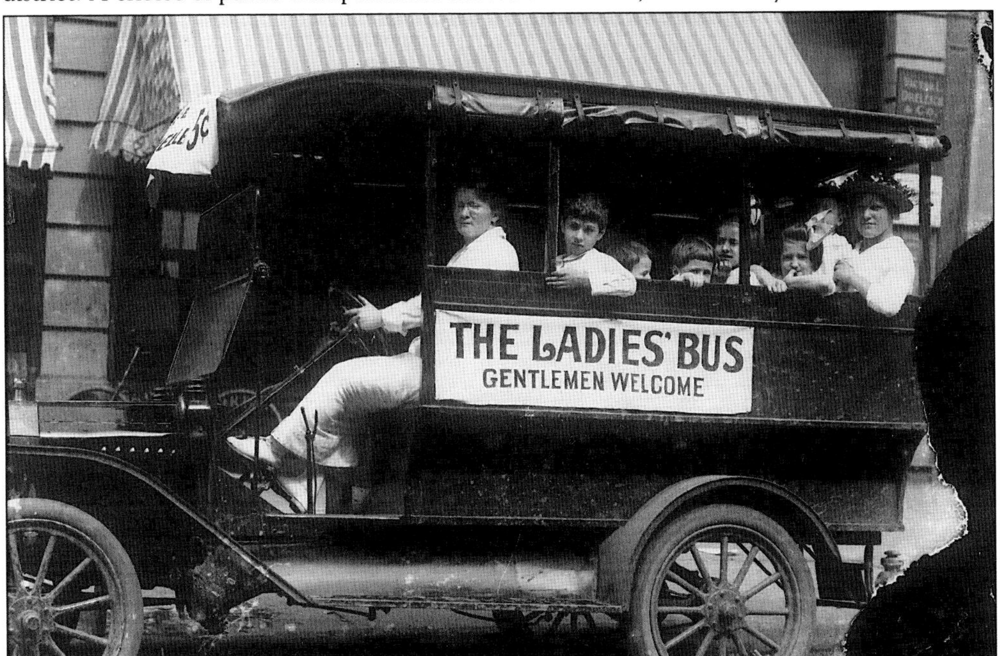

Bus service was private as well as public. Staff and students at Hartridge School had their own means of traveling about town. Privacy gave way to convenience, however, if a likely young fellow should happen by.

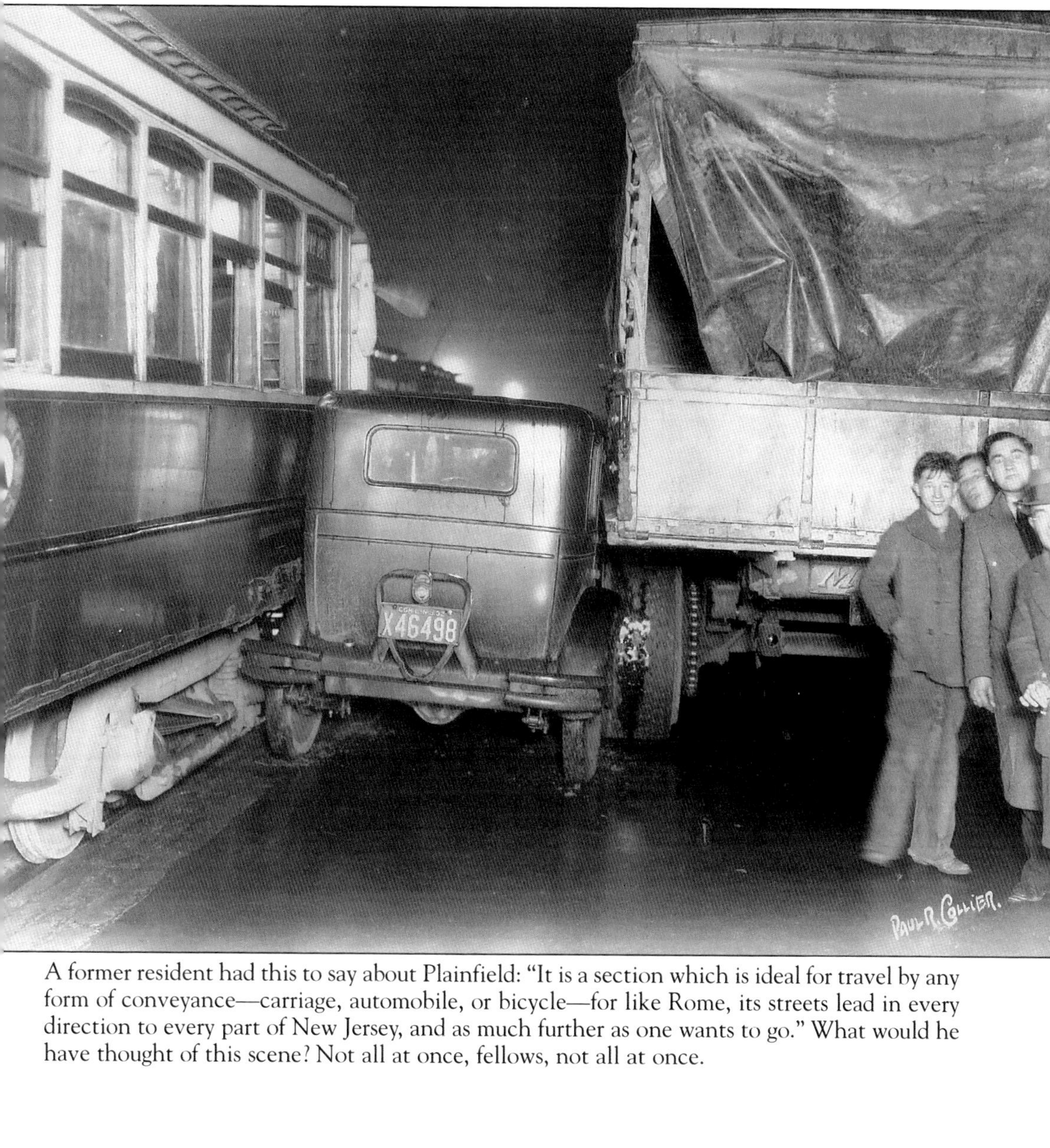

A former resident had this to say about Plainfield: "It is a section which is ideal for travel by any form of conveyance—carriage, automobile, or bicycle—for like Rome, its streets lead in every direction to every part of New Jersey, and as much further as one wants to go." What would he have thought of this scene? Not all at once, fellows, not all at once.

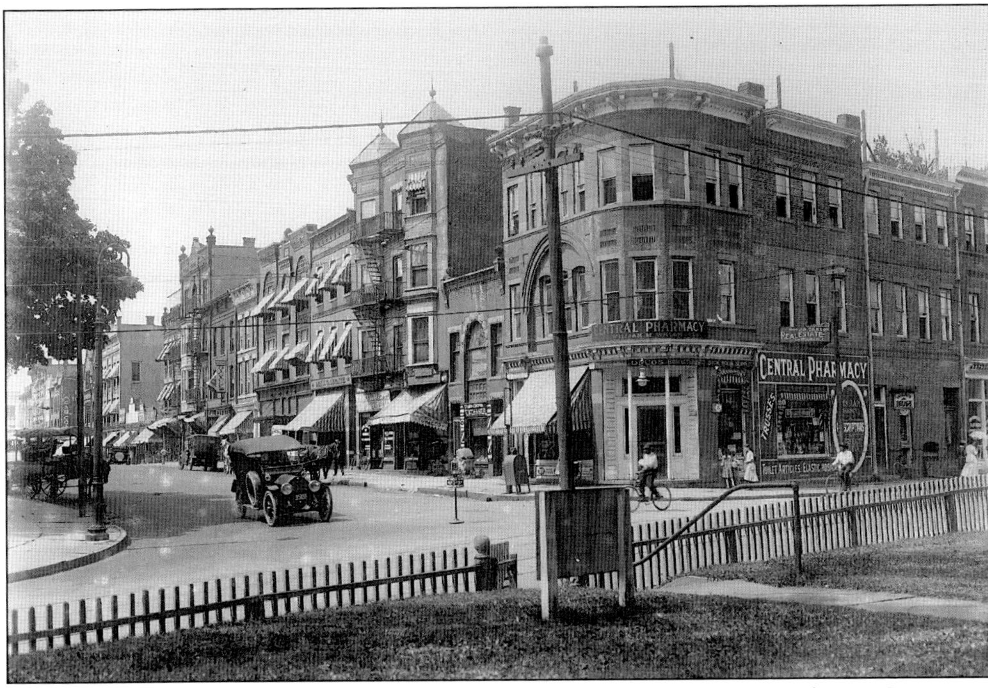

Seen here is a view of North Avenue from the lawn of the Quaker meetinghouse. Impressive Victorian-era commercial buildings line the avenue across from the railroad station. Livery stables were clustered in this hub of transportation. They were replaced at a later date by motorized cab companies.

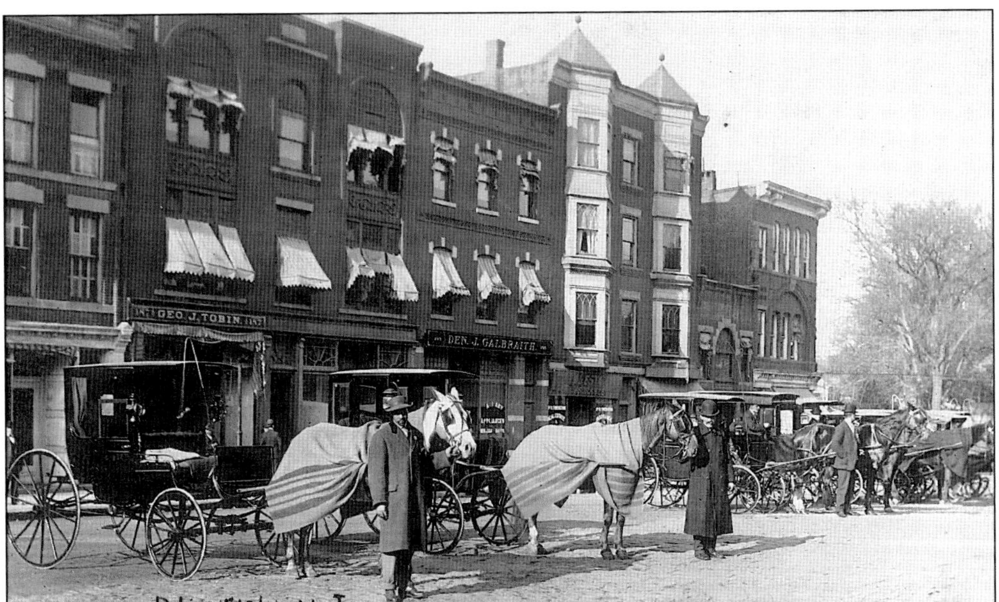

Fancy carriages and handsome horses await patrons at the Plainfield station. In the North Avenue vicinity, livery stables such as Blair's and Robert's stored their buggies and rented and stabled horses for the convenience of all.

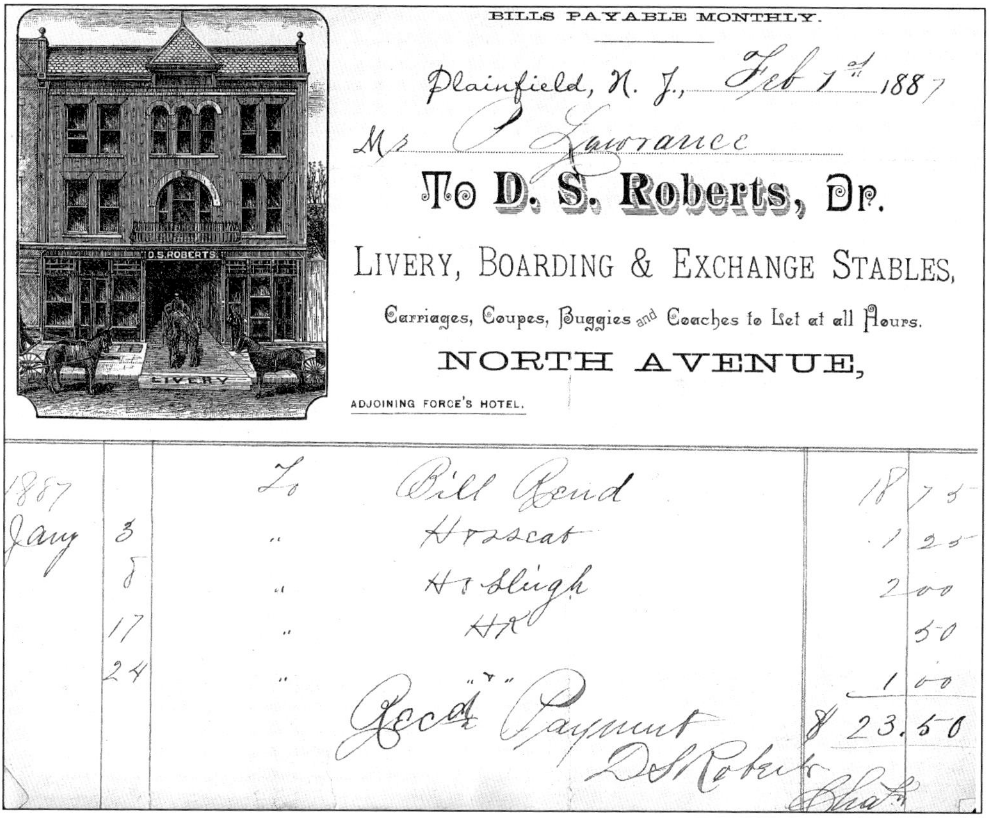

BILLS PAYABLE MONTHLY.

Plainfield, N. J., Feb 1st 1887

Ms P Lawrance

To D. S. Roberts, Dr.

LIVERY, BOARDING & EXCHANGE STABLES,

Carriages, Coupes, Buggies and Coaches to Let at all Hours.

NORTH AVENUE,

ADJOINING FORCE'S HOTEL.

1887		To	Bill Rend	18 75
Jany	3	"	Horsecab	1 25
	8	"	Hs Sleigh	2 00
	17	"	Hs	50
	24	"	"	1 00
			Recd Payment	$ 23.50

D S Roberts

Rates were fairly reasonable. An 1887 billing from D.S. Roberts for the January rental of a horsecab on the third and a horse sleigh on the eighth amounted to $23.50.

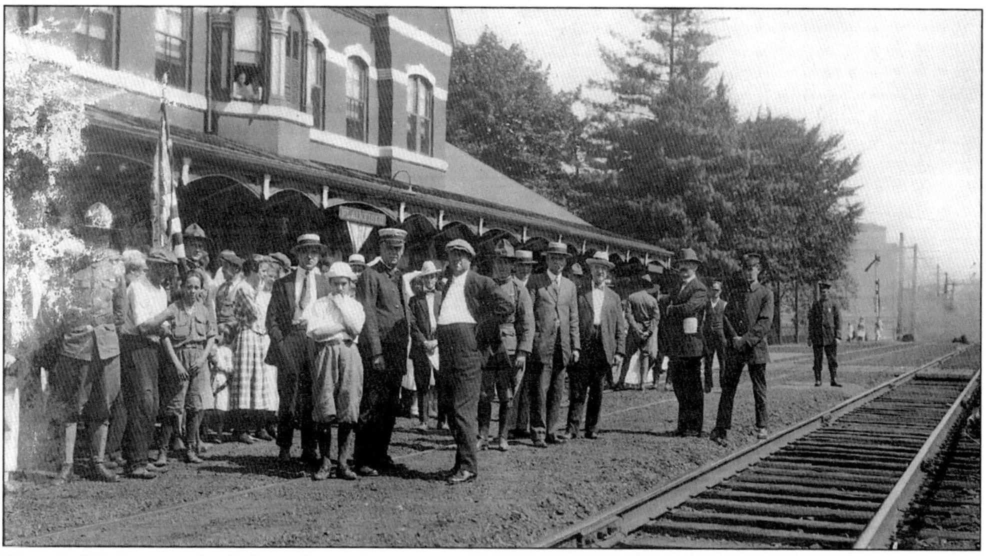

Plainfield's horsecabs did not have long to wait. Business was booming. An observer of the time noted, "More than any other city on the line of the Jersey Central, it has attracted the wealth and fashion of New York to locate here permanently, and its easy access to New York by any one of the 90 trains a day makes the town an ideal place for the busy New York man."

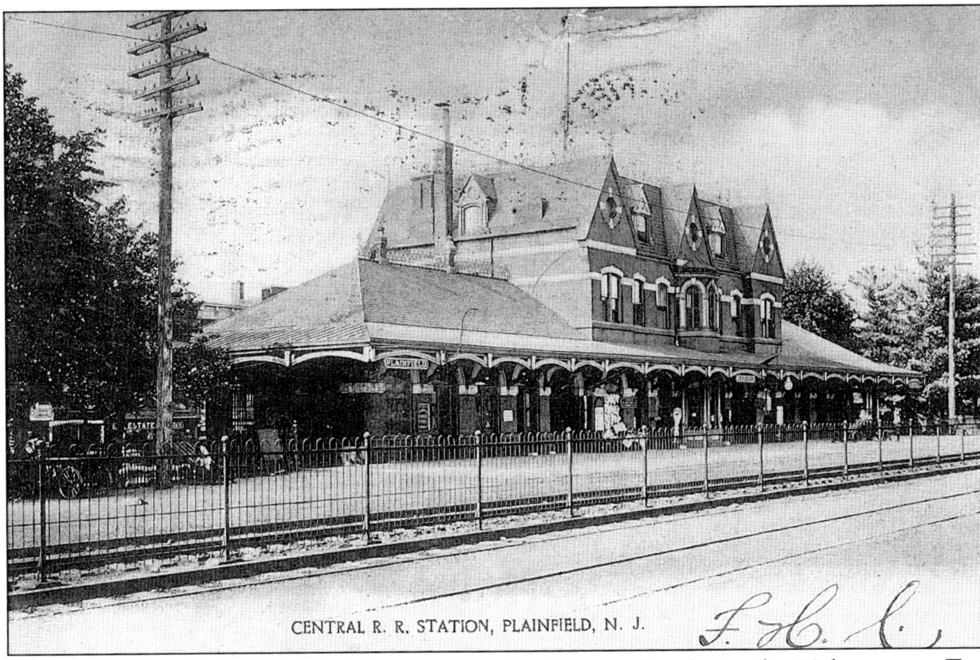

Plainfield had four train stations in a variety of architectural styles in the 19th century. Two stations are pictured here as they appeared in the first decade of the 20th century. The railroad found Plainfield such an important part of its line that it designated club cars exclusively for the use of Plainfield commuters. One resident reminisced, saying, "Father found the daily commute to New York fatiguing despite relaxing games of bridge in the club cars."

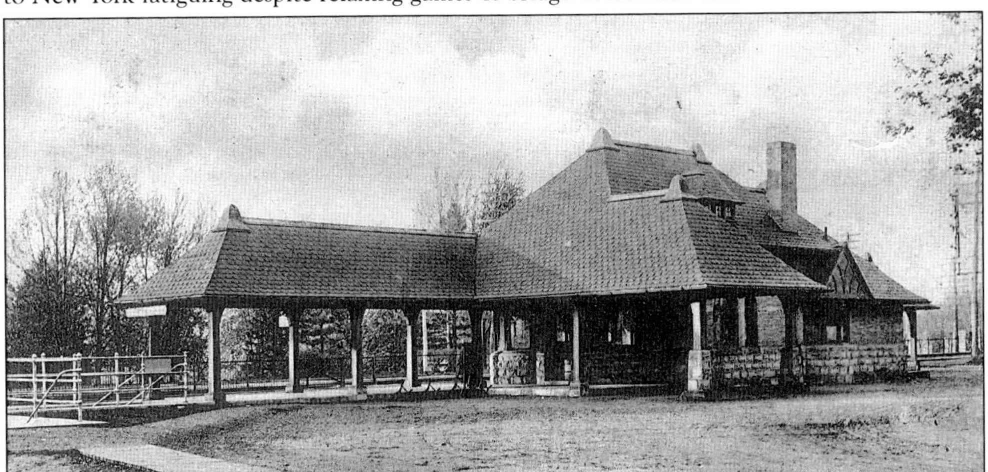

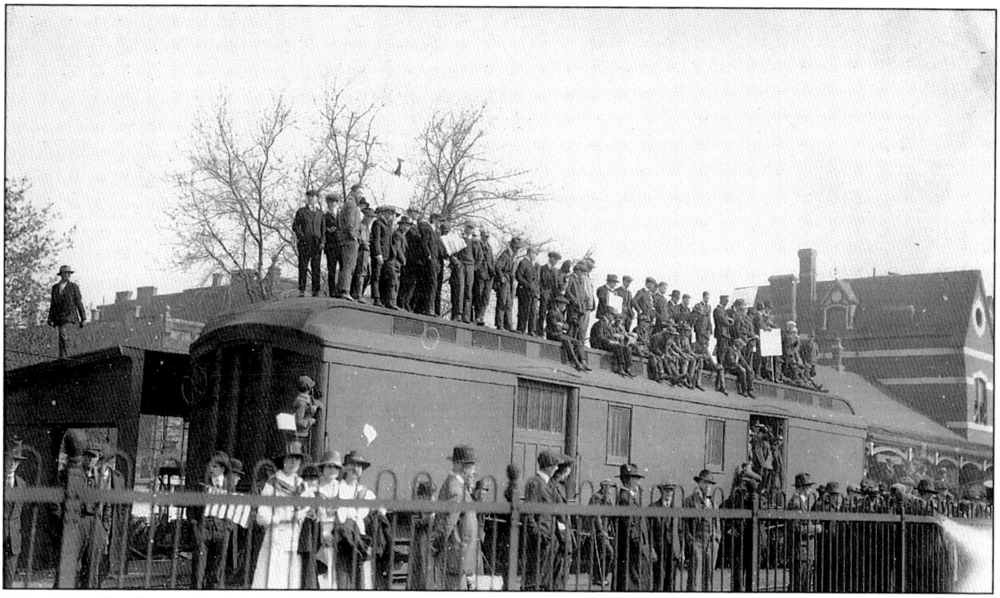

The North Avenue station was attractive both inside and out. By the looks of this large and anxious crowd, someone important must be on the way. Perhaps it was one of the presidential visits—Taft? Teddy Roosevelt? or FDR? It should be noted that while both Roosevelt presidents visited Plainfield, neither one was president at the time.

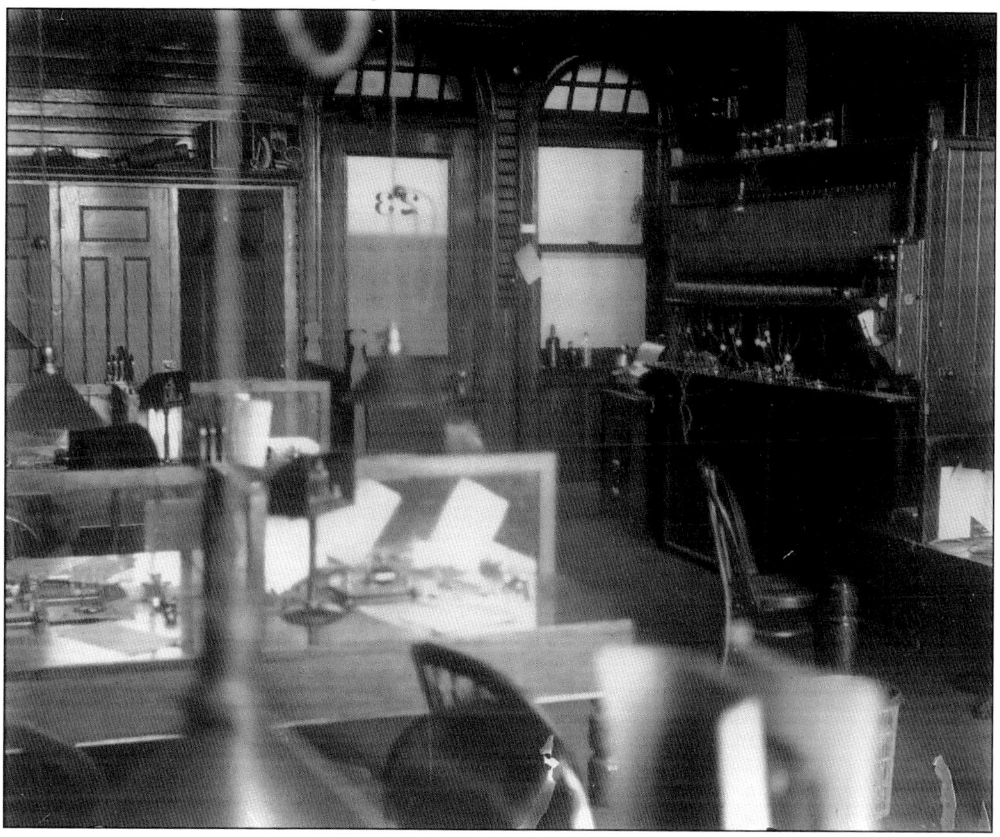

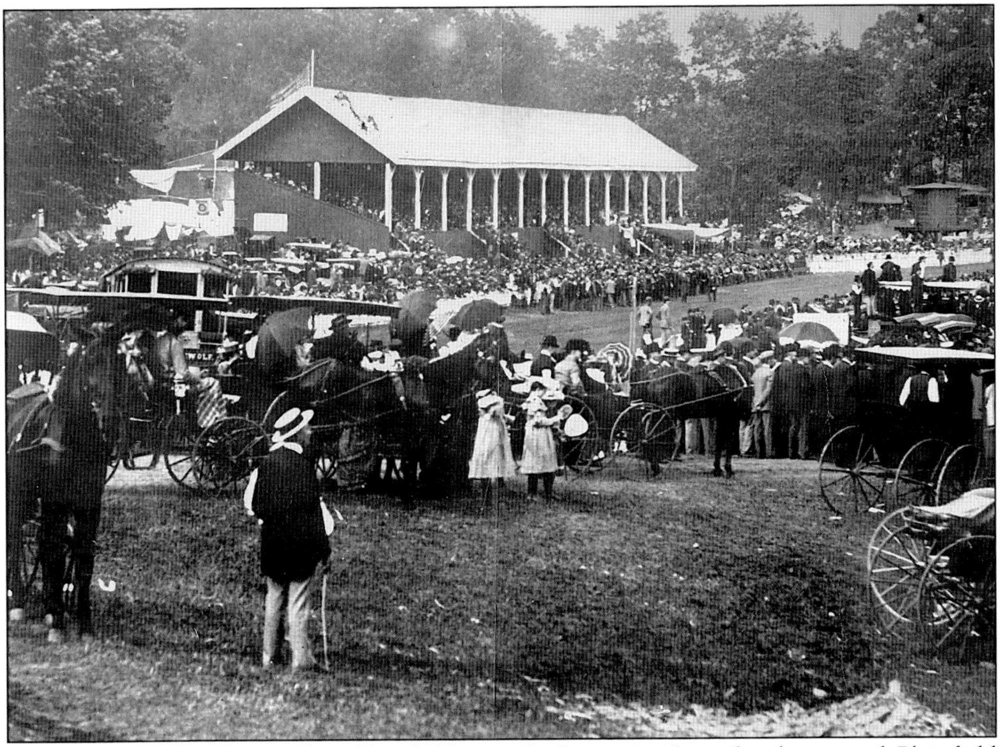

Many visitors who detrained at Plainfield in early June were here for the annual Plainfield Horse Show. This popular, early-1900s event drew hundreds of people from around the country. While it was a fine display of equestrian showmanship, wealth and fashion were strong competitors for attention. The press ran columns on the fashionable gowns worn by the well-to-do.

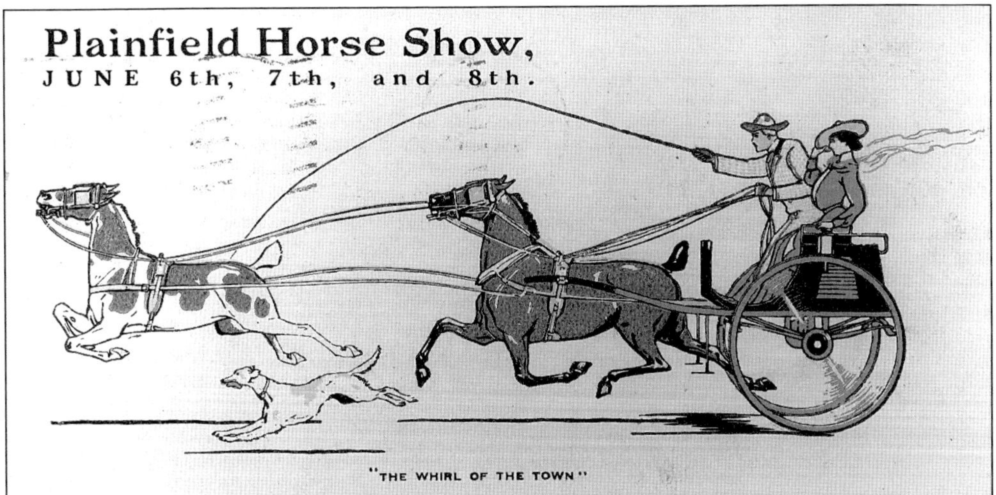

Admission to the horse show was $1. The cost was 50¢ for children, coachmen, and grooms. The grandstand seats were 50¢, and all other seats were free. During the three-day duration of the event, express trains left Liberty Street, New York, at noon and at 1:00 p.m. It was noted that dining cars were attached.

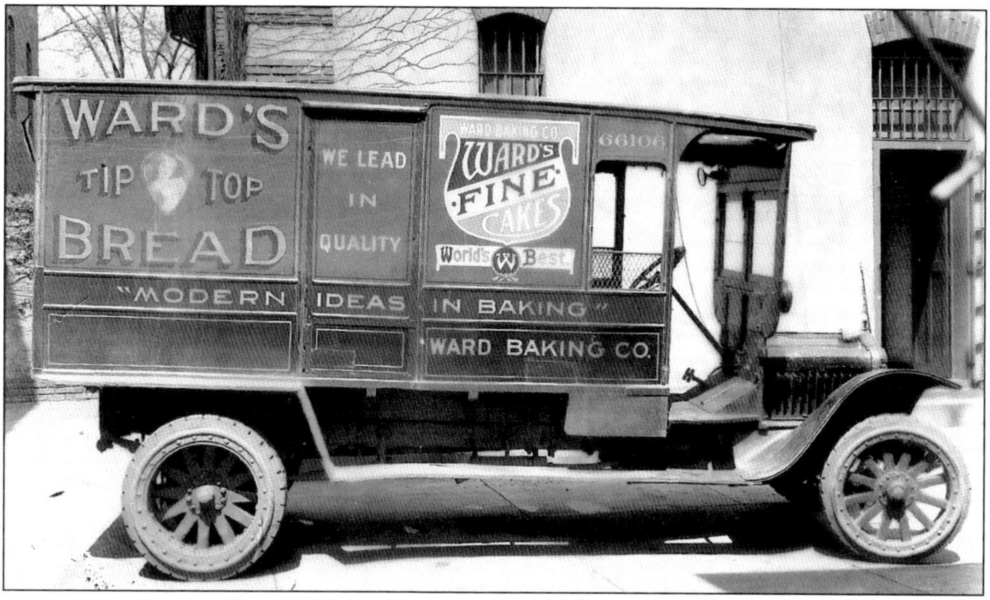

If Omar Khayyam's advice can be taken at face value, downtown Plainfield offered two out of three of life's basic necessities. The loaf of bread was coming in on Ward's delivery truck, while the jug of wine was available at several locations in the neighborhood. Feminine companionship was a different matter. It was and still is a BYOB world—bring your own babe.

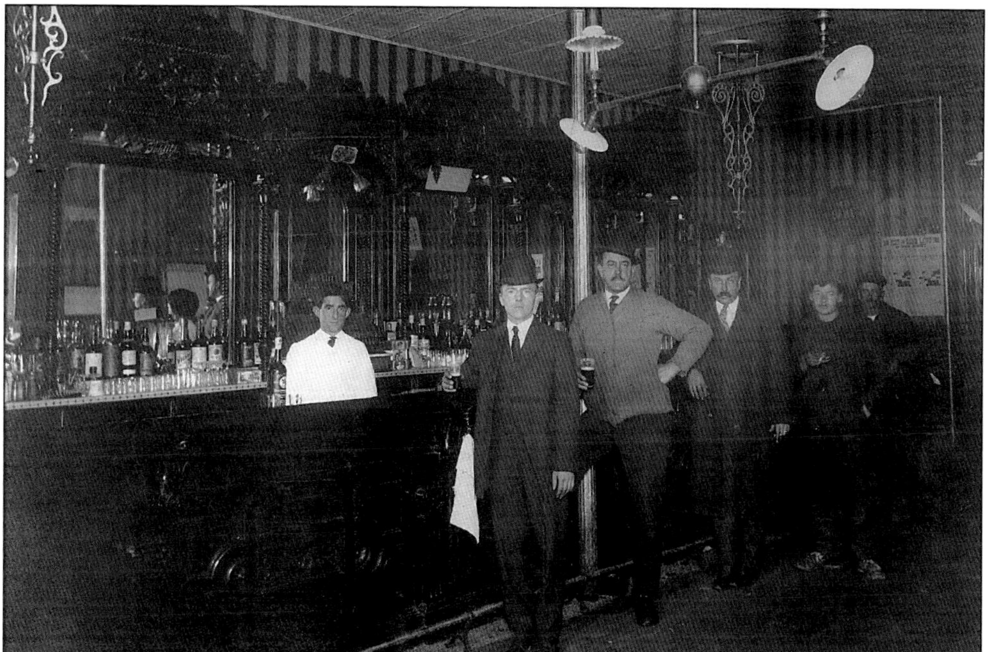

Some visitors to town, however, preferred more sedentary amusement. Plainfield had a number of saloons like this one, on Park Avenue. Owners paid a rather steep $1,000-a-year license fee. However, it was noted that unlike other towns, Plainfield's saloon keepers exhibited a certain esprit de corps. Each keeper was zealous to see that no other one lowered the tone of the business by violations.

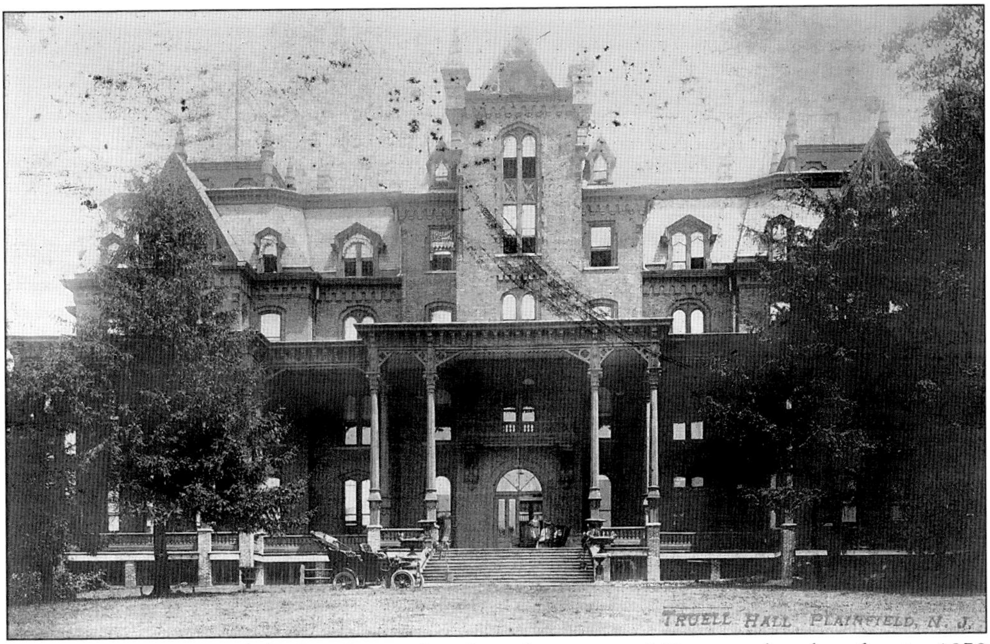

The Netherwood was billed as "a city hotel in the country." For two decades after its 1878 opening, people arrived from New York by parlor car to spend their vacation on the Netherwood Heights. Croquet, danceables, masquerades, tennis, bowling, midnight suppers, and fancy dress balls were the order of the day for the vacationer.

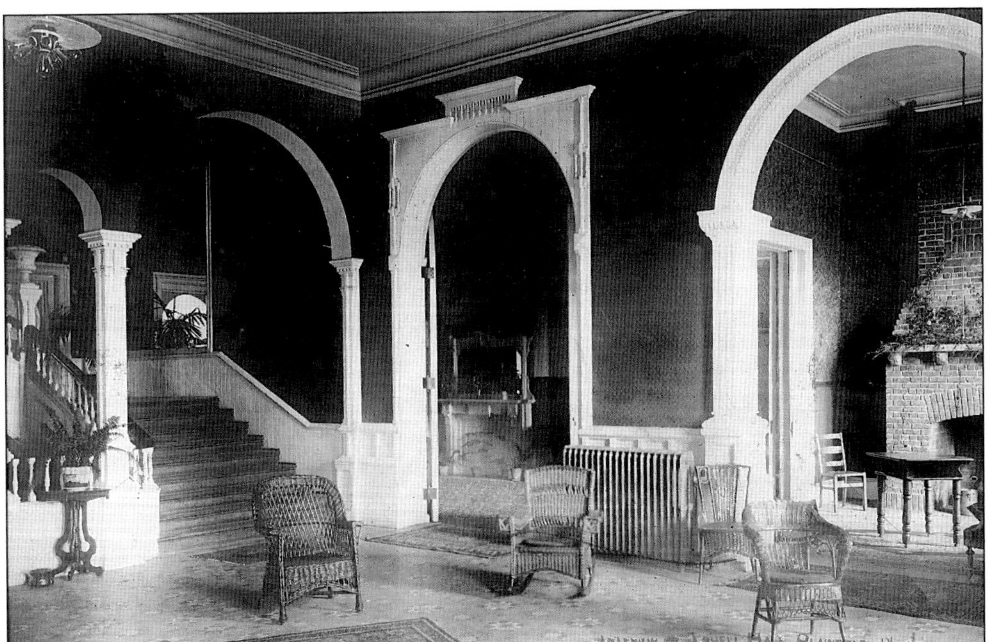

Inside the 200-room hotel were more than 40 suites, all with fireplaces. The ceilings were 16 feet high, and across the front of the building was a 150-foot-long piazza used for strolling and sometimes for roller-skating.

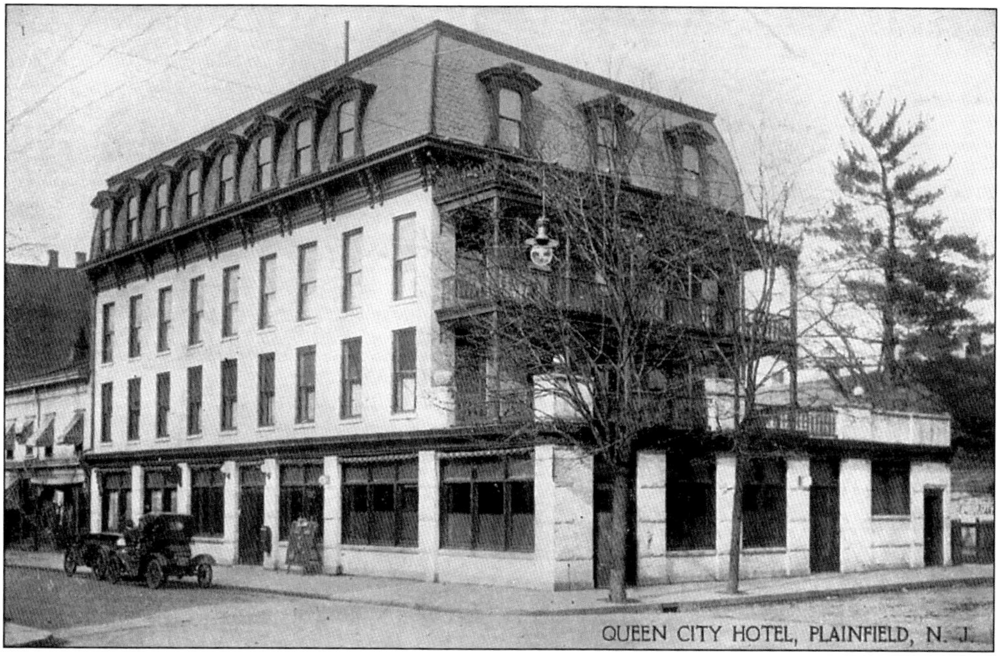

This hotel, known at various times as the Mansion House, City Hotel, and the Iroquois, was reopened under new management by 1911 with the new name Queen City Hotel. Renovated with brown Wilton carpeting to harmonize with the golden oak woodwork, each of the 39 rooms boasted tungsten lights and a telephone. Rooms were 50¢, and meals were an additional 50¢.

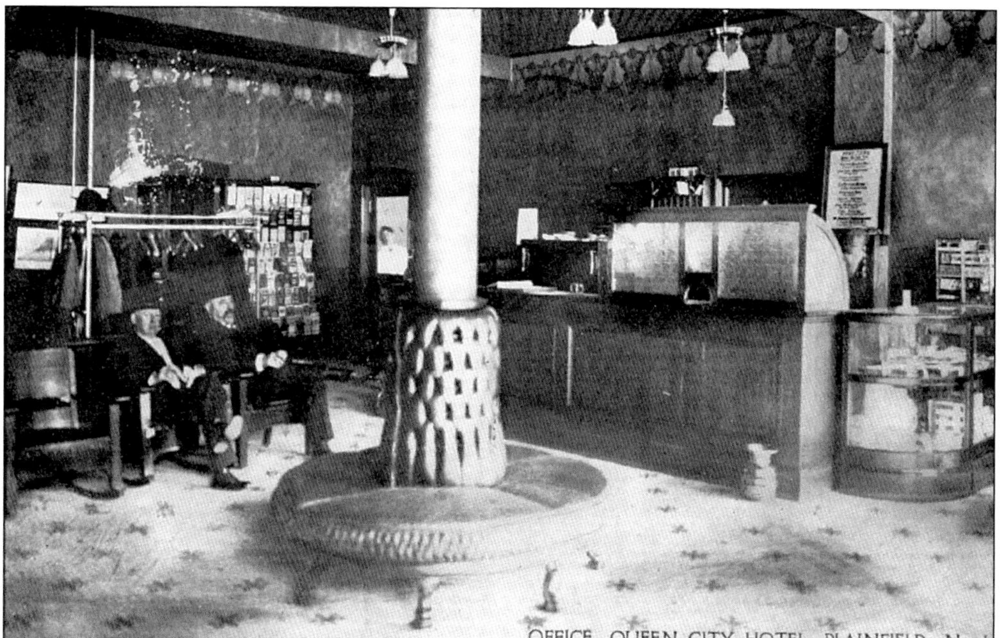

The Queen City Hotel boasted a popular bar that became a political arena for both parties. Nearby, on the porch, was another attraction: the 15-foot oak barrel that Plainfielder Bobby Leach used when he went over the Niagara Falls.

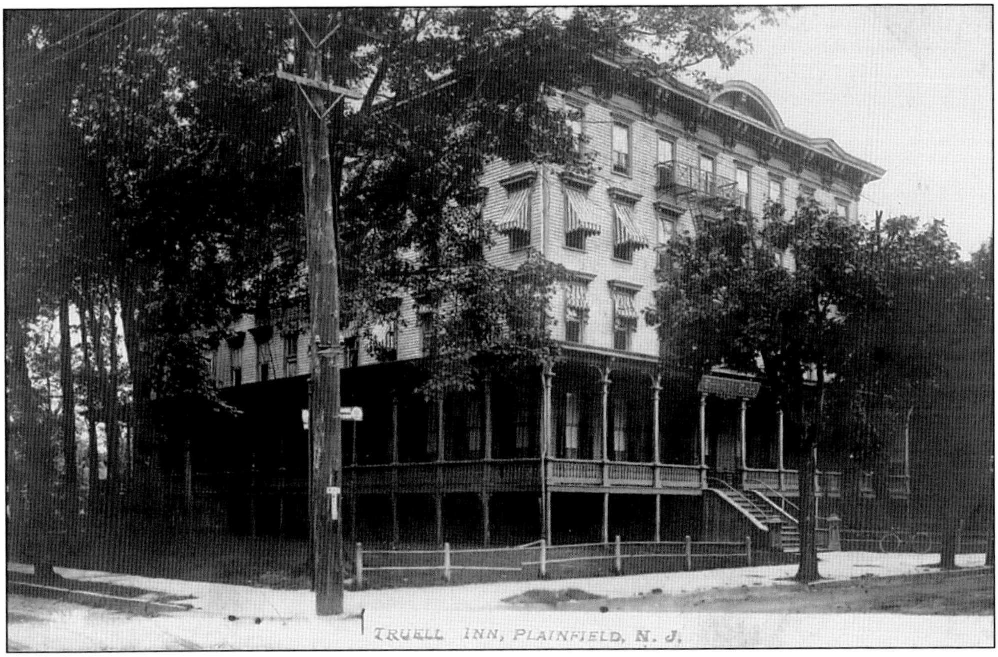

The Park House, with its wonderful wraparound porch, had accommodations for 100 guests. It was opened in 1872 as a "first class family hotel" and became a center for many social activities. For a time, the building was also known as the Revere House and, later, the Truell Inn before closing its doors in 1924.

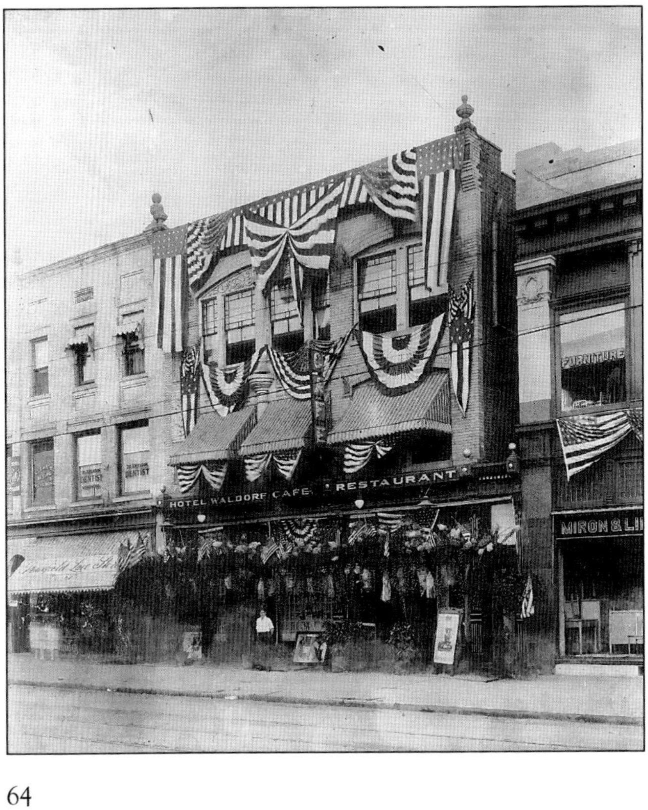

In downtown Plainfield, at 142 East Front Street, was Henry Windham's Waldorf Hotel with adjoining restaurant. At the famous 95-foot-long bar, you could buy a drink of whiskey for 10¢. The hotel was a popular place with businessmen, but it was touched by scandal in 1902, when a Miss Evalyn O'Neil, of questionable character, was found in a side room after drinking carbolic acid.

The last word in hotels was the 1922 Park Hotel, on West 7th Street. This hostelry, built by former Queen City Hotel manager Peter Floersch, cost $250,000. It boasted 25 living suites of three to five rooms each and had 25 transient rooms. The grand opening attracted 240 people. The local paper stated that this was one of the few large public functions in which provision has been made for both genders. The ladies, it was noted, added a certain charm.

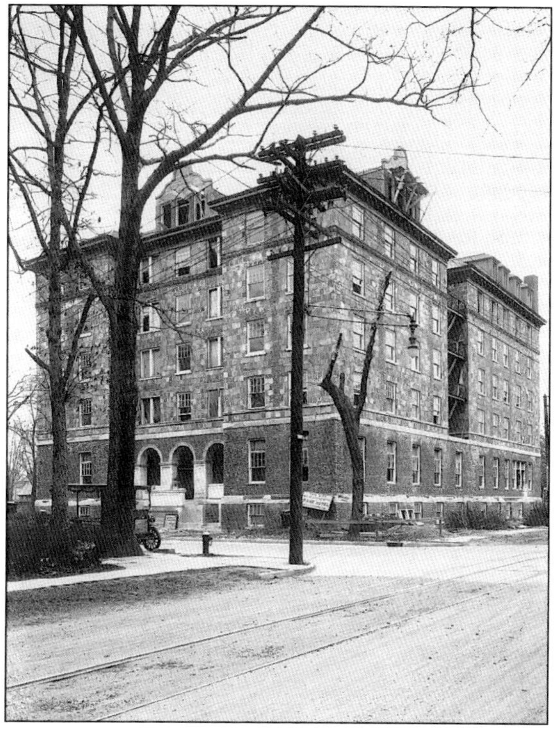

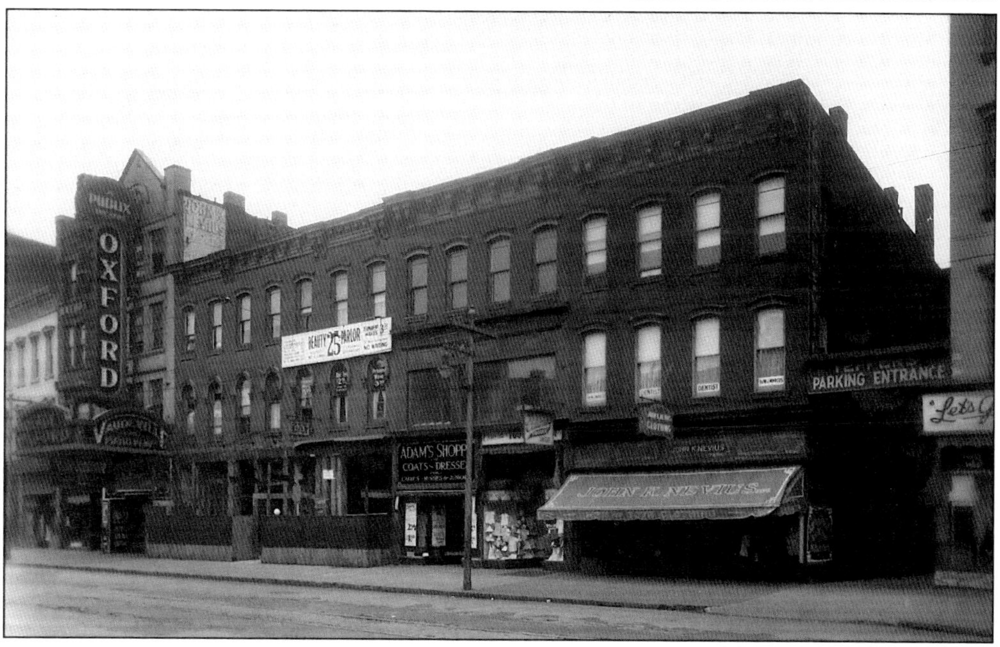

Opened in 1884, the Stillman Music Hall witnessed many well-known performers, such as John Philip Sousa and his band. By 1908, the renamed Proctor's was showing motion pictures and staging an occasional live performance. Among the "photo plays" featured was the locally produced *It Happened in Plainfield*, which was shown in 1916 with Mary Pickford's *Madame Butterfly*, which contained many scenes shot in Plainfield. Under the name Oxford, the theater showed movies until 1955.

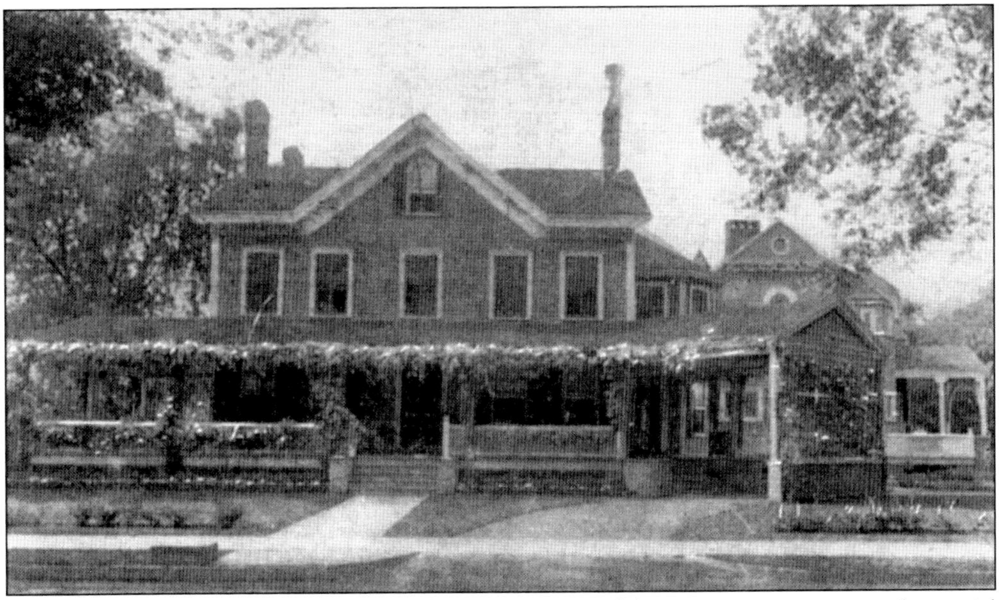

The Plainfield Casino, on West Seventh Street, operated for many years as a popular social club. With a stage and auditorium, the casino provided accommodation for many private and public events. Testimonial dinners, plays by Oshkosh, the opera guild's performance of Gilbert and Sullivan's *Patience*, and an Evening in Spain for the Monday Afternoon Club are just a few of the numerous events that were staged in its commodious premises.

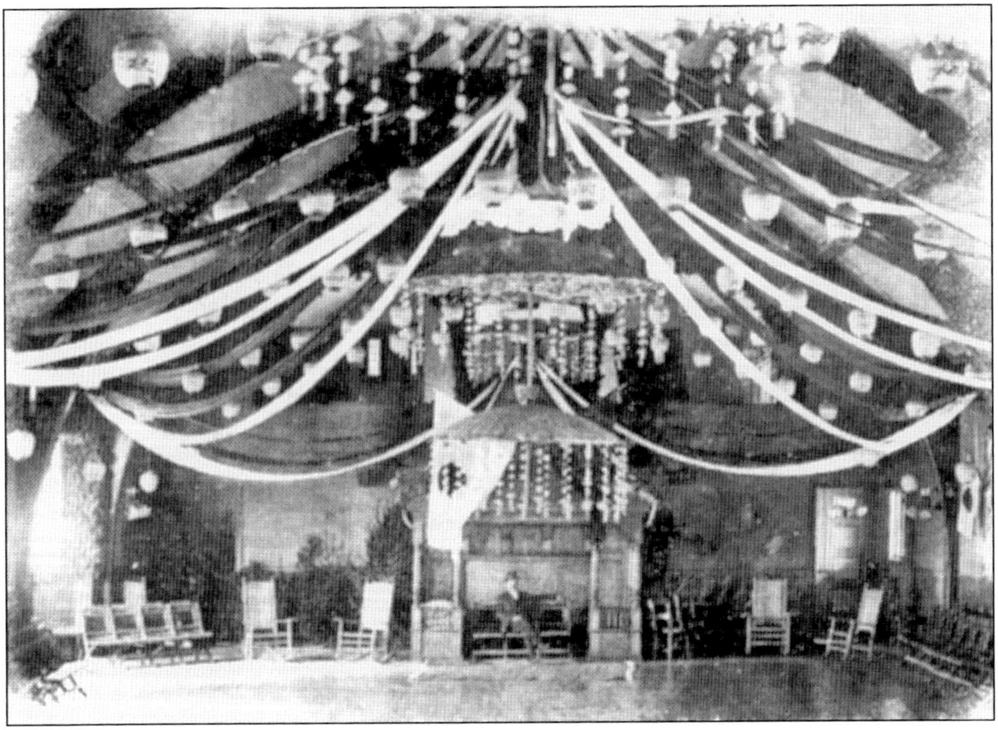

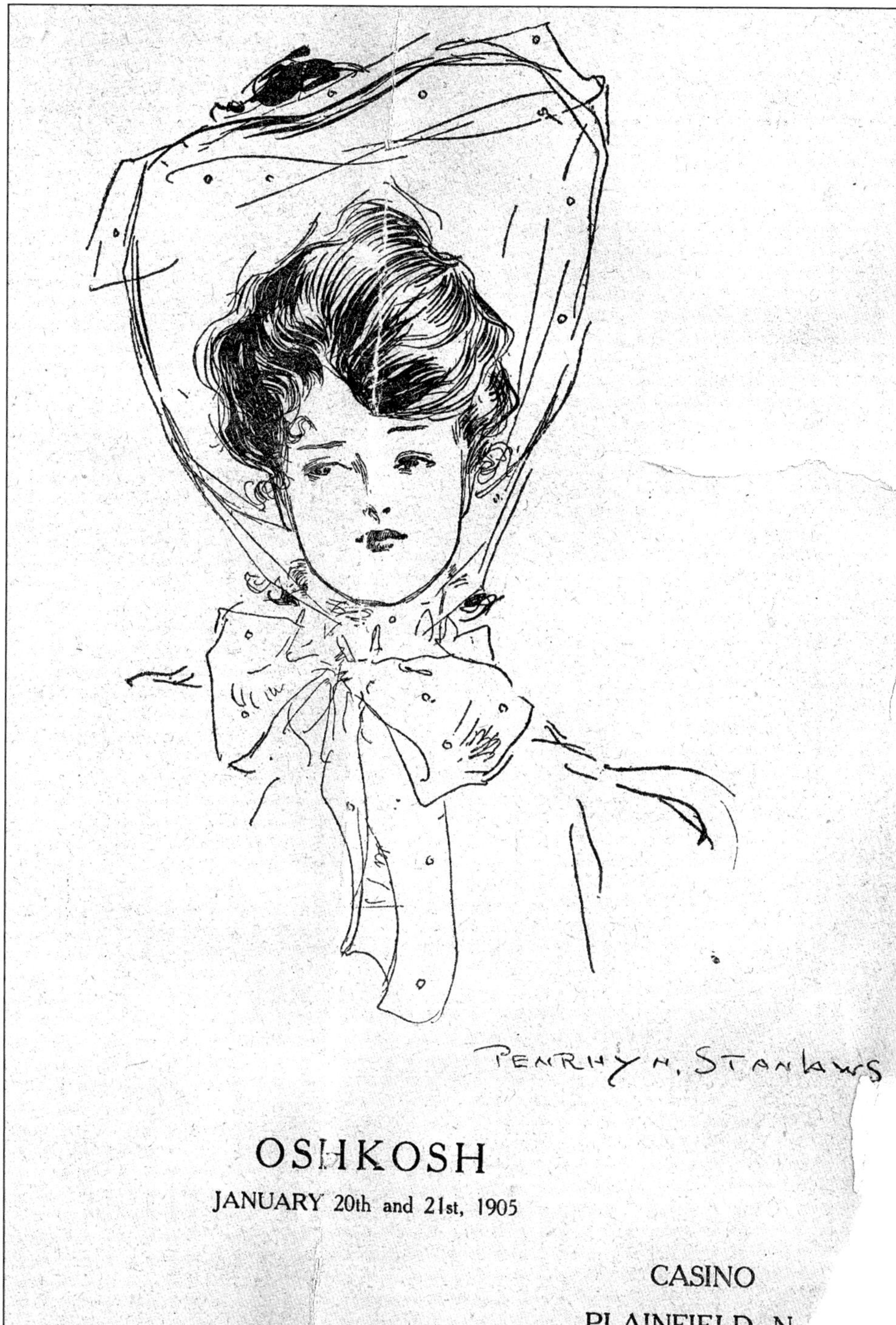

Oshkosh was a local theater group that held annual fund-raising performances entitled "Oshkosh." On January 20–21, 1905, the program was well received. Critics said that the production was splendidly staged and finely acted and sung. It was called "A complete and glittering success."

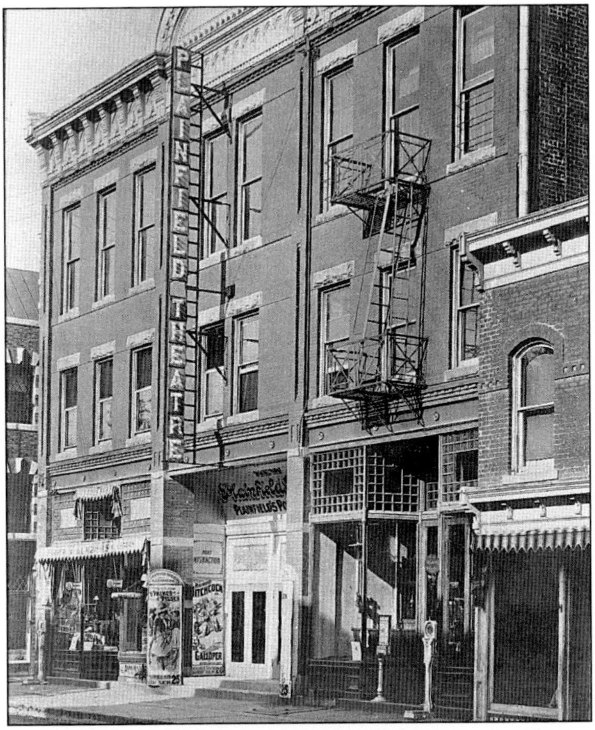

Another popular place for live entertainment was the Plainfield Theater. In August 1910, a performance by Valentine's Athletic Dogs was disrupted by a bat that flew through an open window. The crowd roared with laughter as the dog tried to dodge the bat. By 1916, the Elks ran a more respectable performance of *Mystic Rose*, a Japanese-American opera. The Boola Boola Boys and the Dancing Tea Girls were also a big hit.

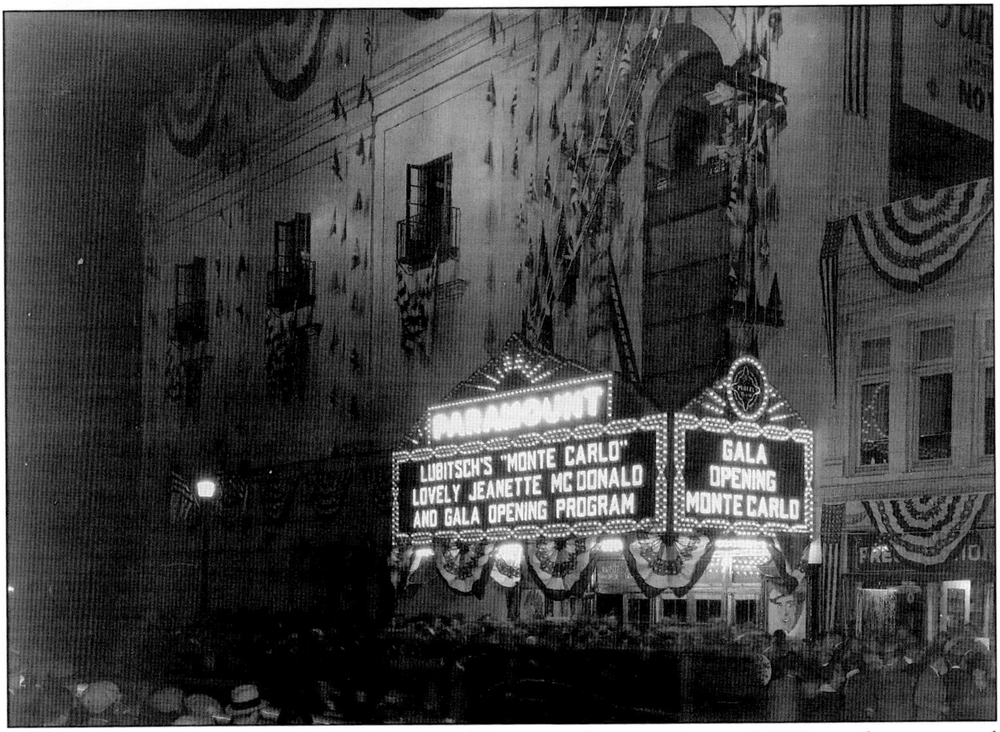

The 1926 opening of another amusement palace created a sensation as 5,000 people attempted to storm the box office. A cordon of police was required to preserve law and order. The lucky 1,300 ticket holders enjoyed a presentation of Jeanette McDonald in *Monte Carlo*.

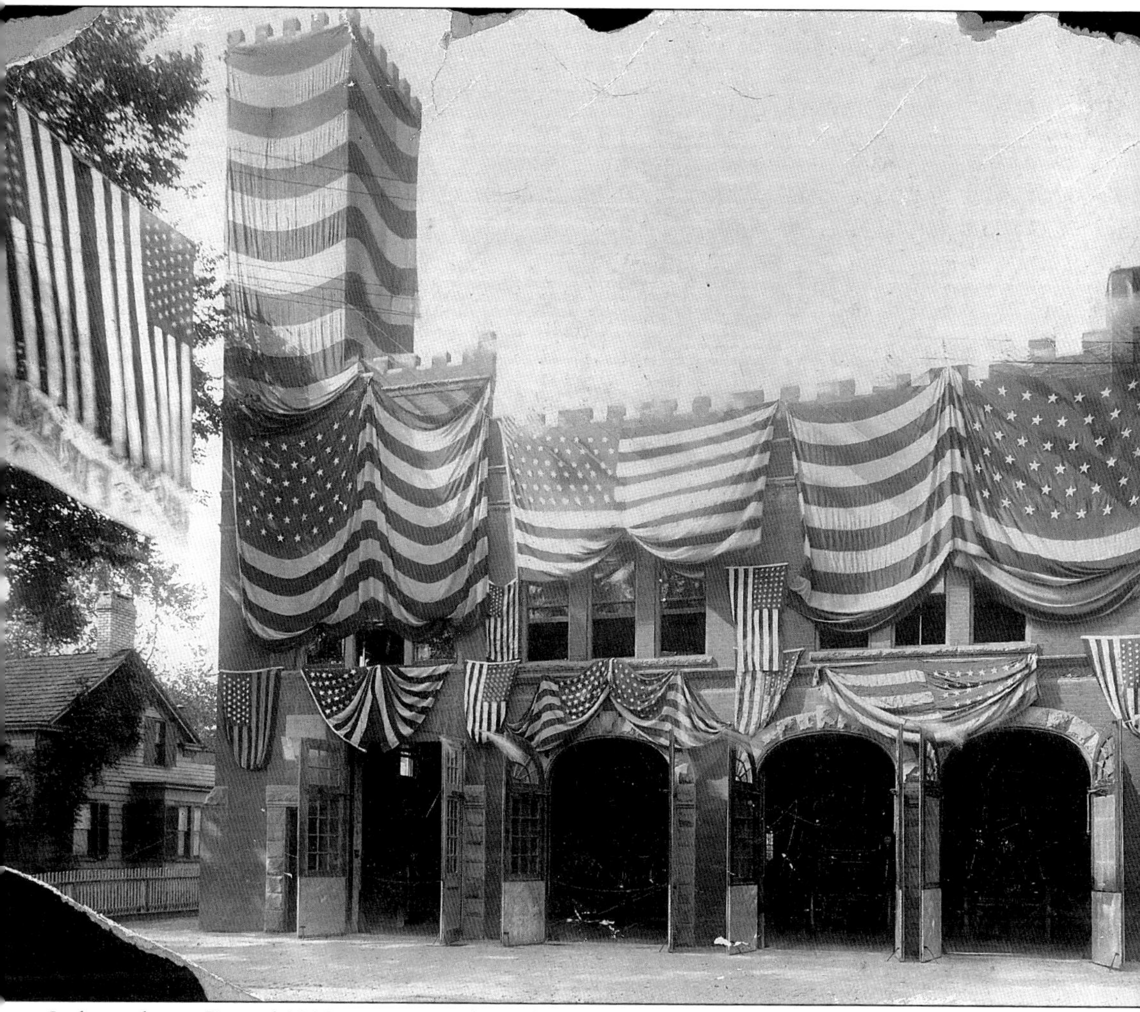

Independence Day of 1909 was an epoch in the city of Plainfield. People draped their homes and businesses in the national colors. Coupled with the Fourth of July was Charter Day, a three-day celebration of the 40th anniversary of the city of Plainfield and a 25th anniversary for the establishment of the borough of North Plainfield.

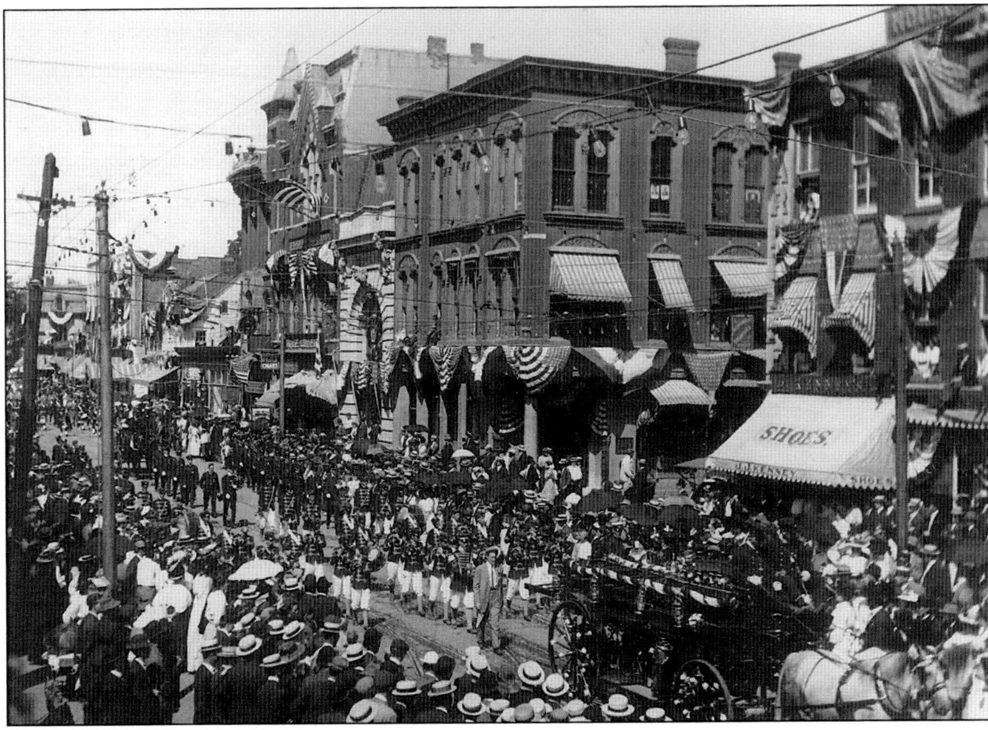

To the beat of drums, 6,000 men fell in line for the start of Charter Day, a three-day event. There were more than 100 floats. The parade, which was over one mile long, took nearly an hour to pass the reviewing stand.

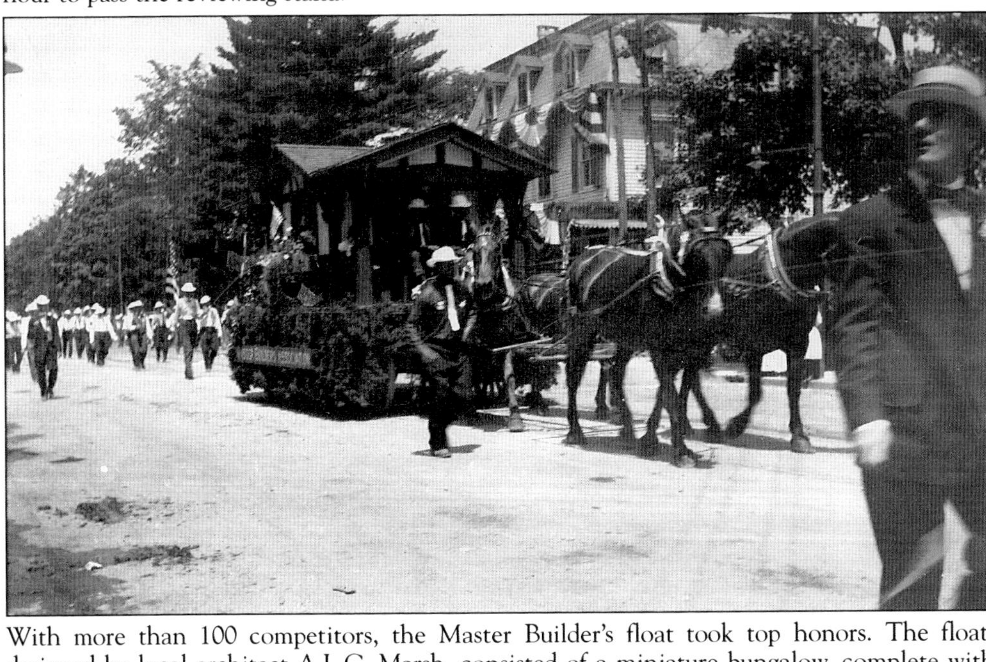

With more than 100 competitors, the Master Builder's float took top honors. The float, designed by local architect A.L.C. Marsh, consisted of a miniature bungalow, complete with running water, electricity, and Colonial trim. Costing $350, the house was later sold to a Berkeley Heights resident as a playhouse for his daughter.

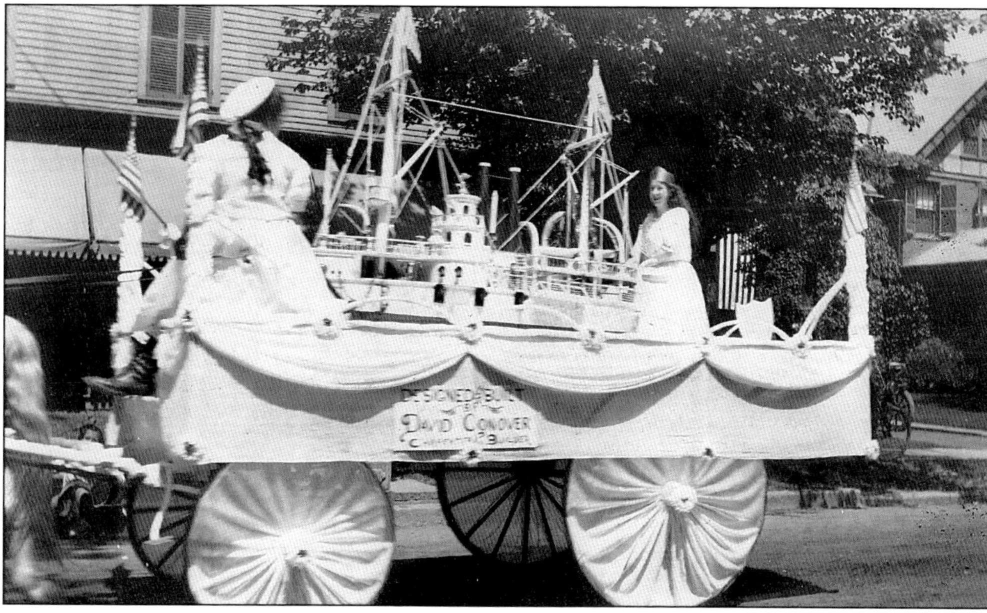

Another prize at the Charter Day festivities was awarded to Conover's gunboat float, which came in first as the most appropriate subject for an Independence Day parade. The boat was a model of the USS *Maine* and was six feet long. Conover tested the boat's seaworthiness on the Green Brook.

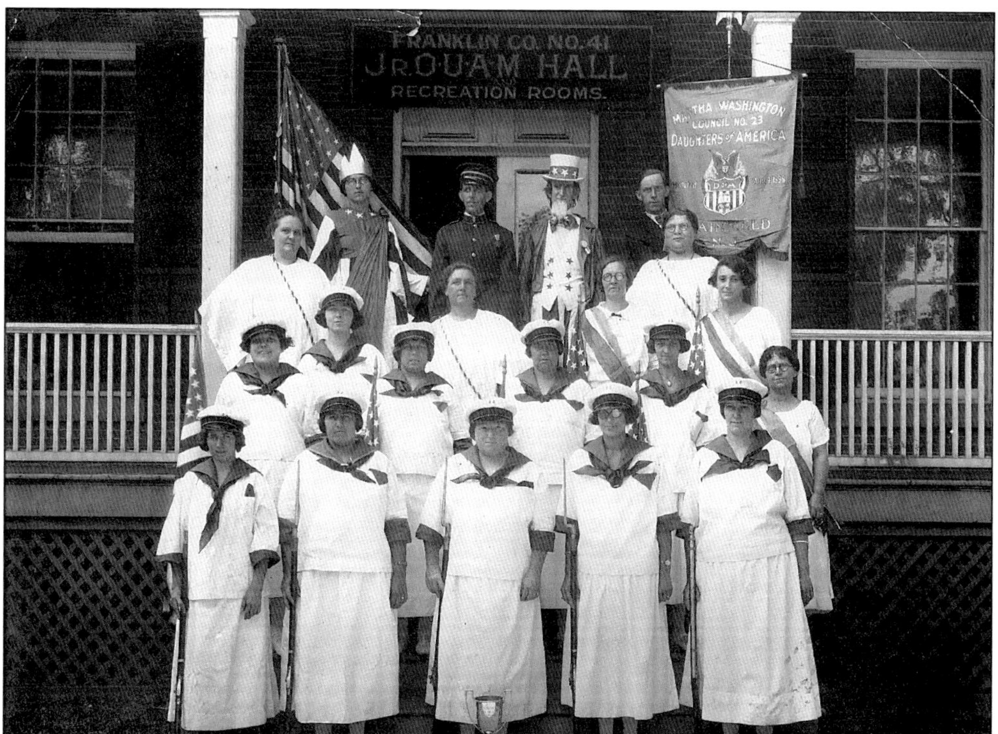

In the spirit of Charter Day, Mr. Conover, himself, dressed up as Uncle Sam. His daughter, Mrs. Charles Wilson, portrayed Liberty. Here, with the Daughters of Liberty, he poses with his cup.

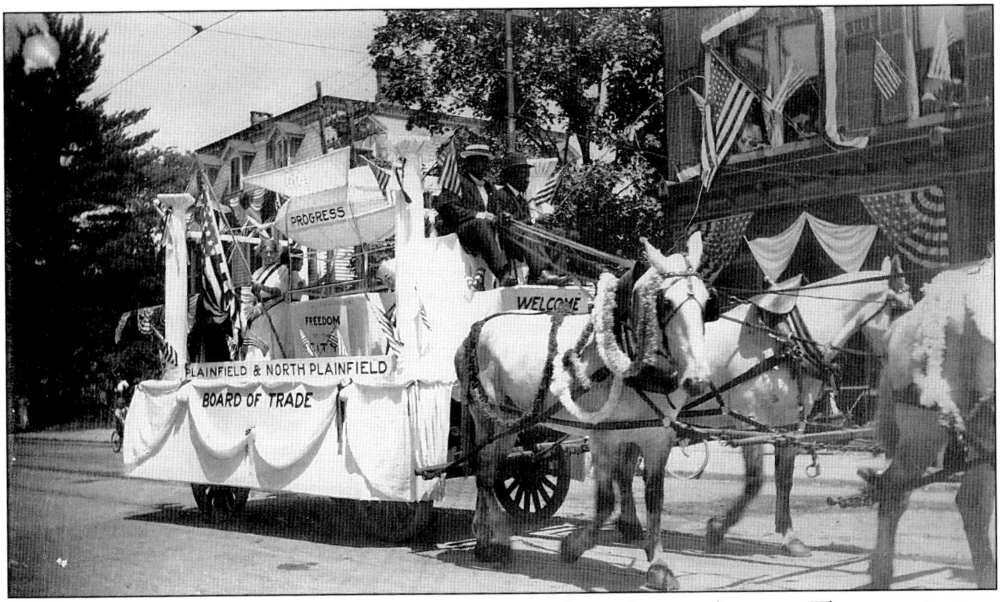

The float of the local board of trade makes its way along the parade route. The organization, sponsor of Charter Day, undertook the gala celebration in response to a local newspaperman's suggestion. We hope the applause was music to the weary members' ears.

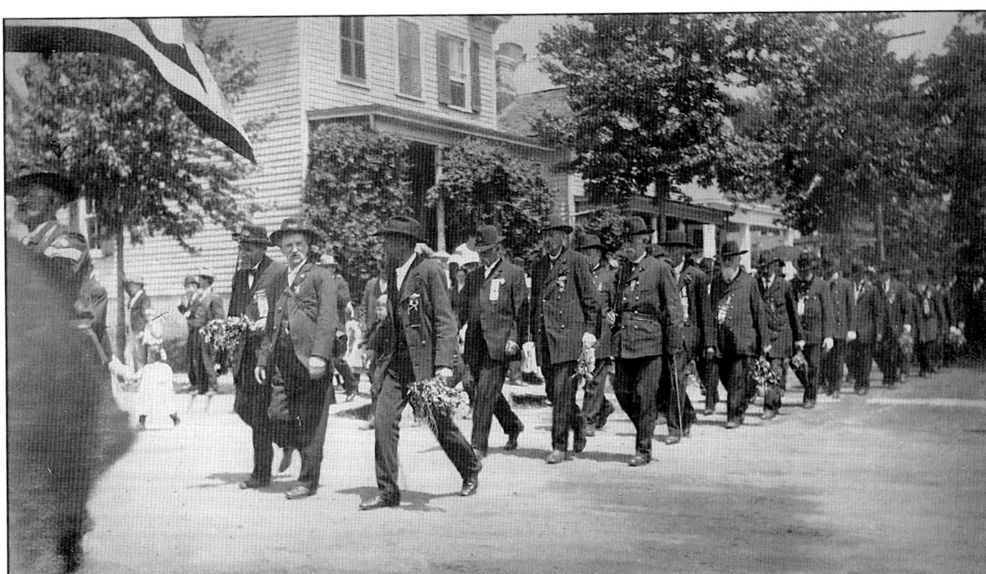

Civil War veterans step smartly past the reviewing stand 44 years after their first participation in an Independence Day parade. Here they come, gallant, bright-eyed, and erect, symbolizing a nation's and a city's pride.

Six

IN THE PUBLIC INTEREST

Charles J. Fisk, mayor of Plainfield, was an extraordinarily active man and a staunch supporter of everything he deemed of lasting value to his community. Without mincing words he stated the following:

"If there is any one thing in which Plainfield excels other cities, it is in its home life. In its early years, Plainfield was designed as a city of homes, and it has since developed along these lines, until it now ranks second to none . . . Plainfield is exceedingly well governed. Its municipal affairs are administered by capable men. In all of its departments the civic government of Plainfield has enlisted the efforts of the best men, the most representative men and the most capable men that can be found. It is a pleasant duty to serve the City of Plainfield in an official capacity and, hence, it is not difficult to secure men of standing to assume the reins of government."—*Plainfield, N.J., the City Beautiful*; City National Bank; Courier-News Publishing Company; Plainfield, N.J.; 1897.

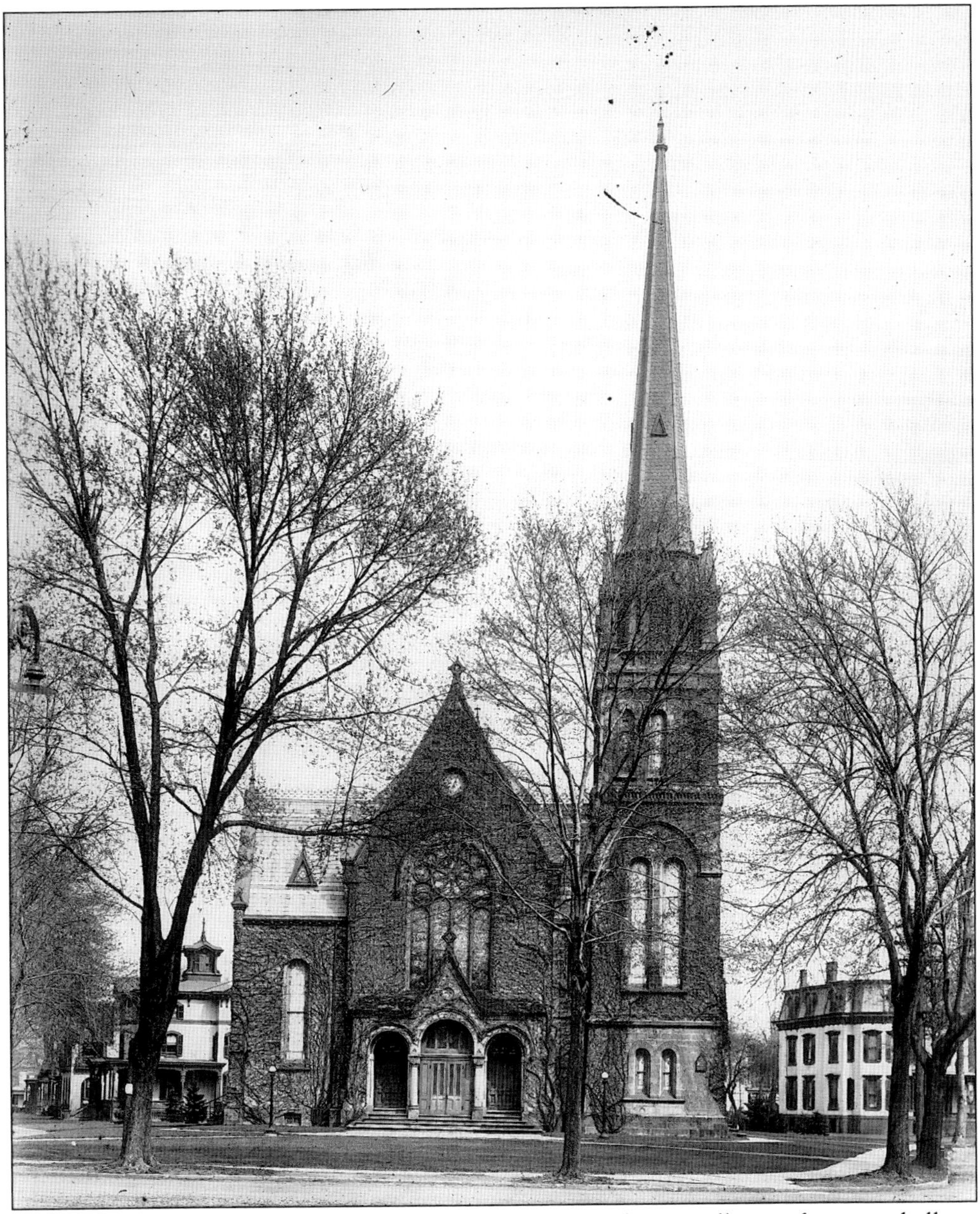

The city of Plainfield has numerous churches; many are architecturally significant, and all are testaments to their parishioners' devotion. Due to its highly visible location at the juncture of three streets, the Crescent Avenue Presbyterian Church is one of the most noticeable in town. Established in 1872, this Gothic structure was built on land donated by Job Male, Plainfield's first mayor.

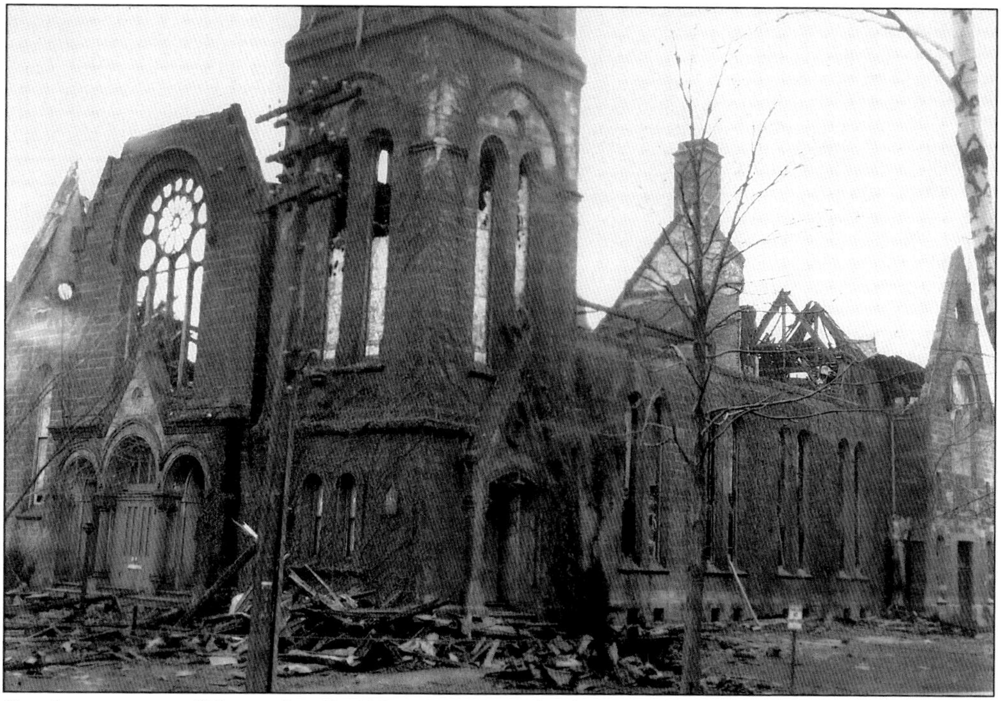

On the evening of November 7, 1931, a "spectacular but appalling blaze" gutted the Crescent Avenue church, causing over $250,000 in damage and resulting in the loss of many fine and valuable Tiffany memorial windows.

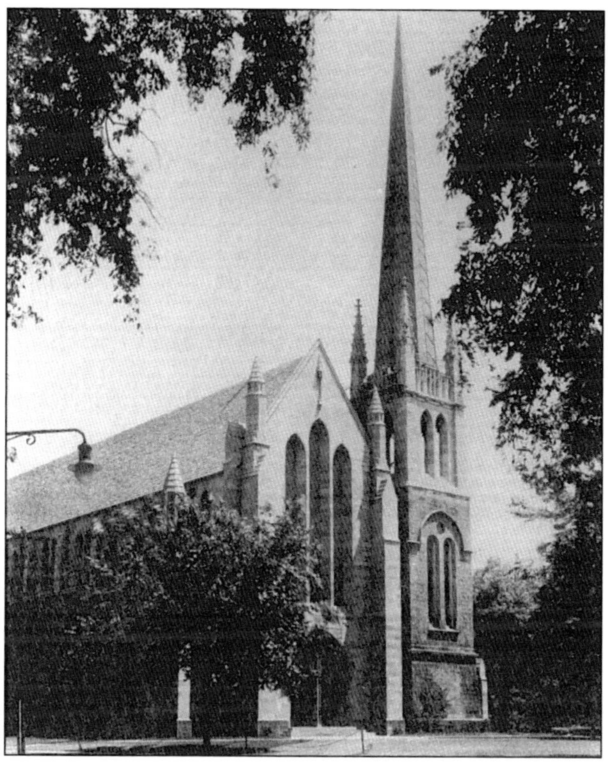

A devastated congregation immediately made plans to rebuild. Like the phoenix, a new and soaring edifice quickly assumed shape. The first service in the new church was held on Sunday, February 25, 1934.

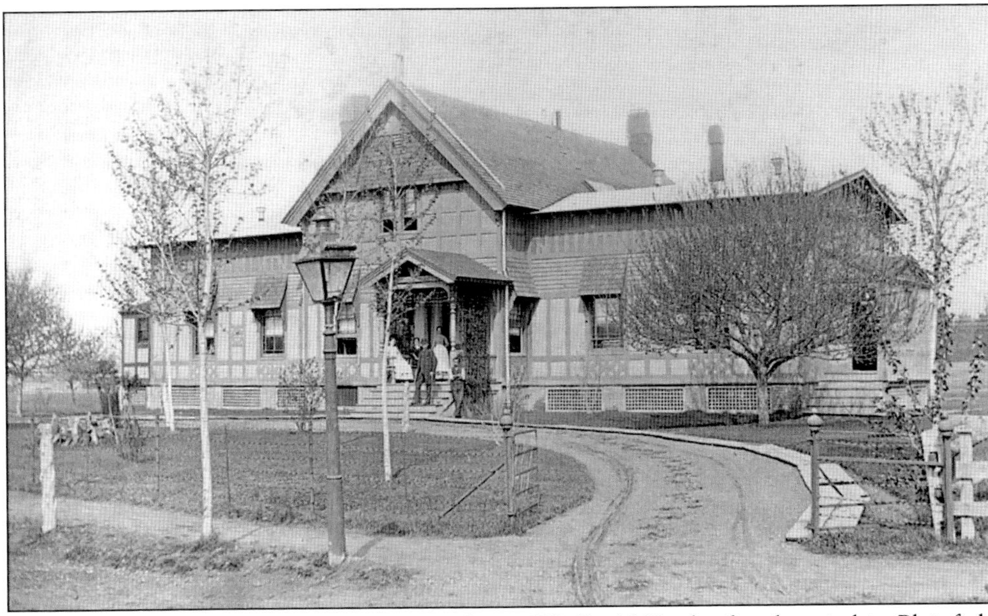

The Muhlenberg Hospital was incorporated in 1877. By 1880, the first hospital in Plainfield was located on Muhlenberg Place, in Plainfield's west end. Built on land donated by Job Male, the hospital had room for 20 beds and was staffed by a handful of employees. Financially, the hospital was assisted by an annual collection from the churches.

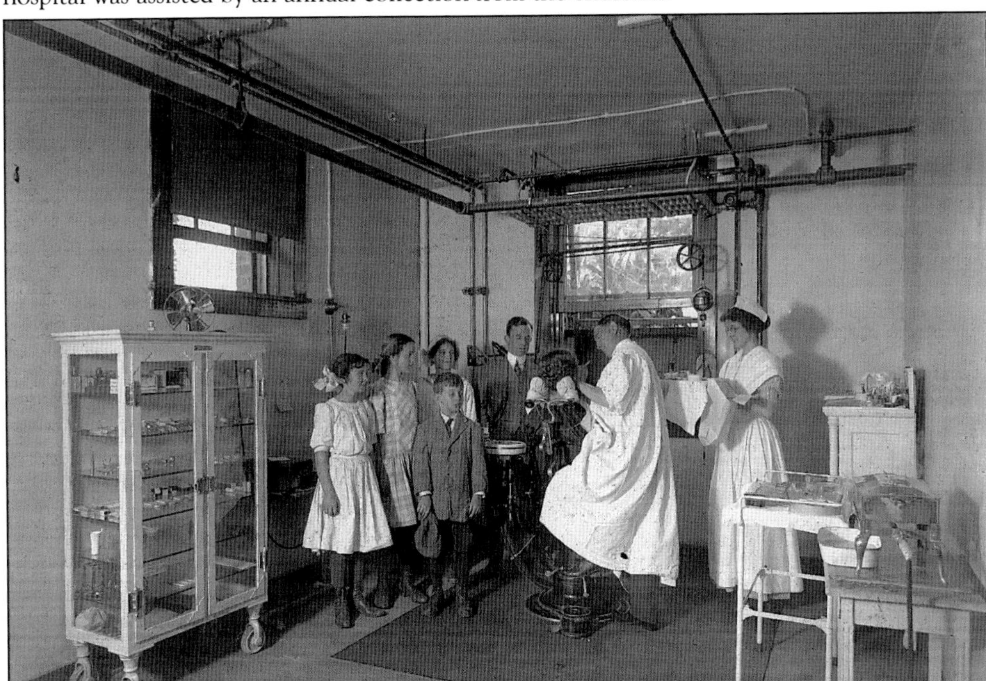

By 1900, the use of dental drills had become widespread and principles for filling teeth had been established. Anesthetics such as nitrous oxide and cocaine were commonly used. Perhaps a growing awareness of the importance of dental hygiene led to the Plainfield Free Dental Clinic in 1913.

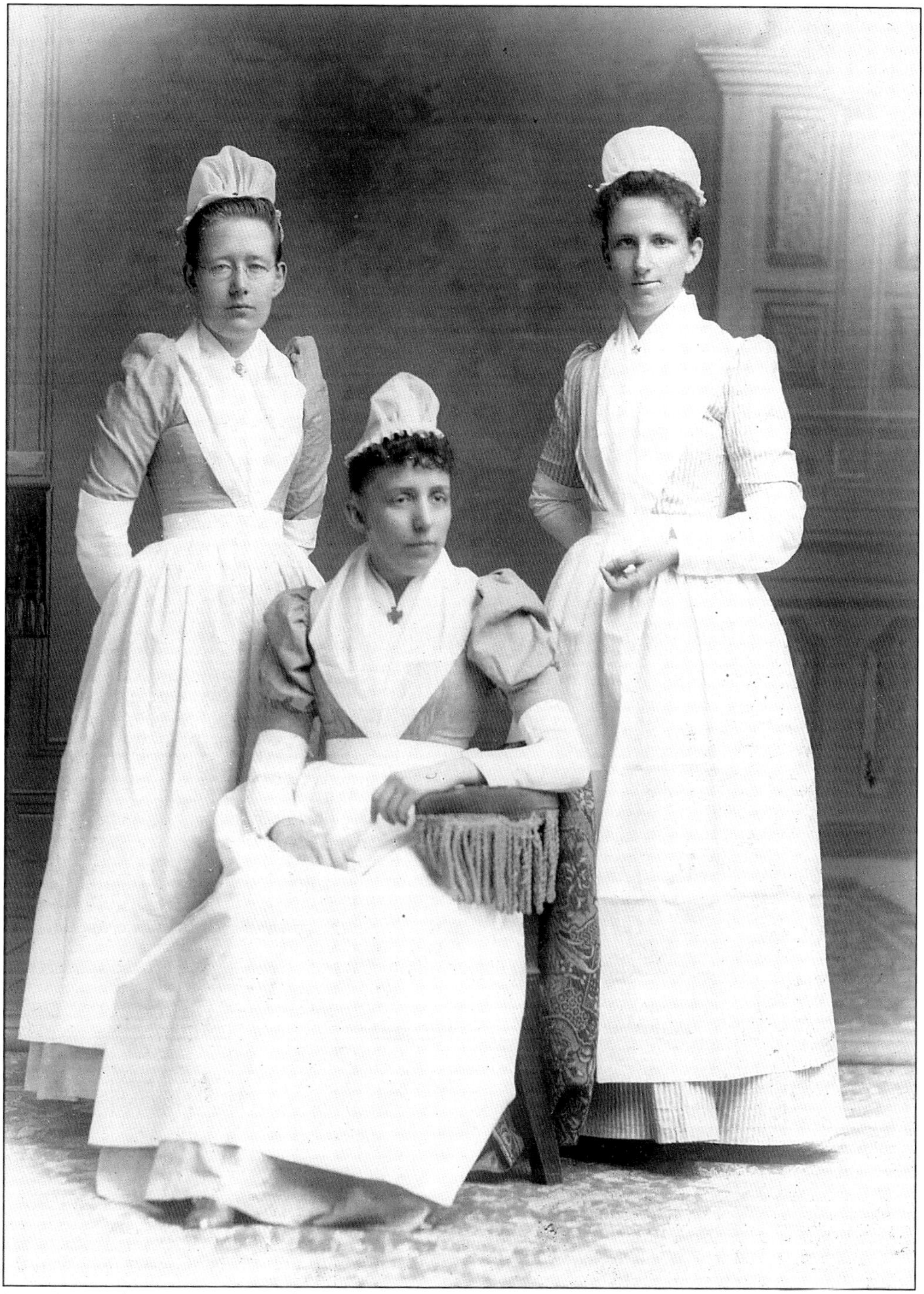

In 1900, three nurses graduated from the Muhlenberg Training School for Nurses. Commencement exercises were held at the Crescent Church chapel, amid banks of flowers and backdrops of American flags. Each graduate was formally presented with a pin bearing the red cross. In those days, nursing duties included not only patient care but also food preparation, care of wards, stoking of the furnace, surgical preparation, and application of leeches.

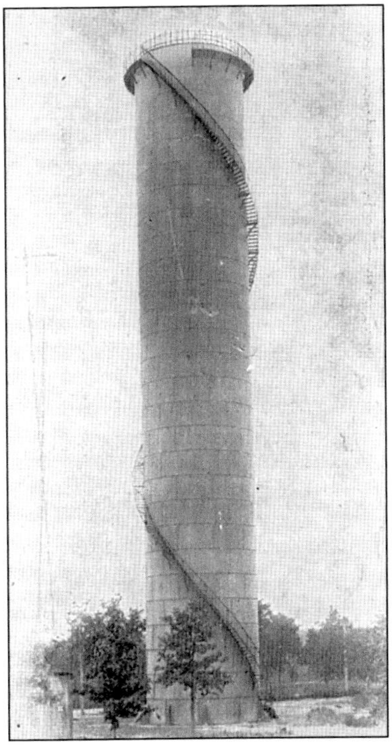

Touted as pure, Plainfield's water came from an underground river in the Netherwood area and was tapped by deep wells by the water company. The water tower pictured here was 25 feet in diameter and 140 feet high. It stood on elevated ground, which ensured a uniform system of pressure throughout the city at all times.

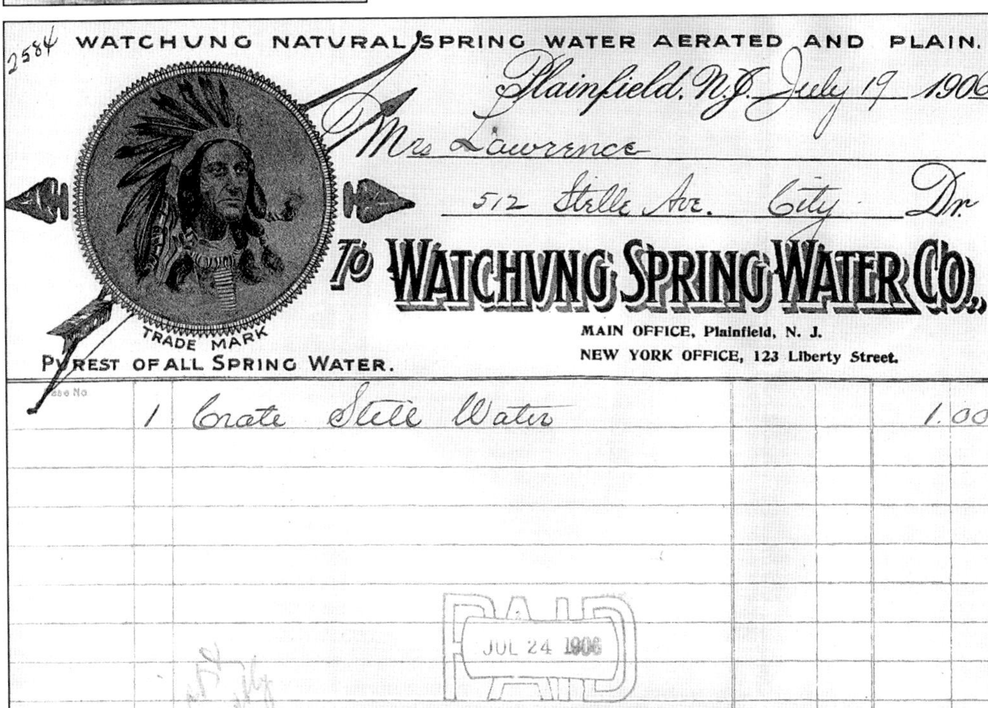

2584 WATCHUNG NATURAL SPRING WATER AERATED AND PLAIN.

Plainfield, N.J. July 19 1906

Mrs Lawrence

512 Stelle Ave. City Dr.

To WATCHUNG SPRING WATER CO.,

TRADE MARK

PURIST OF ALL SPRING WATER.

MAIN OFFICE, Plainfield, N. J.

NEW YORK OFFICE, 123 Liberty Street.

1	Crate Stele Water			1.00

PAID JUL 24 1906

The Watchung Spring Water Company's product flourished for a time as the popular drink for sportsmen. When it was exhibited at a sports show in Madison Square Garden in the early 1900s, everyone who tried it declared the water to be as good a thirst quencher as any previously tried.

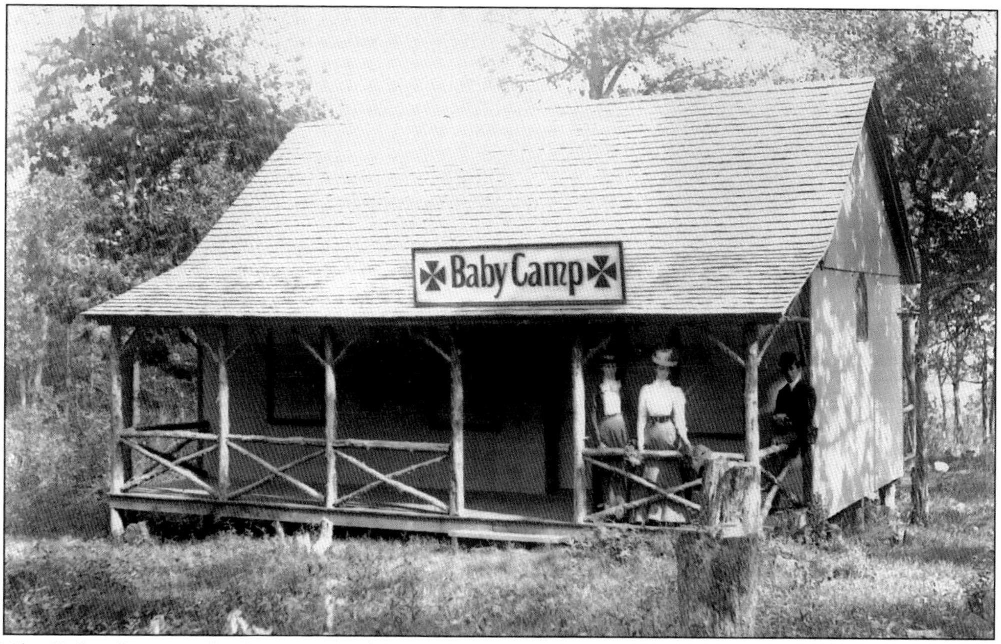

The Baby Camp, a fresh-air camp for underprivileged children, was located on Leland Avenue on the old Brisbane Estate. Children and their mothers were allowed to live in the country for the summer. Weekend visits allowed father to escape the heated city and spend quality time with his family, thus ensuring domestic happiness.

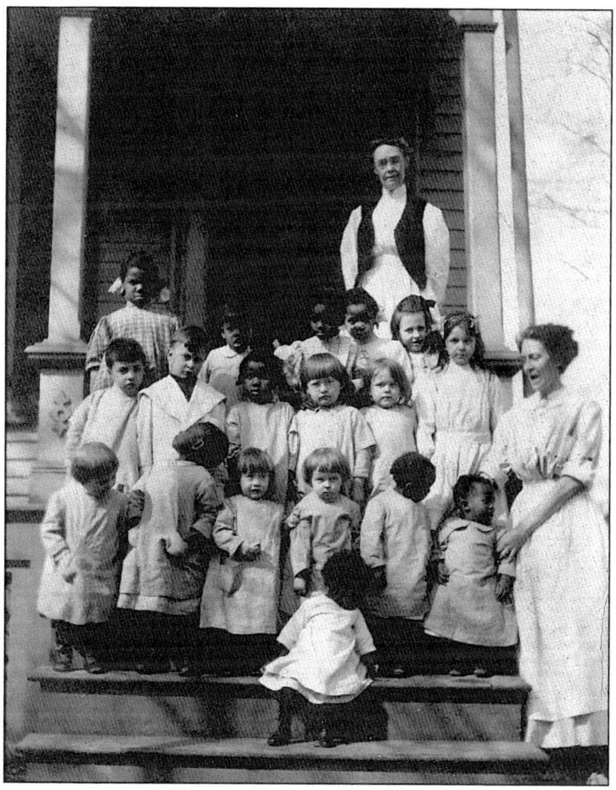

In 1892, the King's Daughters Day School was founded in Plainfield and by 1906, the organization was operating out of a small house on West Third Street. The school's purpose was to "keep the children off the streets." Today, the King's Daughters Day School still serves the community in a modern facility on West Front Street.

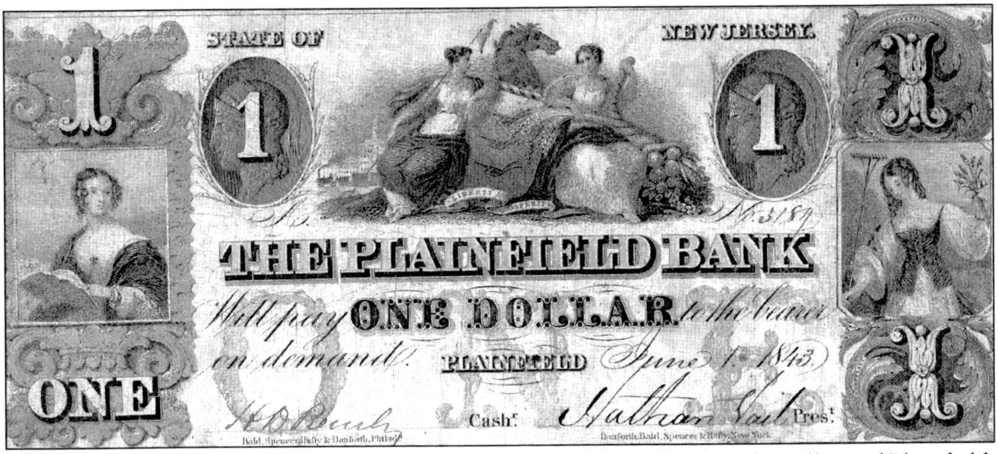

In 1837, the Plainfield Bank became the first institution of its kind in the village of Plainfield. As did many banks, companies, and municipalities, the Plainfield Bank issued its own redeemable bank notes. This 1843 bill is a florid example of the engraver's skill.

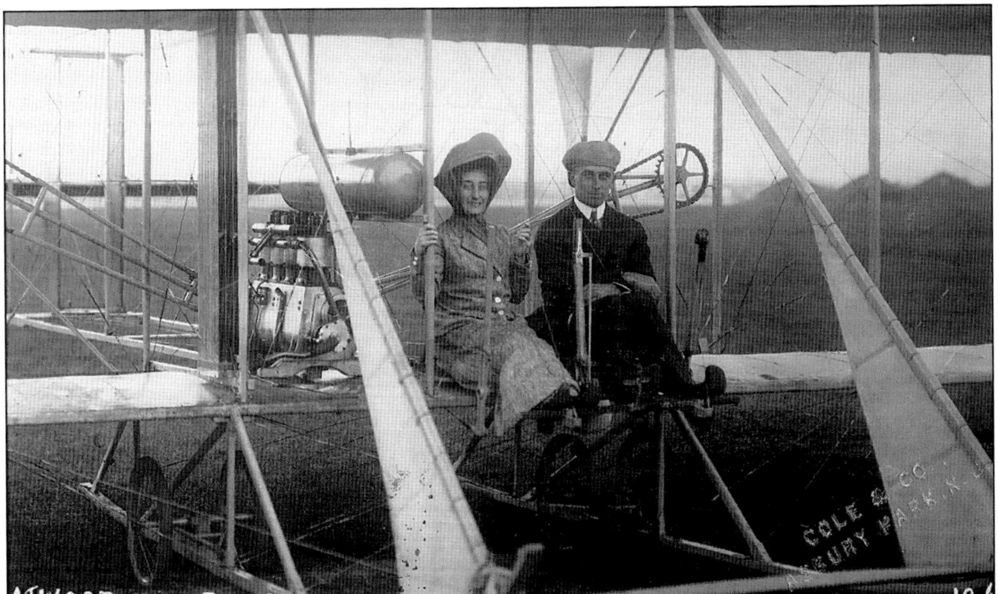

The post office in Plainfield was established in the early 1800s and little more than a century later, airmail was becoming a reality. In August 1912, the famous aviator Lincoln Beachey gave an aerial show at the Riding and Driving Club. For the first time, spectators could send airmail cards. This card is one of 1,351 that were sent that day. It went to Mrs. W.E. Stewart, 526 West Seventh Street.

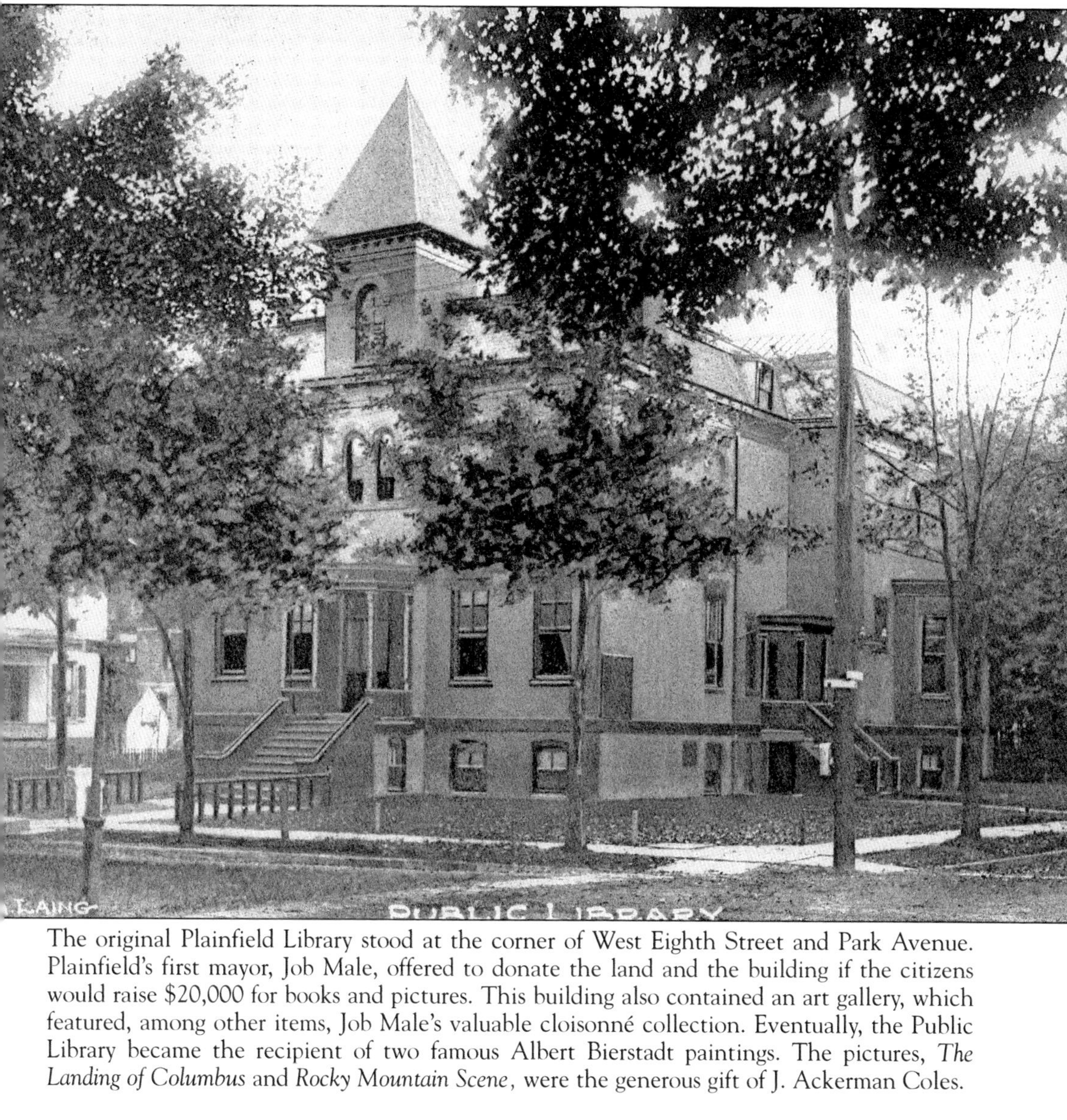

The original Plainfield Library stood at the corner of West Eighth Street and Park Avenue. Plainfield's first mayor, Job Male, offered to donate the land and the building if the citizens would raise $20,000 for books and pictures. This building also contained an art gallery, which featured, among other items, Job Male's valuable cloisonné collection. Eventually, the Public Library became the recipient of two famous Albert Bierstadt paintings. The pictures, *The Landing of Columbus* and *Rocky Mountain Scene*, were the generous gift of J. Ackerman Coles.

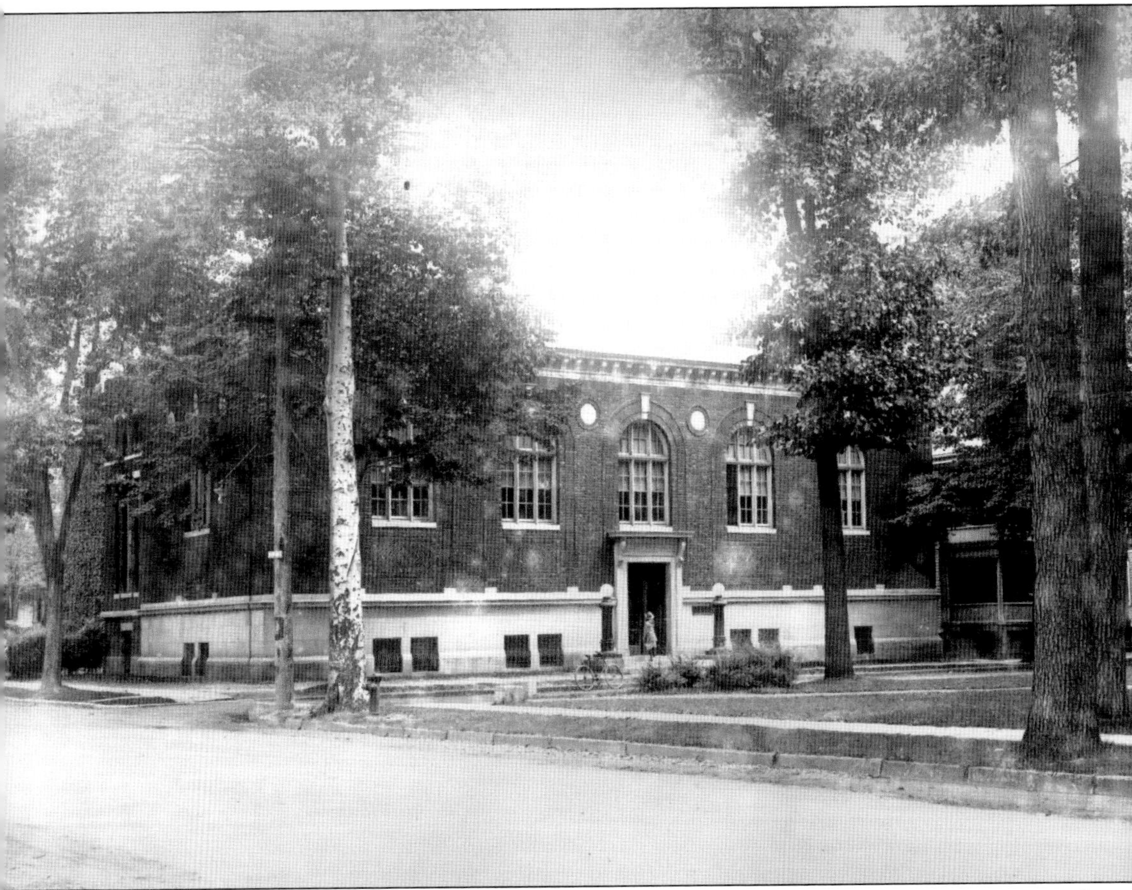

In January 1915, Andrew Carnegie gave $50,000 to the city of Plainfield for construction of a new addition to the cramped quarters in the old Job Male building. The new structure of Italian Renaissance style was designed by New York architects Wilder and White and contained a reading room 30 feet wide with 22-foot ceilings. The exterior, constructed of limestone and tapestry brick, "will be handsome and striking, and still restrained and dignified."

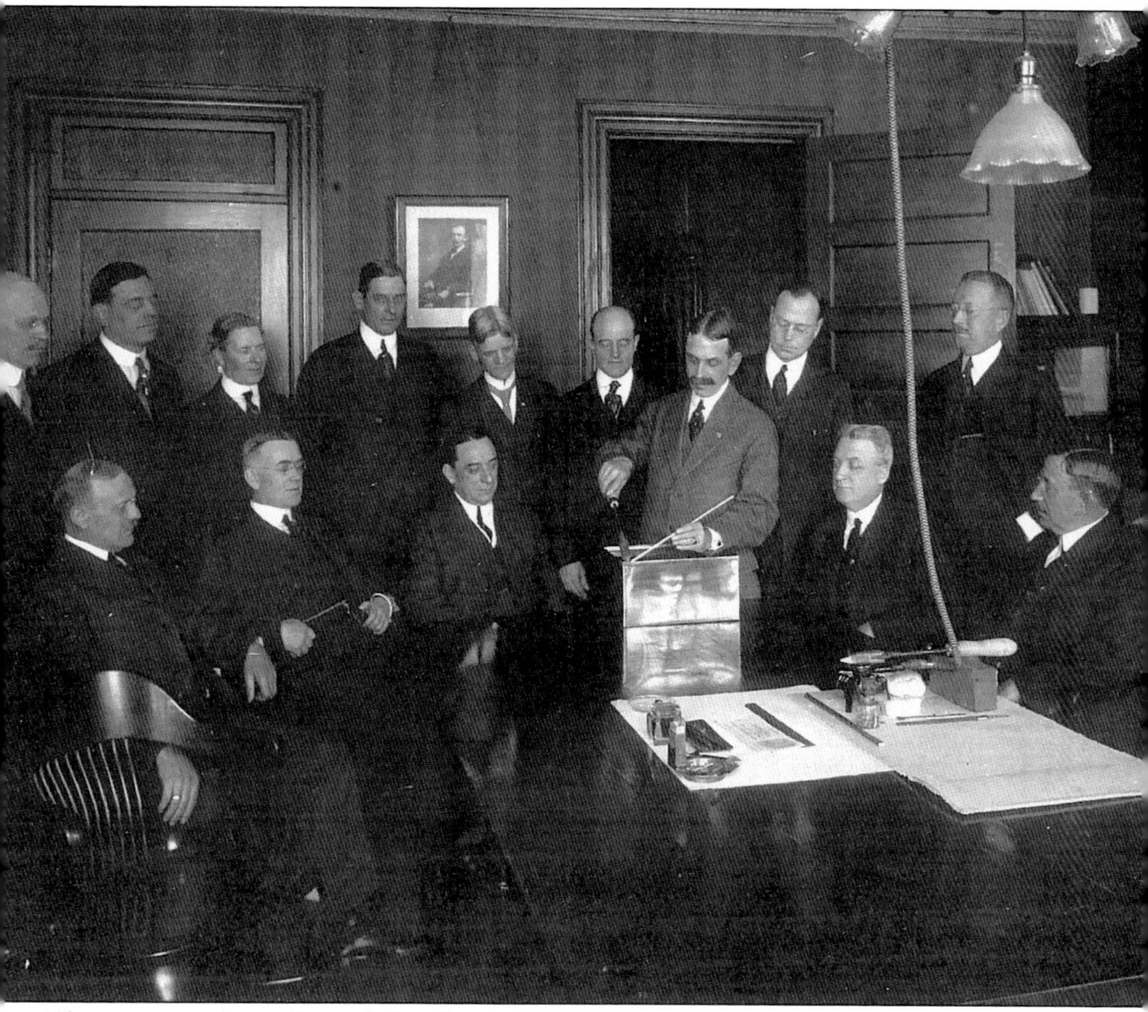

The mayor and members of the Common Council seal the document box before the cornerstone-laying ceremony. In reality, the men were simply posing. Photographer Paul Collier took the picture at 1:50 p.m., dashed home, and developed the film. He then returned at 2:37 p.m. so the print could be put in the box. The copper box was then sealed and ready for the 3:00 p.m. cornerstone ceremony. Shown are the following: (seated) Elias H. Bird, Juan A. Babcock, Francis J. Blatz, Thomas F. Hylan, and Charles C. Graves; (standing) G. Herbert Condict, Theodore A. Martin, John J. Carroll, John Cose, Charles S. Sminck, Arthur Crone, David Dunavan, Lewis M. Booth, and Leighton Calkins.

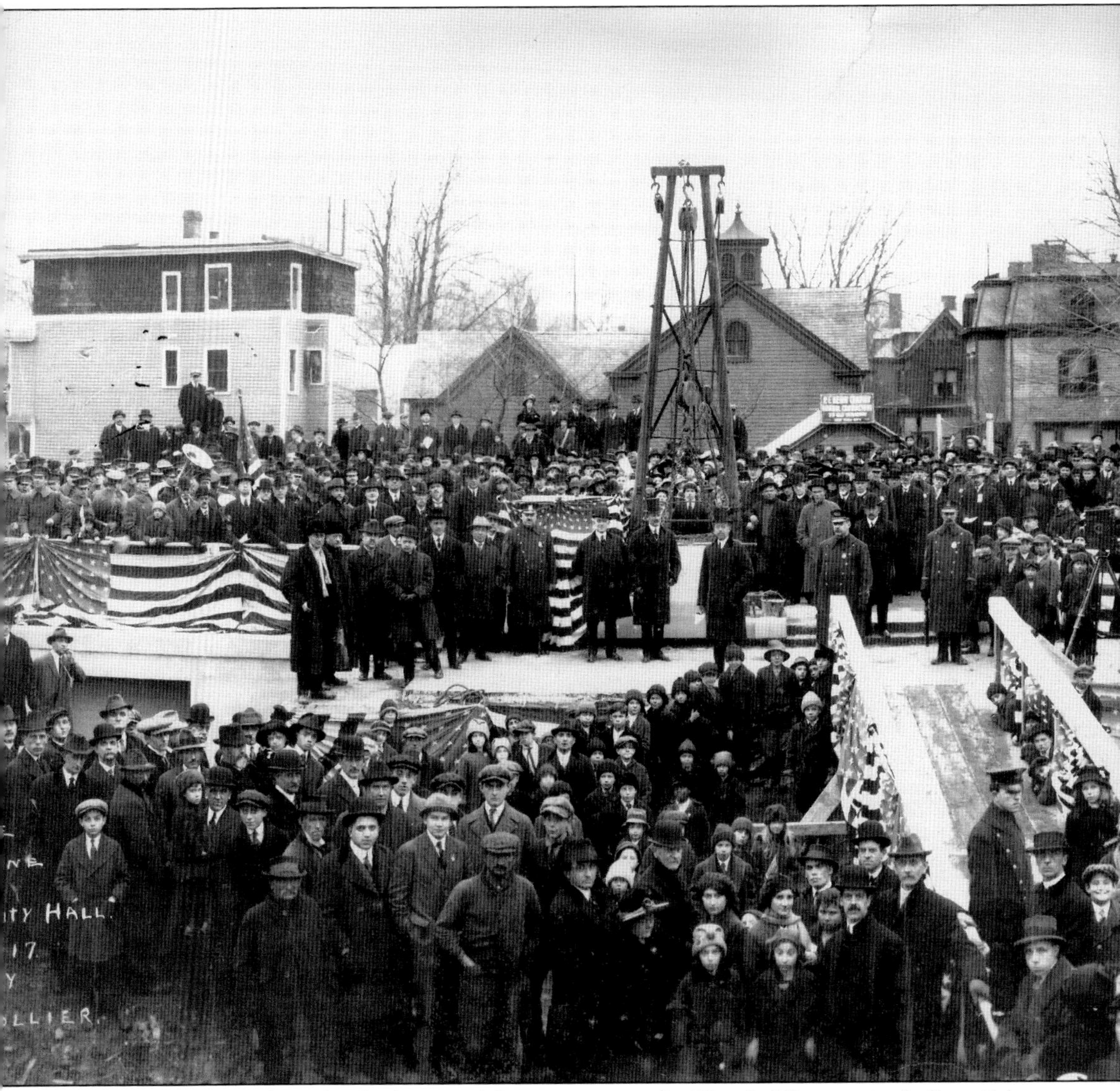

Hundreds turned out for the laying of the cornerstone for Plainfield's new city hall on February 17, 1917. Despite the winter weather, there were speeches and music. Mayor Leighton Calkins said: "Here will be performed the duties of the servants of the people. Let this building be a

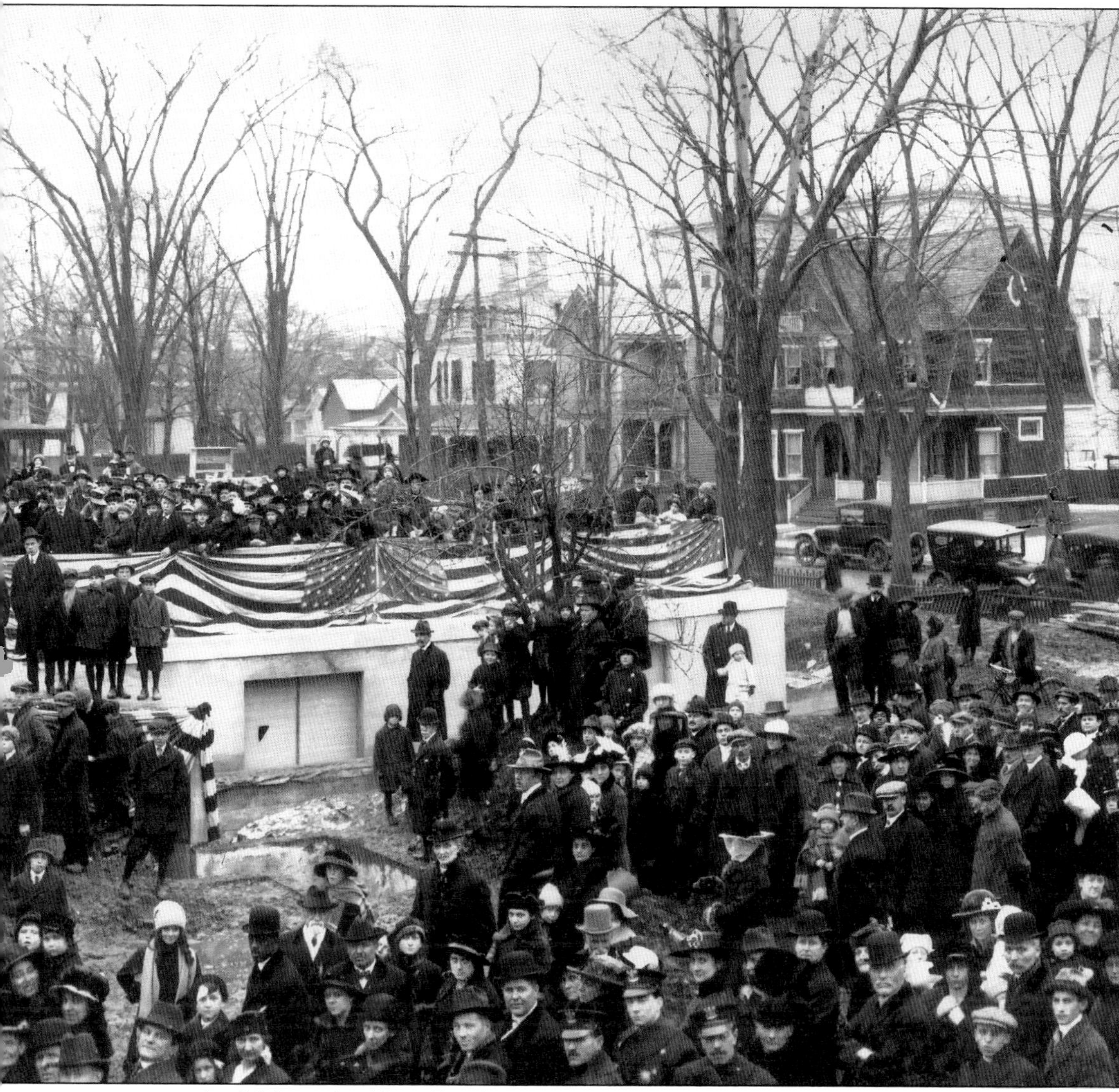

monument to the fidelity of public officials sworn to the service of this community. . . . Better that this building should never be erected than it should be desecrated by unworthy use."

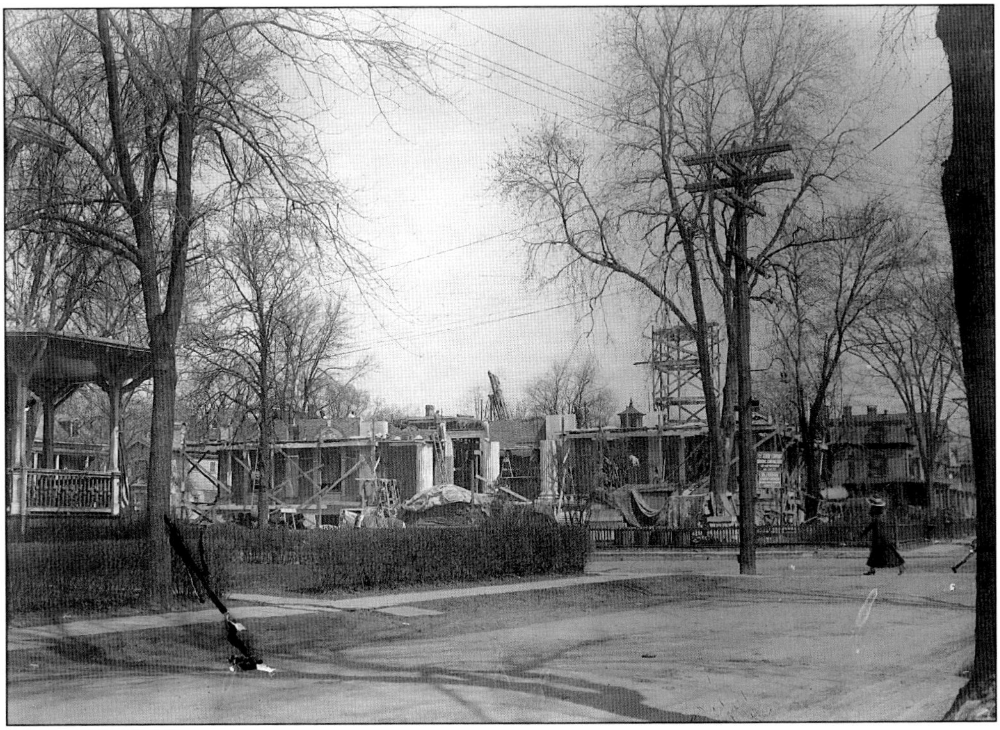

It had been deemed that all construction work on the new city hall should be performed by union labor. The laying of the cornerstone and the mayor's role were actually considered part of the construction process. In the ultimate politically correct move, Mayor Leighton Calkins was sworn in as an honorary member of the bricklayers union.

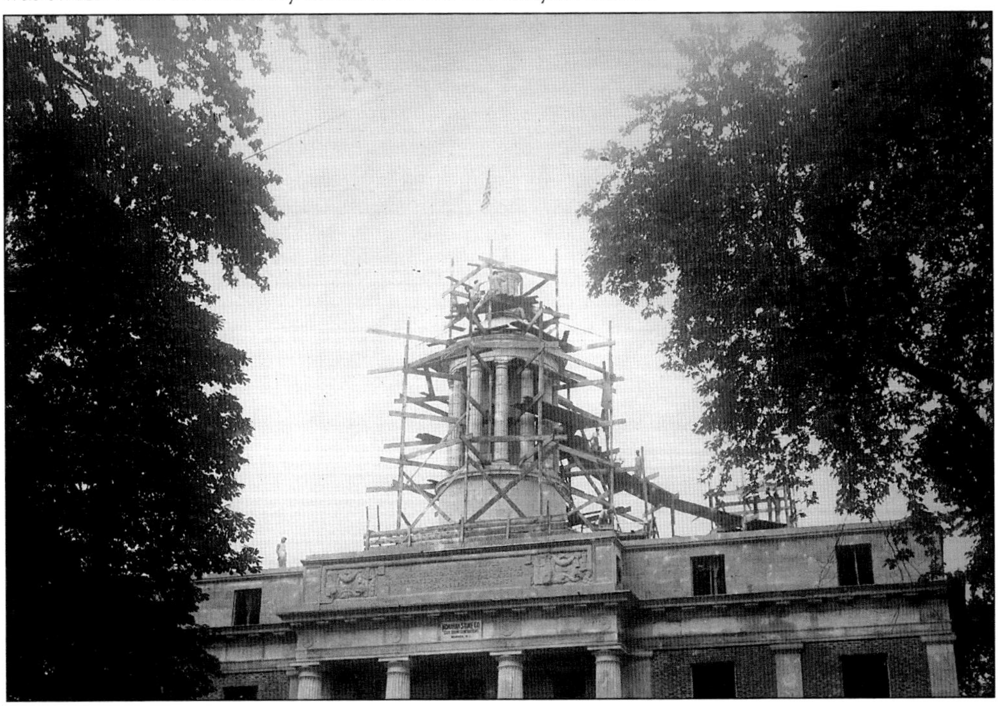

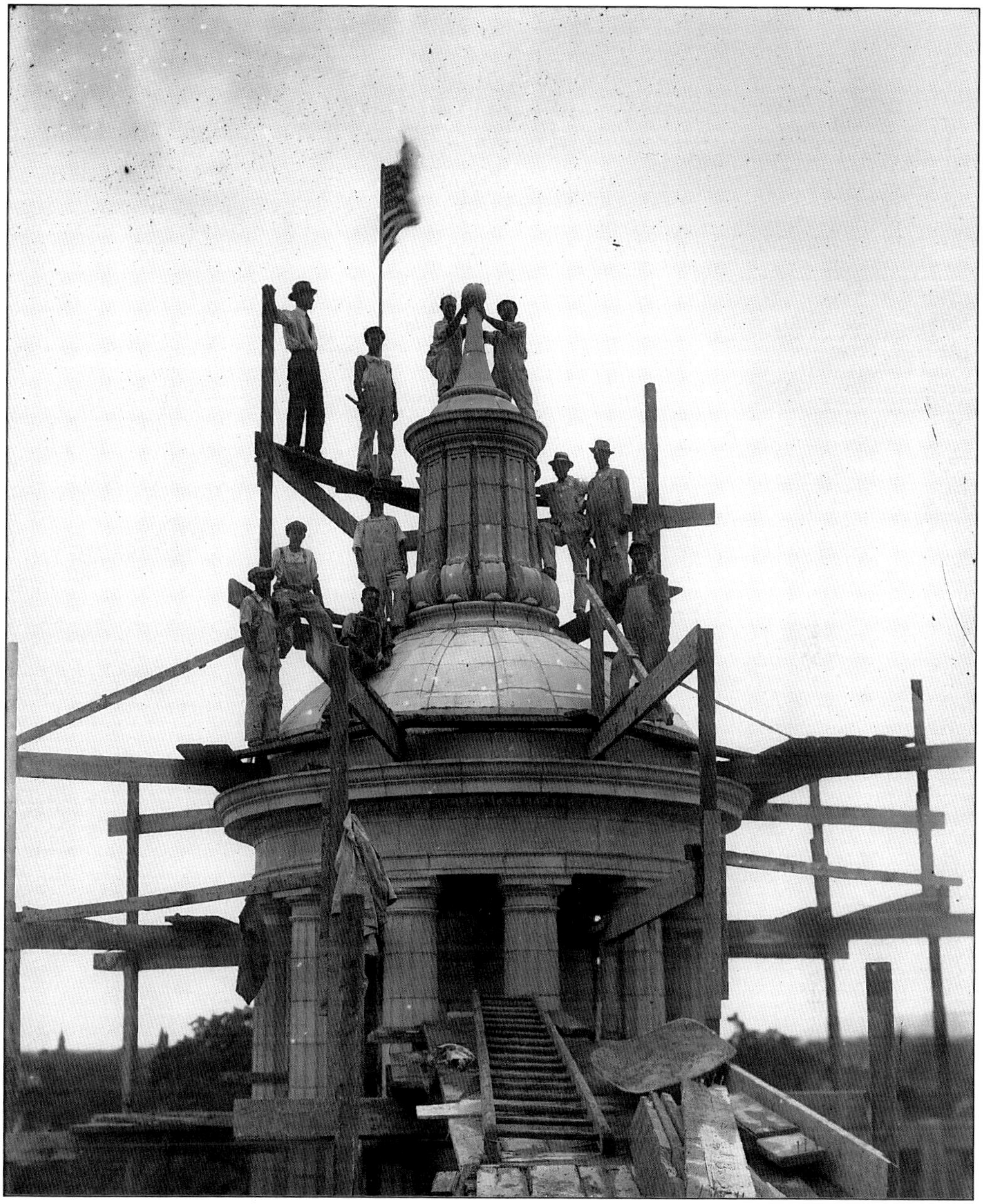

Workmen look to the camera as they complete the cupola atop Plainfield City Hall. This crowning touch to Plainfield's monument of civic pride recalls what Abraham Lincoln once said: "I like to see a man proud of the place in which he lives. I like to see a man who lives in it so that his place will be proud of him."

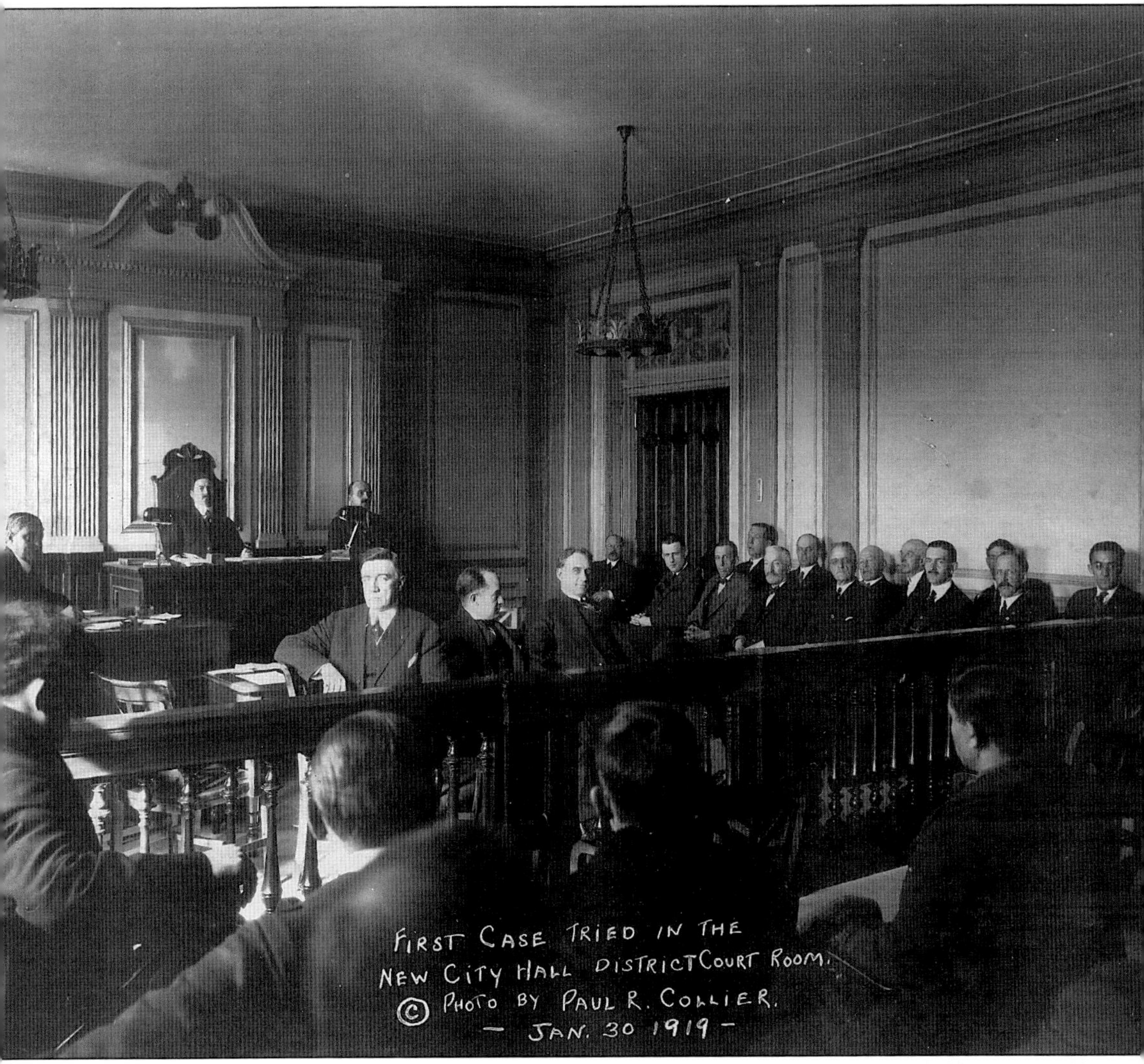

Photographer Paul Collier captures the first case tried in the new Plainfield City Hall. Many photographers, both amateur and professional, have captured Plainfield's history on film. Some of their names are unrecorded in history. We are grateful to all of them. However, a very special thanks to Collier, who so thoroughly recorded the events of everyday life in the city of Plainfield.

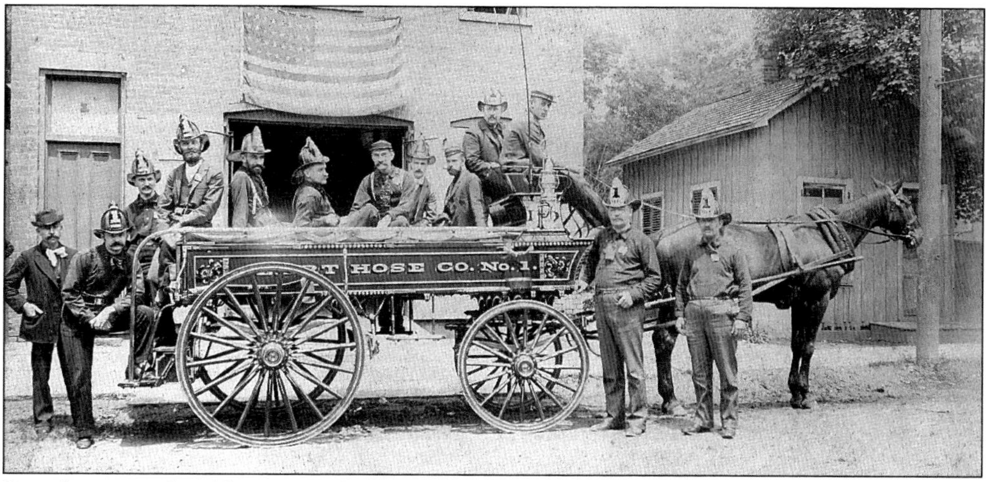

Seen here are the Alert Hose Company in 1891 (above) and Plainfield's original firehouse (below). Fire protection developed in a tradition of communities guarding themselves against the ever-present threat of fire. However, in the 1870s, national boards were being organized and equipment was being standardized. Many early companies were volunteer groups composed frequently of prominent citizens. In some cases, these groups became powerful social and political forces.

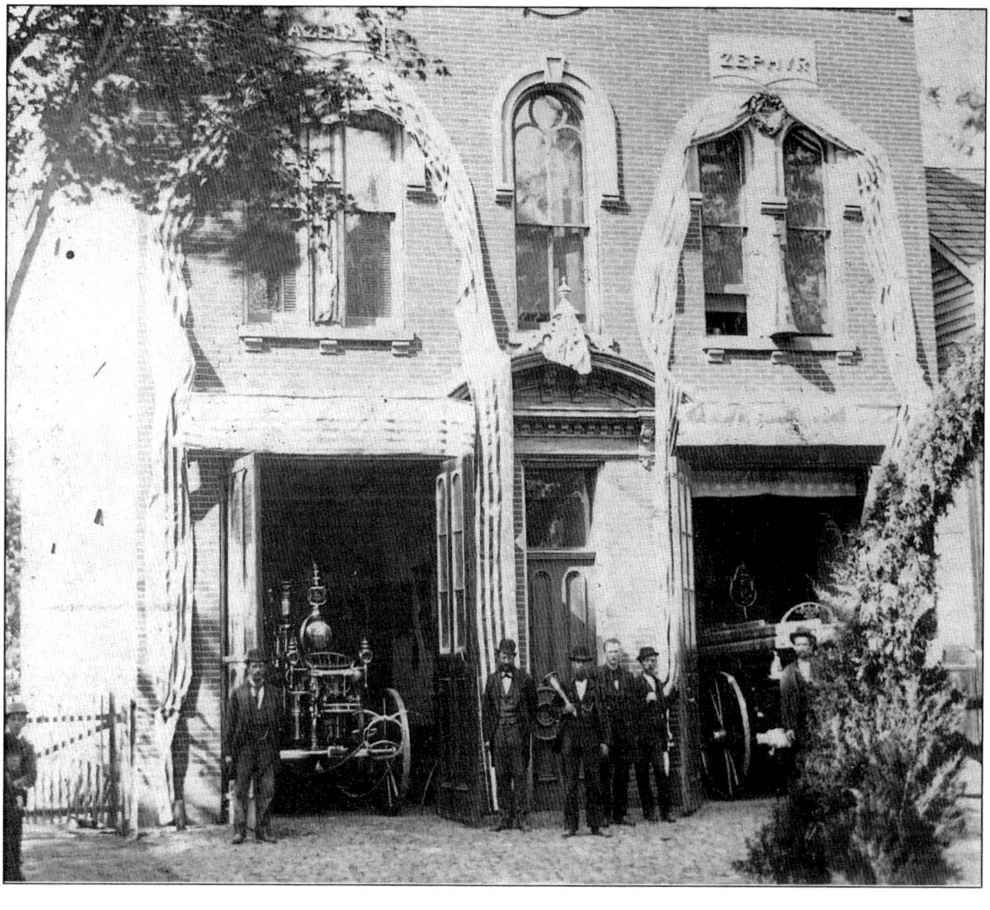

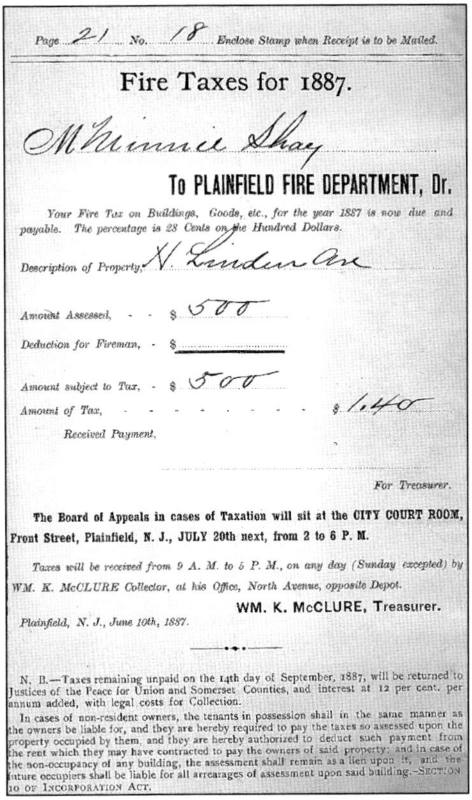

Page 21 *No.* 18 *Enclose Stamp when Receipt is to be Mailed.*

Fire Taxes for 1887.

M Minnie Shay

To PLAINFIELD FIRE DEPARTMENT, Dr.

Your Fire Tax on Buildings, Goods, etc., for the year 1887 is now due and payable. The percentage is 28 Cents on the Hundred Dollars.

Description of Property, N. Linden Ave

Amount Assessed, $ 500

Deduction for Fireman, $

Amount subject to Tax, $ 500

Amount of Tax, $ 1.40

Received Payment,

For Treasurer.

The Board of Appeals in cases of Taxation will sit at the CITY COURT ROOM, Front Street, Plainfield, N. J., JULY 20th next, from 2 to 6 P. M.

Taxes will be received from 9 A. M. to 5 P. M., on any day (Sunday excepted) by WM. K. McCLURE Collector, at his Office, North Avenue, opposite Depot.

WM. K. McCLURE, Treasurer.

Plainfield, N. J., June 10th, 1887.

N. B.—Taxes remaining unpaid on the 14th day of September, 1887, will be returned to Justices of the Peace for Union and Somerset Counties, and interest at 12 per cent. per annum added, with legal costs for Collection.

In cases of non-resident owners, the tenants in possession shall in the same manner as the owners be liable for, and they are hereby required to pay the taxes so assessed upon the property occupied by them, and they are hereby authorized to deduct such payment from the rent which they may have contracted to pay the owners of said property; and in case of the non-occupancy of any building, the assessment shall remain as a lien upon it, and the future occupiers shall be liable for all arrearages of assessment upon said building.—SECTION 10 OF INCORPORATION ACT.

Plainfielders can be a cantankerous lot. Many disliked their separation from Essex County in 1857, and many more opposed the name Union County, preferring Rock County with its Revolutionary War associations. They also took exception to the legality of a municipal fire tax in 1887. That time, they won.

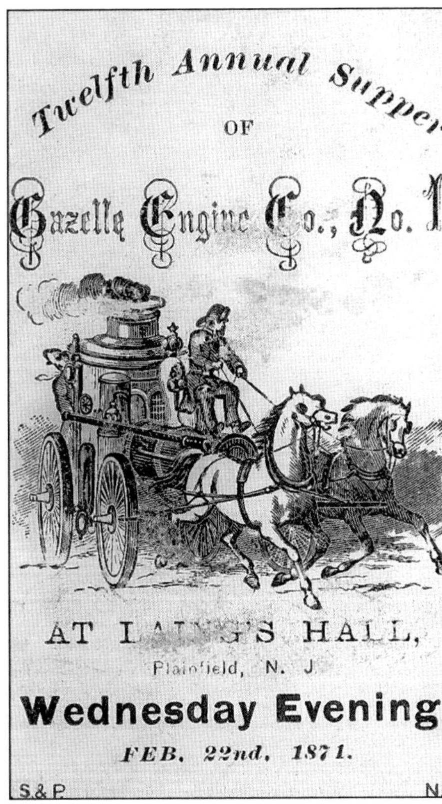

With open flame such an everyday part of life, firefighters took their duties seriously. There was, however, time for relaxation at the annual firemen's ball, held in the popular Laing's Hotel, on West Front Street. If the alarm had rung, Laing's would have been half-empty in minutes.

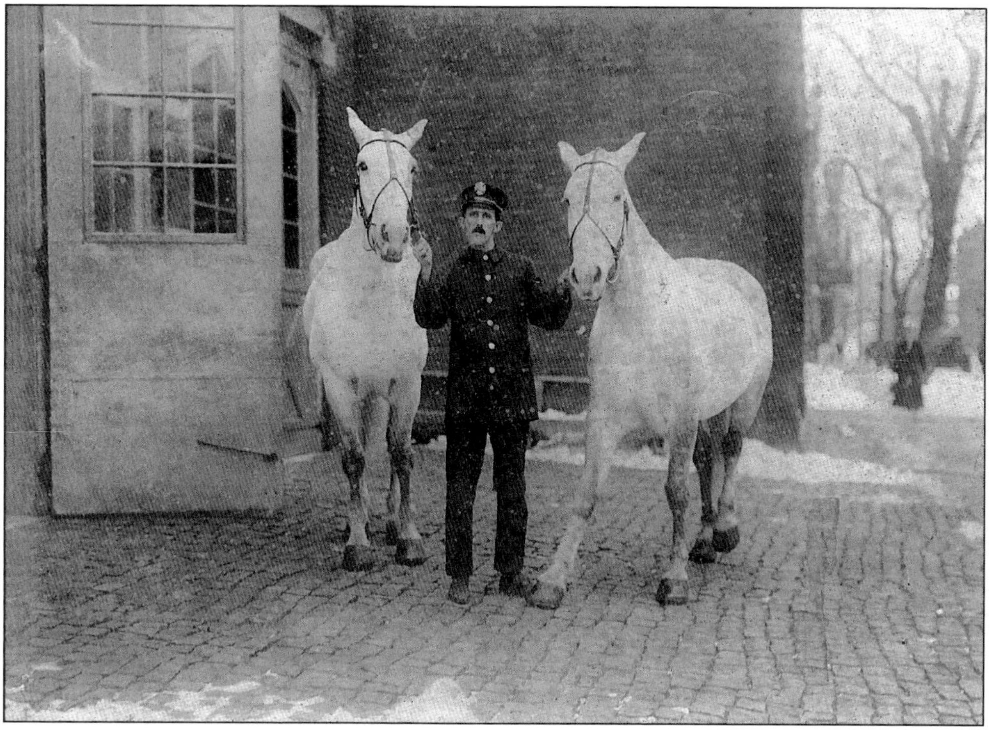

The unsung heroes of the fire department were the hardworking horses. When the city street department was short on steeds, the fire horses were frequently pressed into service, hauling dump carts of gravel or sprinkler wagons around Plainfield's dusty streets.

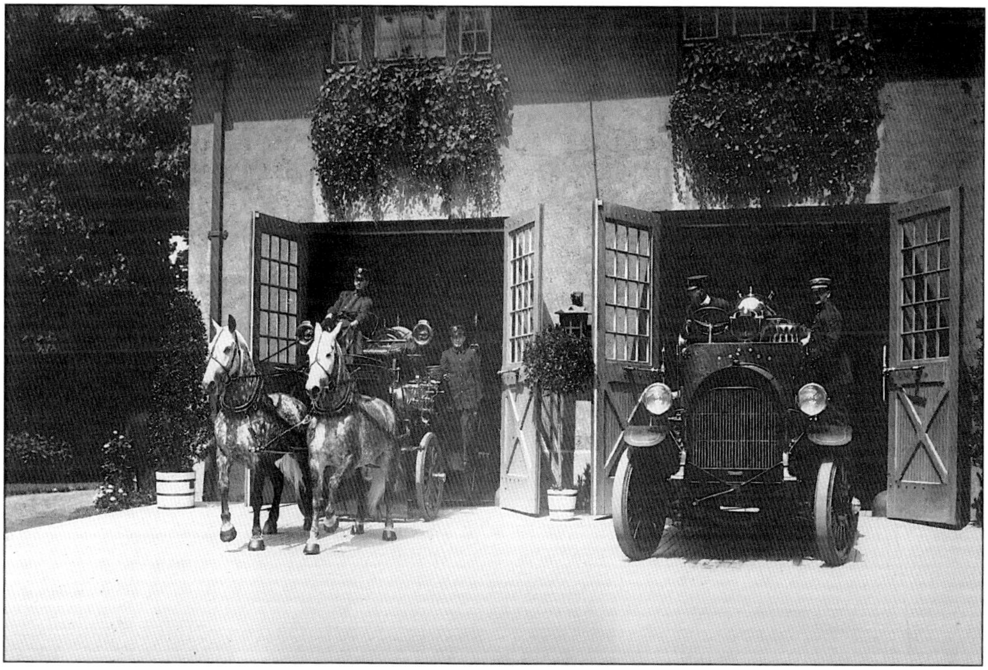

In 1909, the Netherwood firehouse, on South Avenue, was completed, but the transition had yet to be finalized with mechanized transportation.

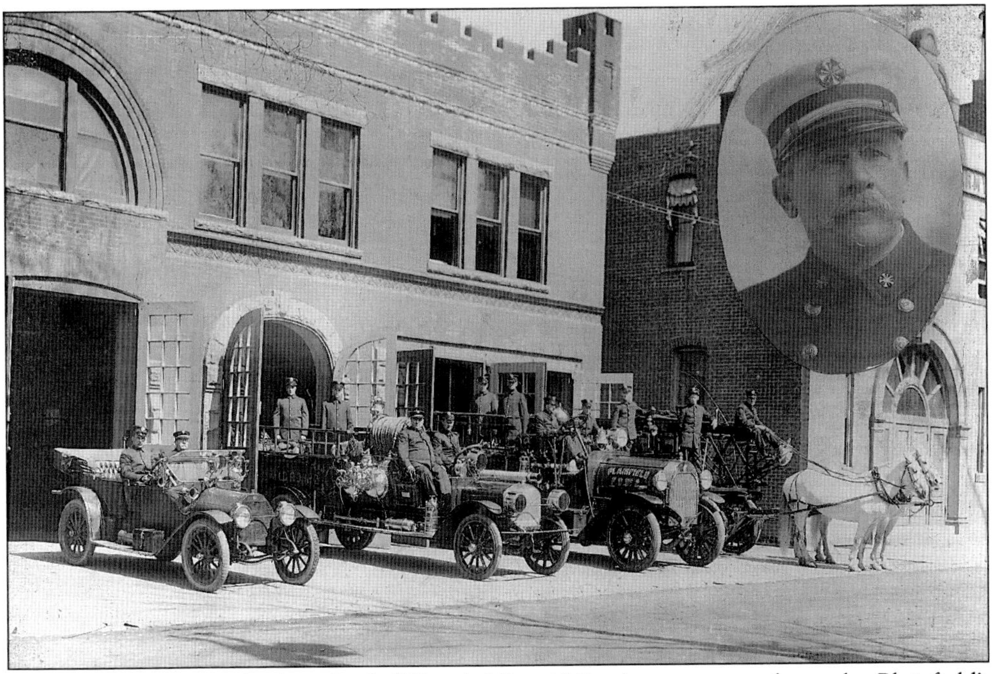

Thaddeus Doane was the first chief of Plainfield's paid fire department and was also Plainfield's building inspector. A Civil War veteran, Doane retired in 1916 and continued to live in Plainfield until his death in 1928 at age 84.

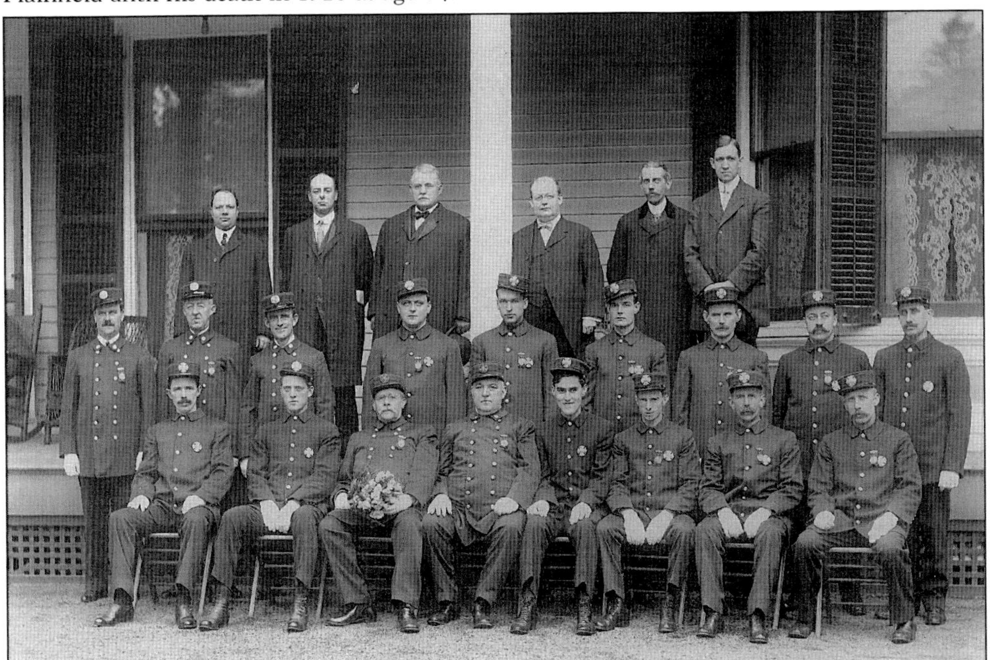

Mayor Fisk (to the right of the column) was a great advocate of the fire and police departments. Each year, both departments were inspected and reviewed on the front lawn of his West Seventh Street mansion. Fisk took all of his responsibilities seriously, especially public safety issues.

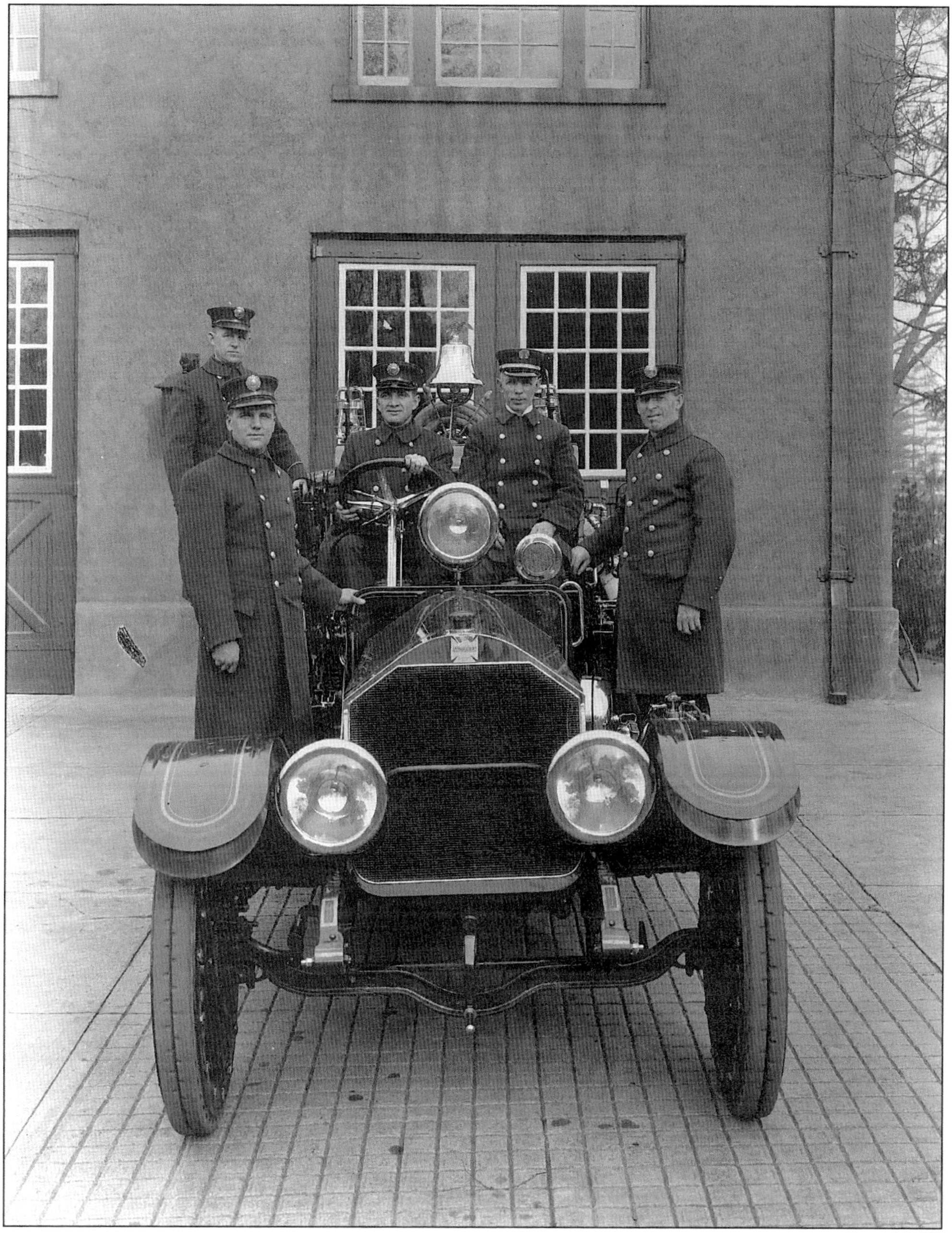

The men of the Netherwood Company posed for a formal portrait to show off their well-maintained engine, firehouse, and uniforms on November 1, 1921. Spit and polish was the order of the day.

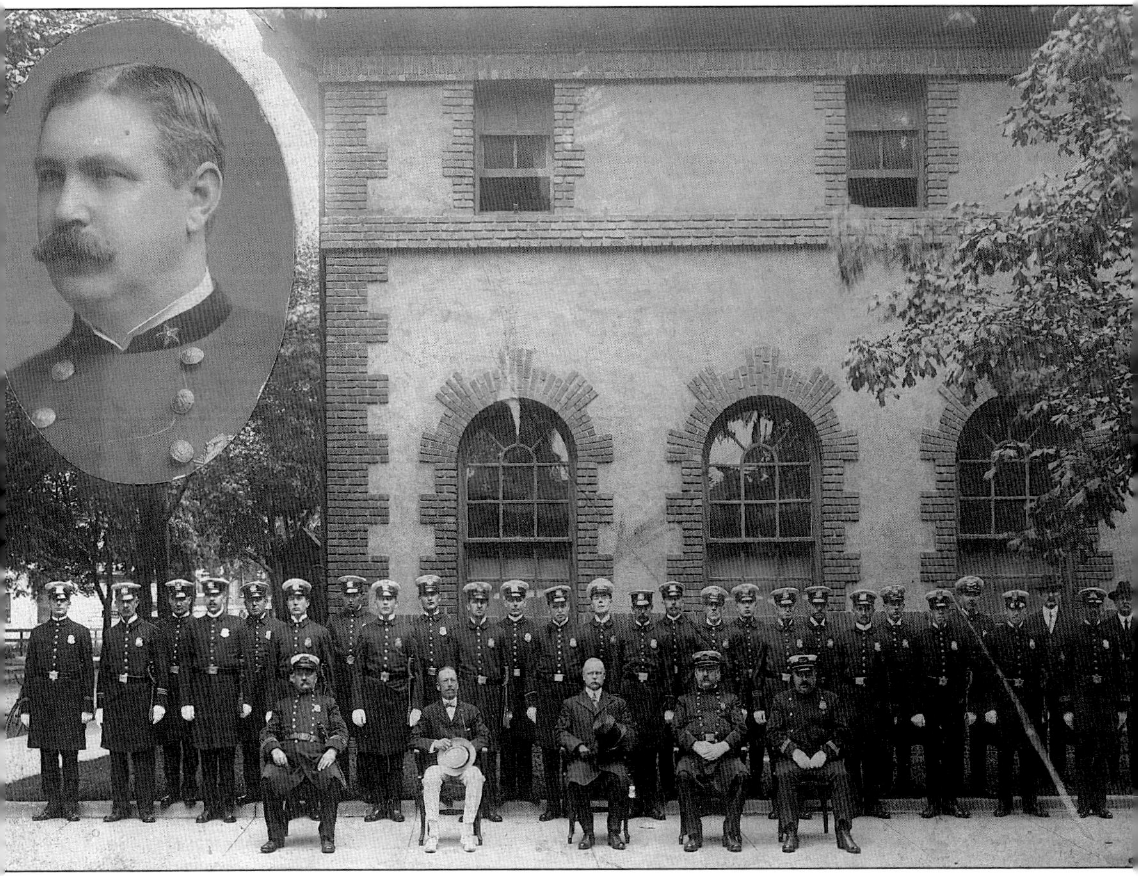

The police force, under the direction of Chief Kiely, poses in front of its headquarters on Sycamore and West Fourth Streets. It was reputedly the best force to be found in any city of comparable size at the time this photograph was taken, c. 1916.

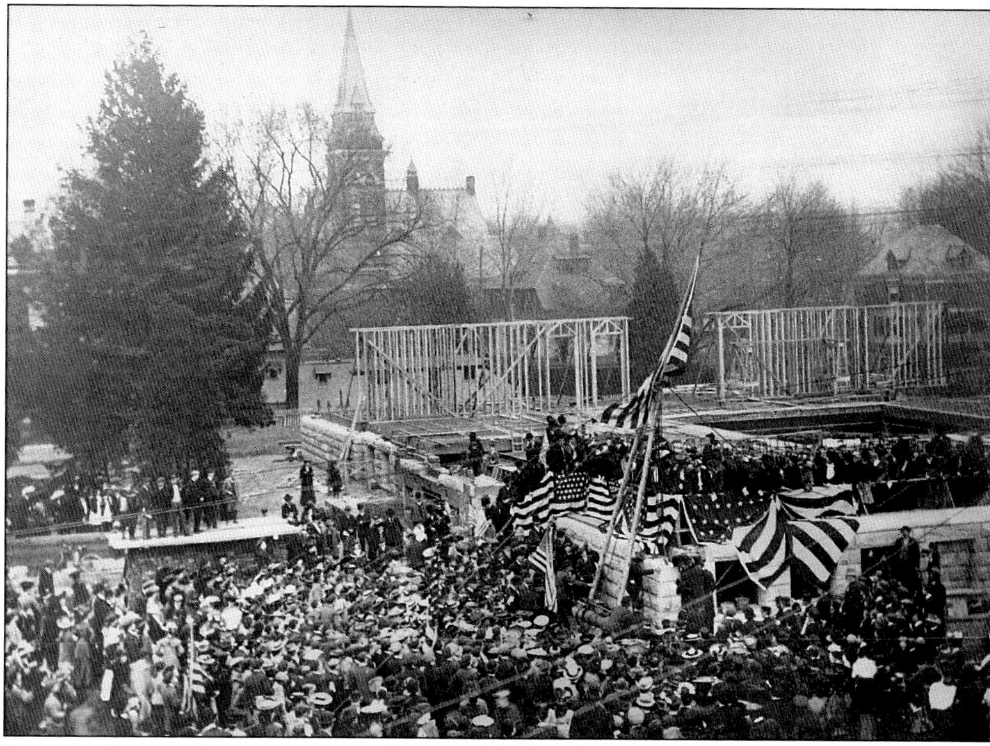

Ever popular was the construction of new public buildings and their attendant festivities. On November 3, 1904, the cornerstone was set for the new high school. Mayor Olin Jenkins, member of the Class of 1869, presided and spoke before a crowd of 2,500 people.

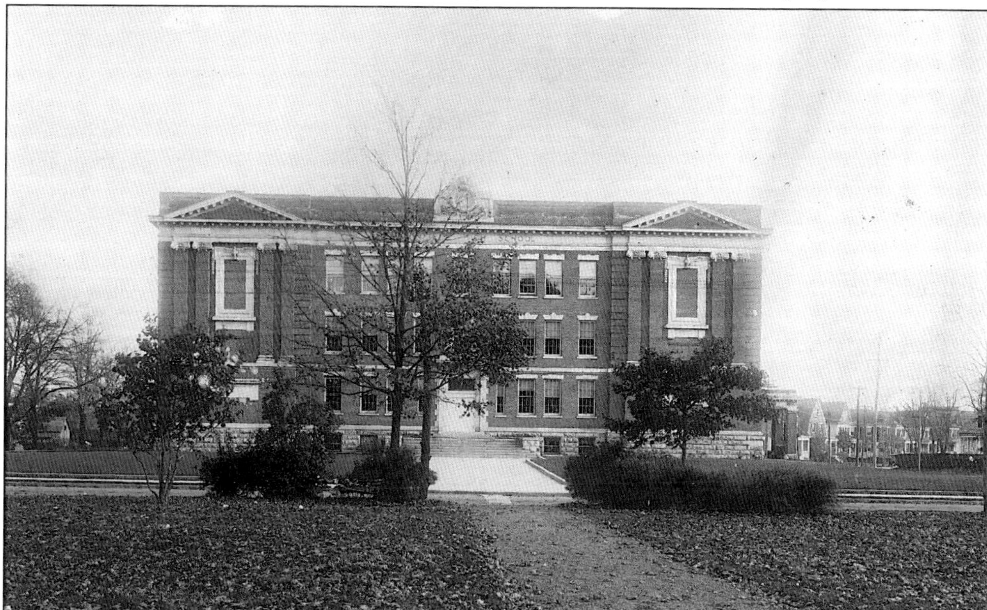

The new high school was dedicated on February 23, 1906. The building was open from early morning until after midnight to accommodate the hundreds who came to marvel at the up-to-date educational facility.

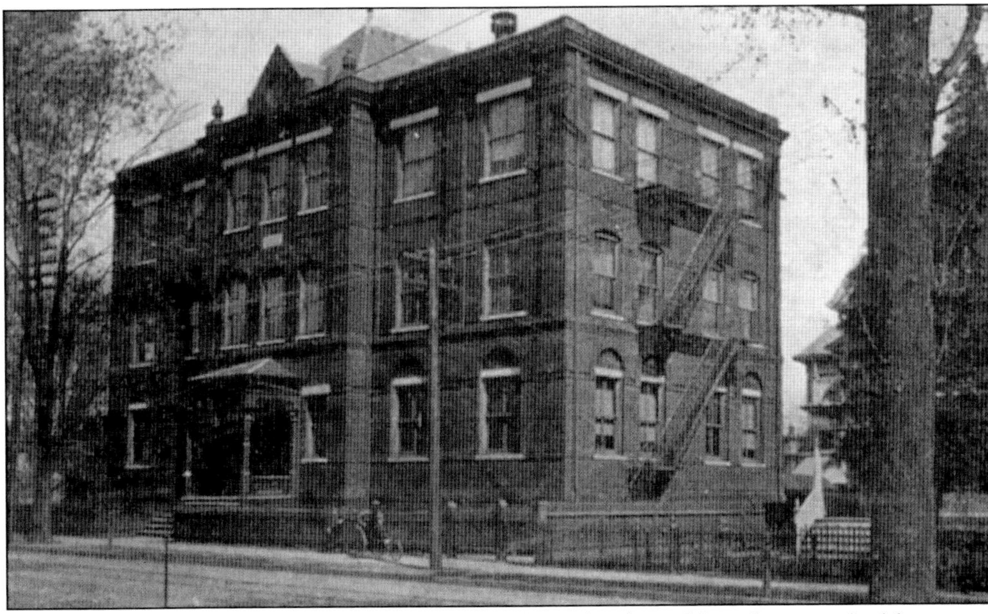

By 1909—the date of this class picture at Franklin School—public education had become a matter of great community pride, as evidenced by the 10 public schools in town. Children of the rising generation, it was pointed out, had facilities for learning far ahead of those that their fathers enjoyed.

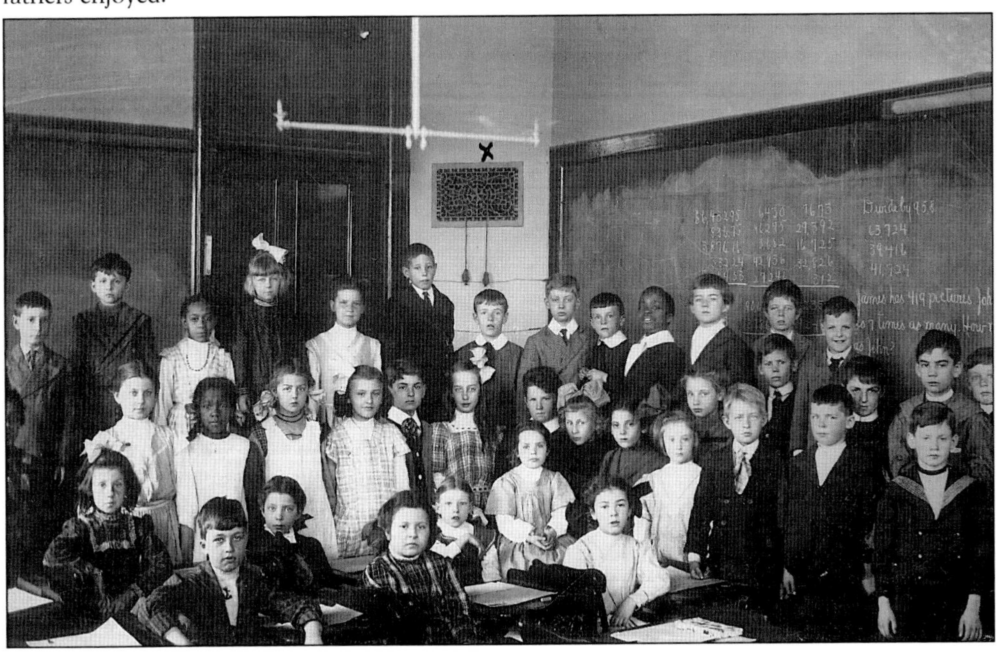

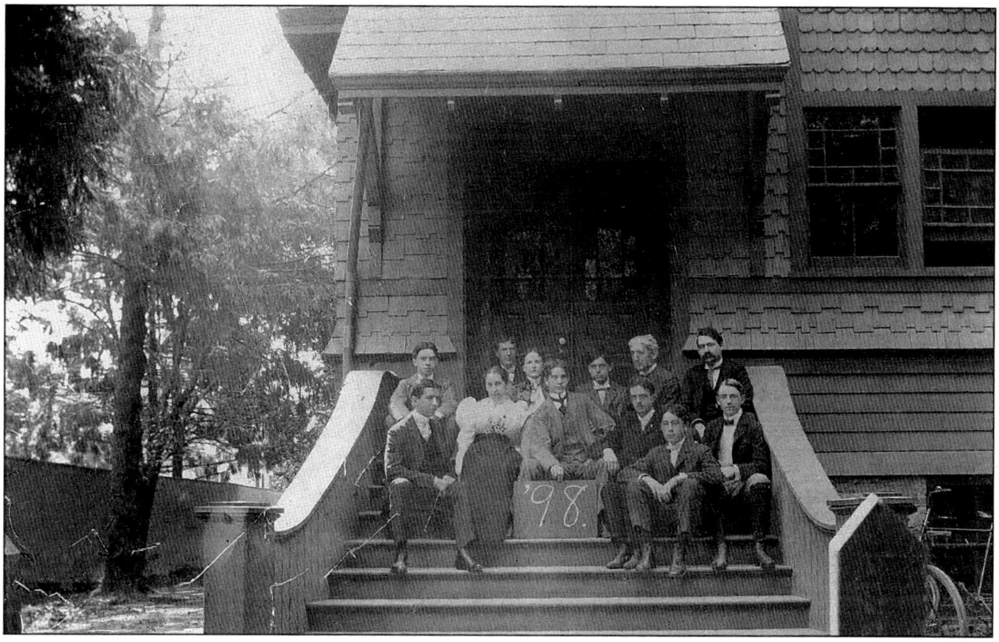

By the time the Class of 1898 sat for this picture, Mr. Leal's School for Boys was well established. The West Front Street location had historical associations, in that it was the first plot of ground to be set aside for educational purposes in Plainfield. For more than 100 years, it had been known as "Academy Lot."

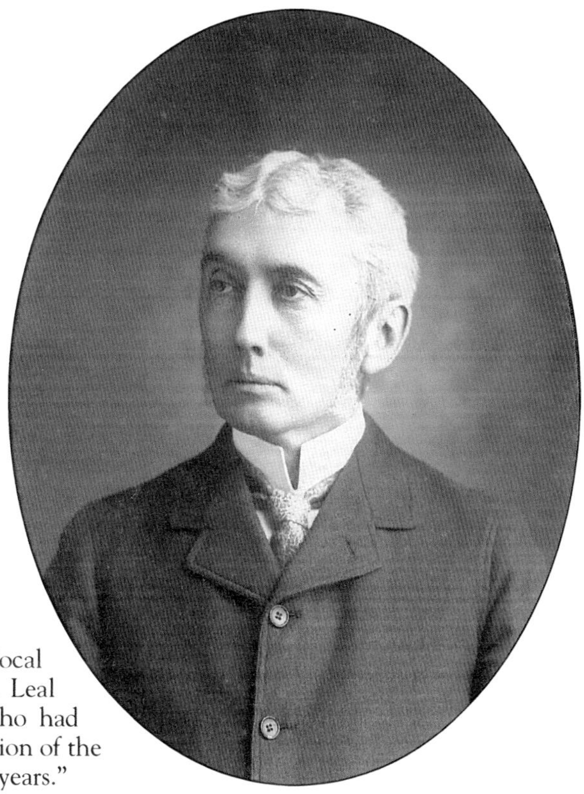

When John Leal died in 1936, the local press stated that "The passing of Mr. Leal removes from the community one who had been an important factor in the education of the youth of Plainfield over a period of 34 years."

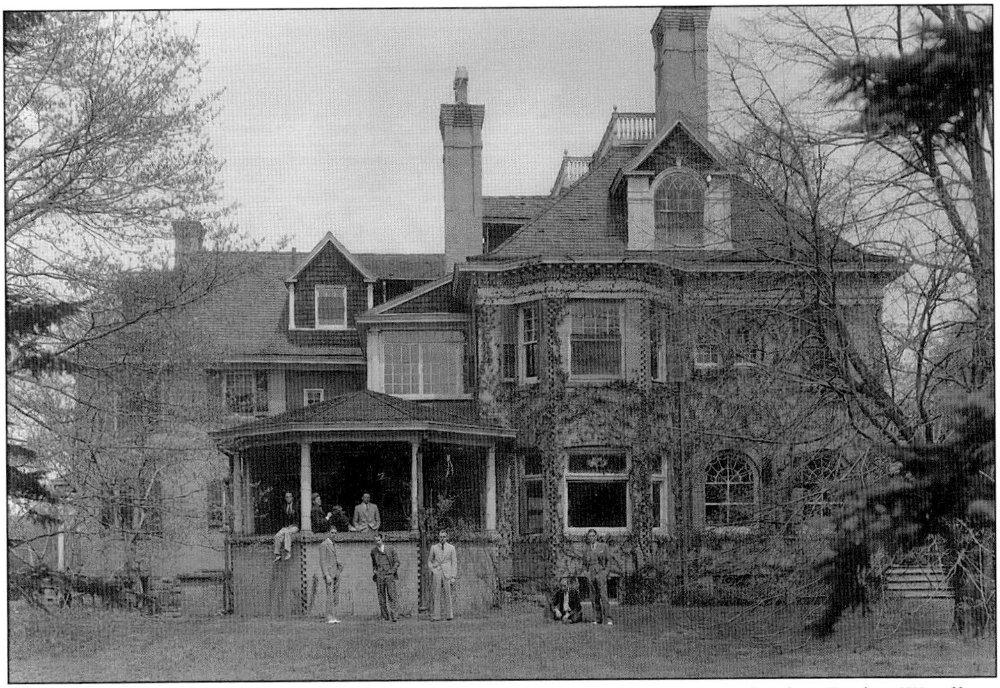

After Mr. Leal's 34-year tenure, the tradition was carried on by Charles Digby Wardlaw. Wardlaw renamed the school the Wardlaw Country Day School and moved classes to Park Avenue. In 1932, Wardlaw acquired the Strong mansion (above), on Central Avenue, which proved adequate for many years. Today, the home is known as the DuCret School of Art.

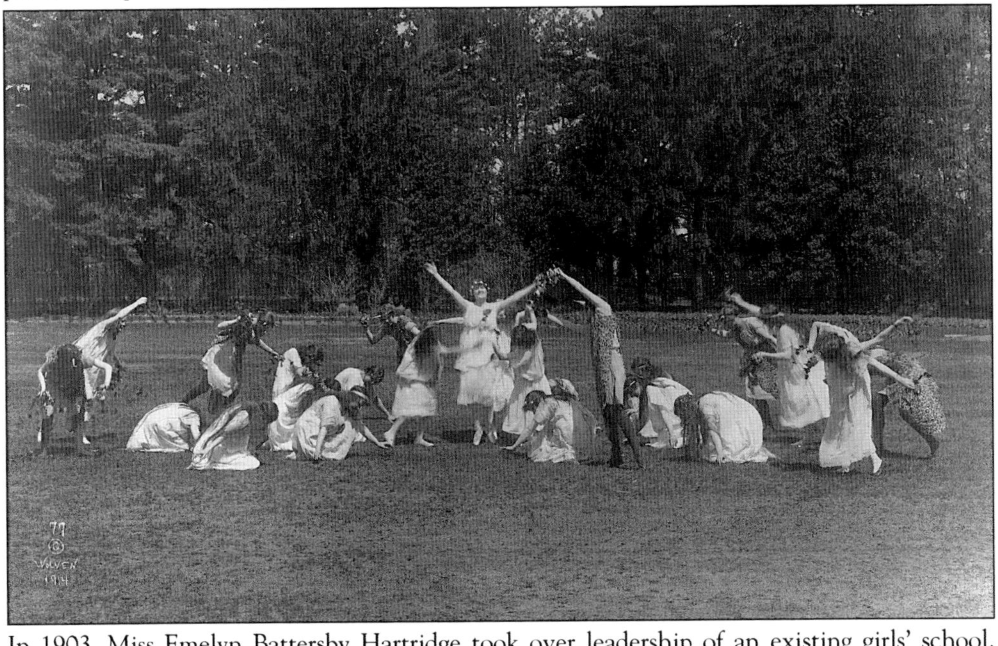

In 1903, Miss Emelyn Battersby Hartridge took over leadership of an existing girls' school. Hartridge established the Hartridge School for Girls at the old Oakwood estate on Plainfield Avenue. An annual event at the school was a presentation on the green *of A Midsummer Night's Dream*. Pictured here are the young women from the Class of 1914.

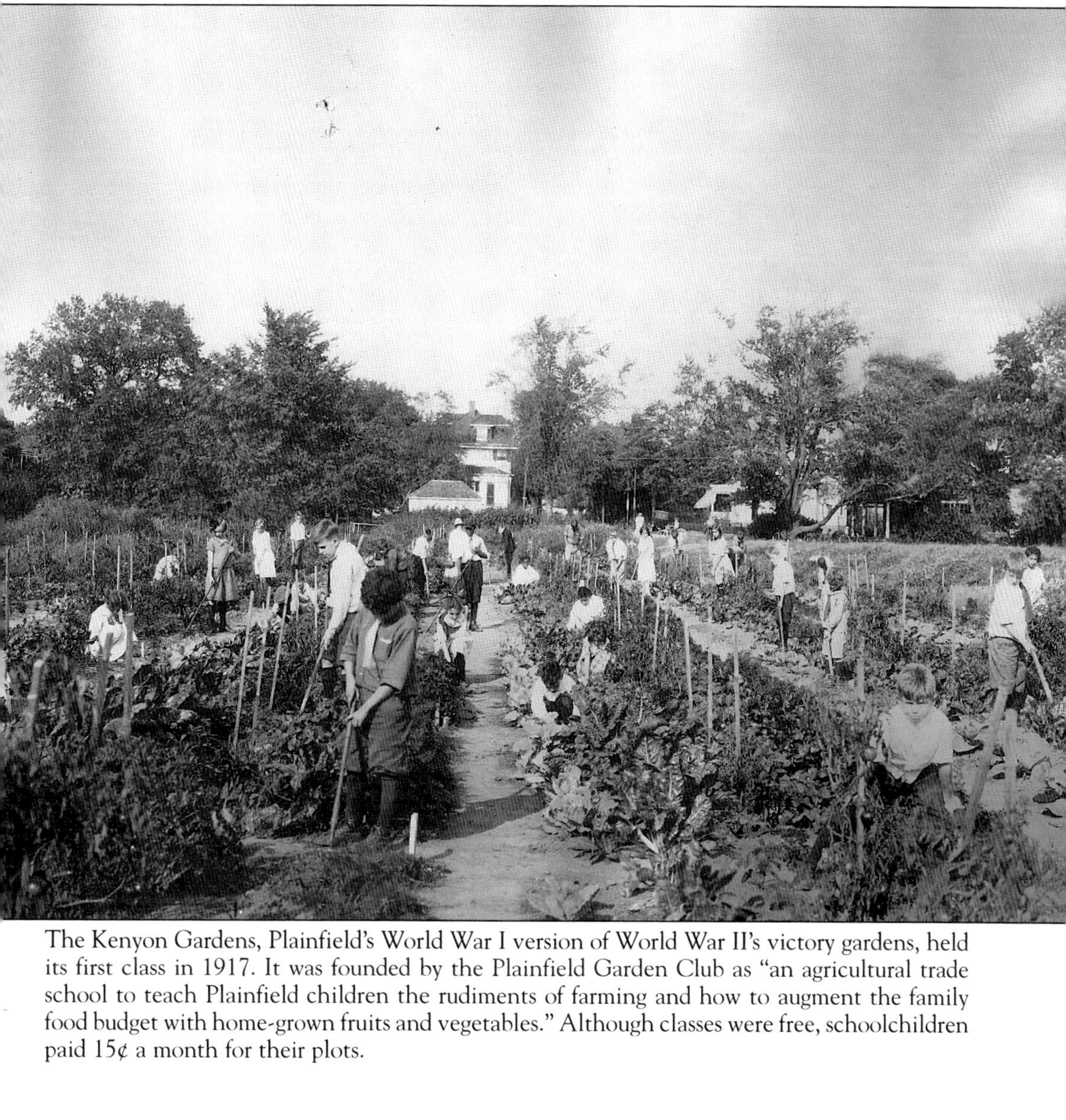

The Kenyon Gardens, Plainfield's World War I version of World War II's victory gardens, held its first class in 1917. It was founded by the Plainfield Garden Club as "an agricultural trade school to teach Plainfield children the rudiments of farming and how to augment the family food budget with home-grown fruits and vegetables." Although classes were free, schoolchildren paid 15¢ a month for their plots.

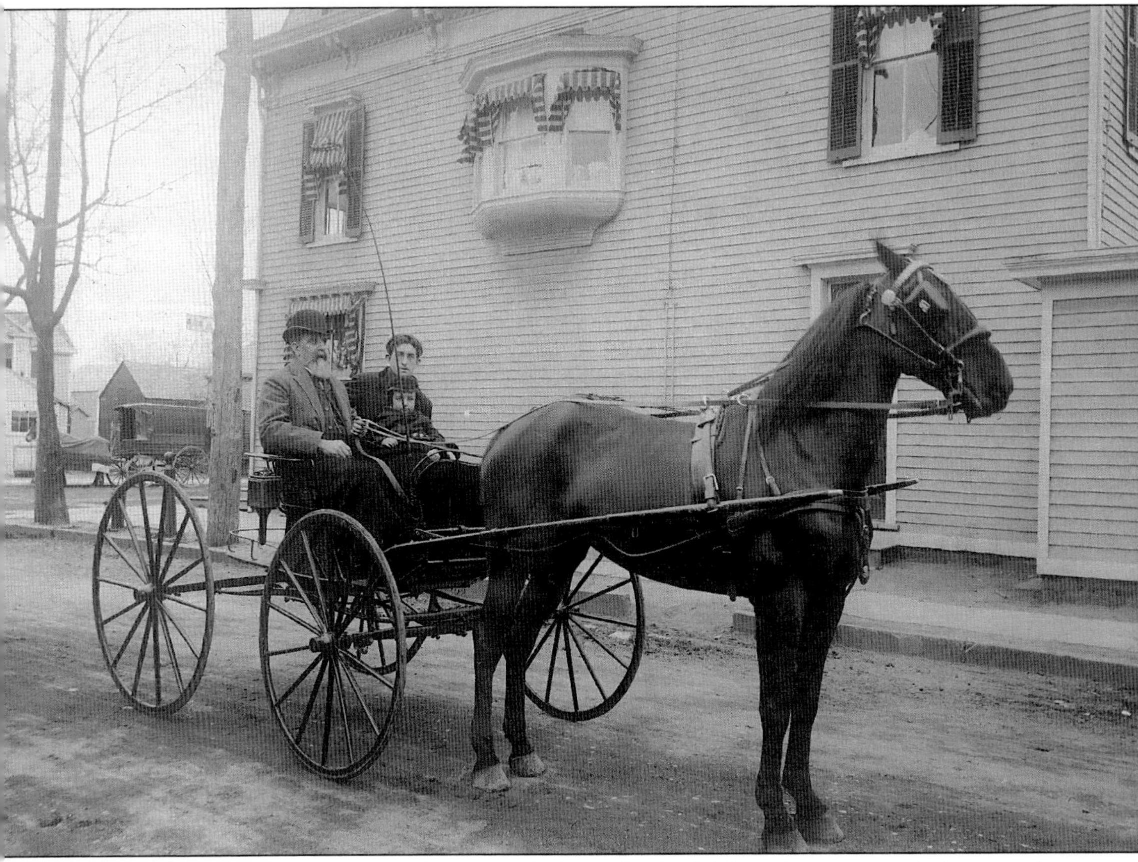

Commitment to a community begins with the individual. Here, in an unusual photograph, we find not only three generations of the Blatz family, but a tradition of community service that still carries through today. The youngest in the carriage, Frank Blatz, later became father to the current Frank Blatz Jr., attorney and former Plainfield mayor.

Seven

I DREAMT THAT I DWELT

Fantasy fails in comparison with Pulitzer Prize-winning author Van Wyck Brooks's memories of childhood days on West Eighth Street during Plainfield's gilded age. He wrote as follows:

"By this time the quiet Quaker village where Woolman had preached in the meetinghouse had become a full-blown Wall Street Suburb. Even the name of Peace Street had vanished forever . . . Vast red sandstone houses rose, like so many Kenilworth castles, with turrets, verandahs, balconies and porte-cocheres, with arches, fountains, coach-houses, kennels and stables . . . In any case . . . it seemed to be a stable world, permanently supported by cast iron customs . . . The grinding sound of the coffeemill that rose early from the kitchen mingled with the other summer sounds, the mowing of the lawn and the far away beating of the carpets, the whirring of the water sprinklers, the rocking of hammocks, bespeaking not only security but endless time for everything."—From *Scenes and Portraits, Memories of Childhood and Youth*; Van Wyck Brooks; E.P. Dutton & Company, New York; 1954.

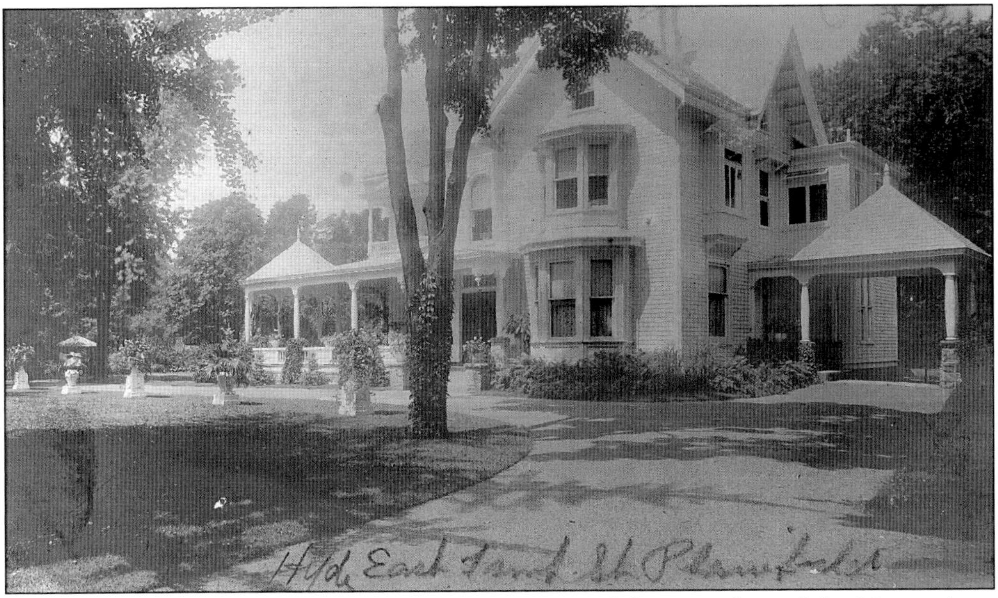

The president of the Central Railroad of New Jersey and first president of the Metropolitan Museum of Art, John Taylor Johnston maintained his summer home here from 1863 to 1895. After Johnston's death, the 100-plus-acre estate was passed to his daughter, Frances Mali, wife of the Belgian consul general Pierre Mali. The estate remained intact until 1936, when the property was subdivided into building lots and the house was demolished.

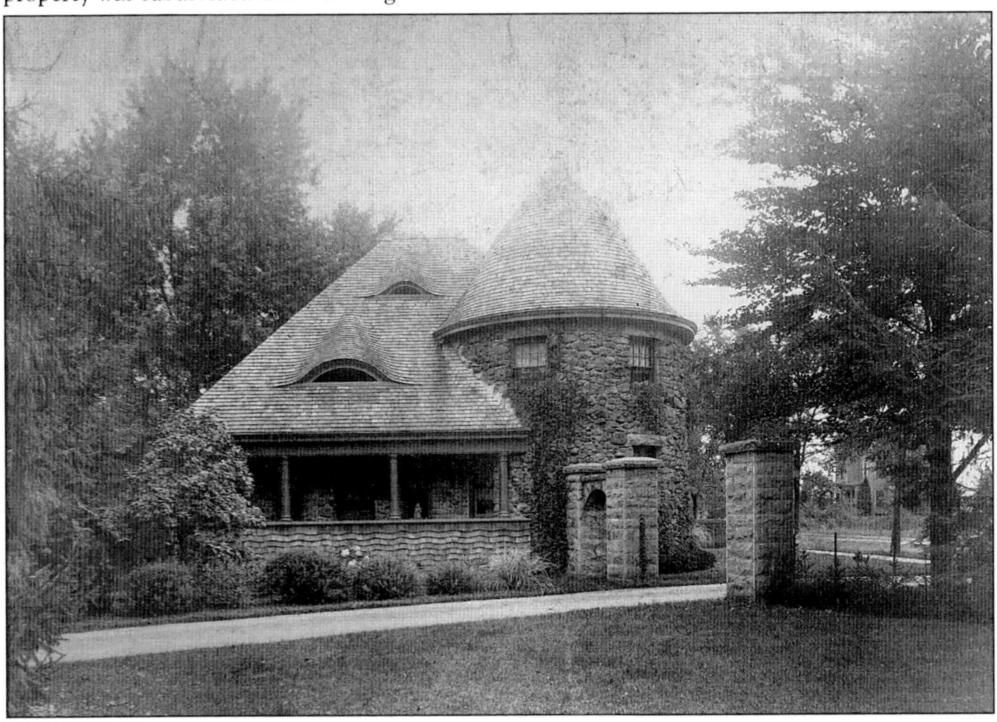

The port of entry to the Johnston estate was this still extant gatehouse built in the Richardsonian Romanesque style. Many a finely appointed equipage must have passed by its door on the way to one of Mrs. Mali's many soirees.

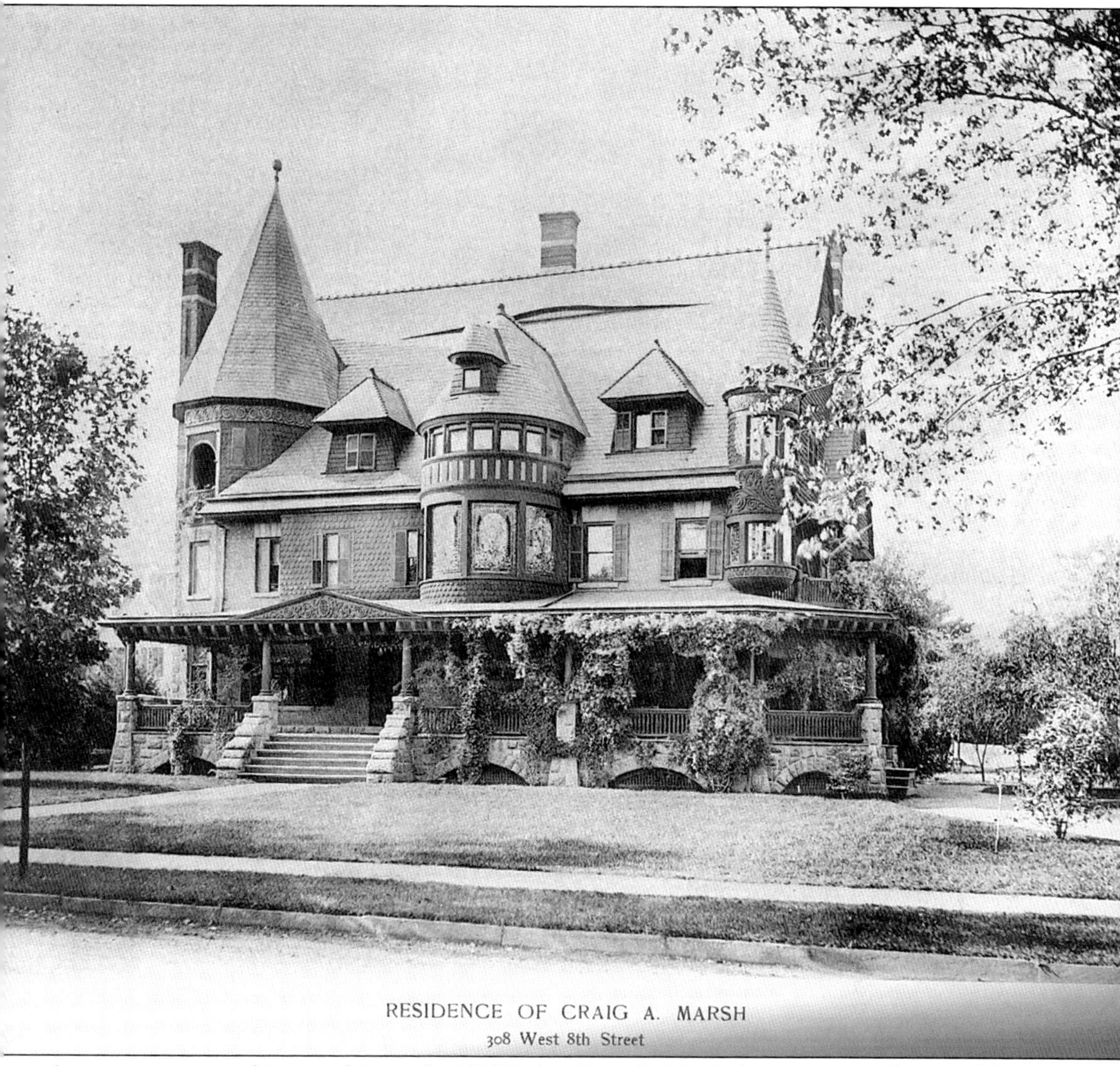

RESIDENCE OF CRAIG A. MARSH
308 West 8th Street

Appearing in an architectural journal of 1893, the Craig A. Marsh home is certainly one of the most flamboyant examples of Queen Anne architecture still standing in Plainfield. With its advancing and receding forms and variety of surface materials, the home makes an impressive statement of industrial-age technologies. An exact copy of this residence was built in India.

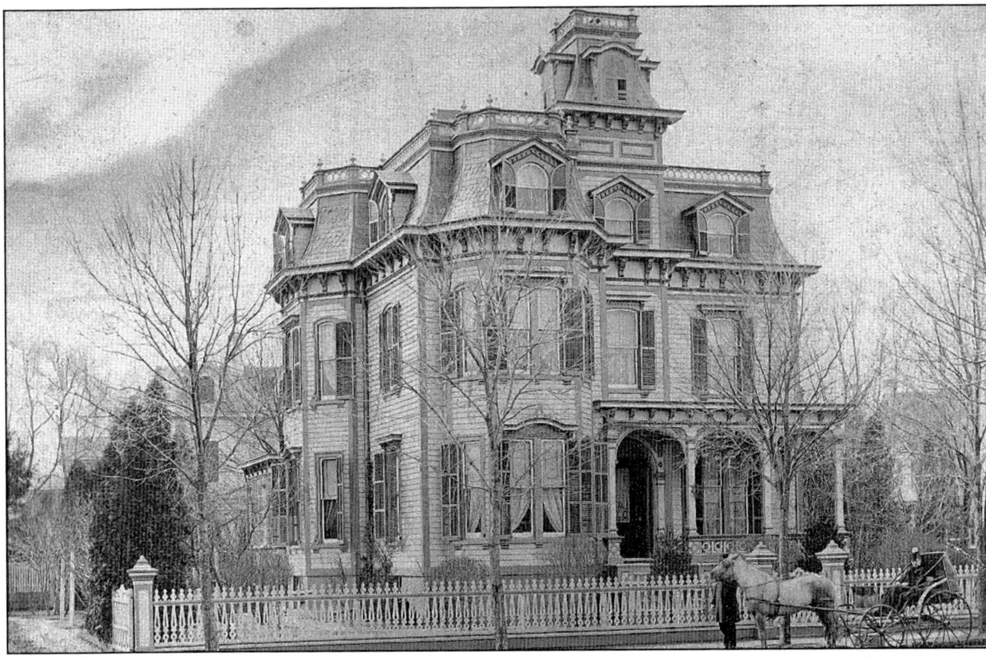

This imposing Second Empire-style home belonged to the David Demarest family. Demarest was a partner in the New York concern of Demarest and Jeroloman, makers of twine and netting. Demarest was also president of the Irving Savings Bank of New York. This site, on the corner of Seventh Street and Crescent Avenue, is now occupied by an apartment building.

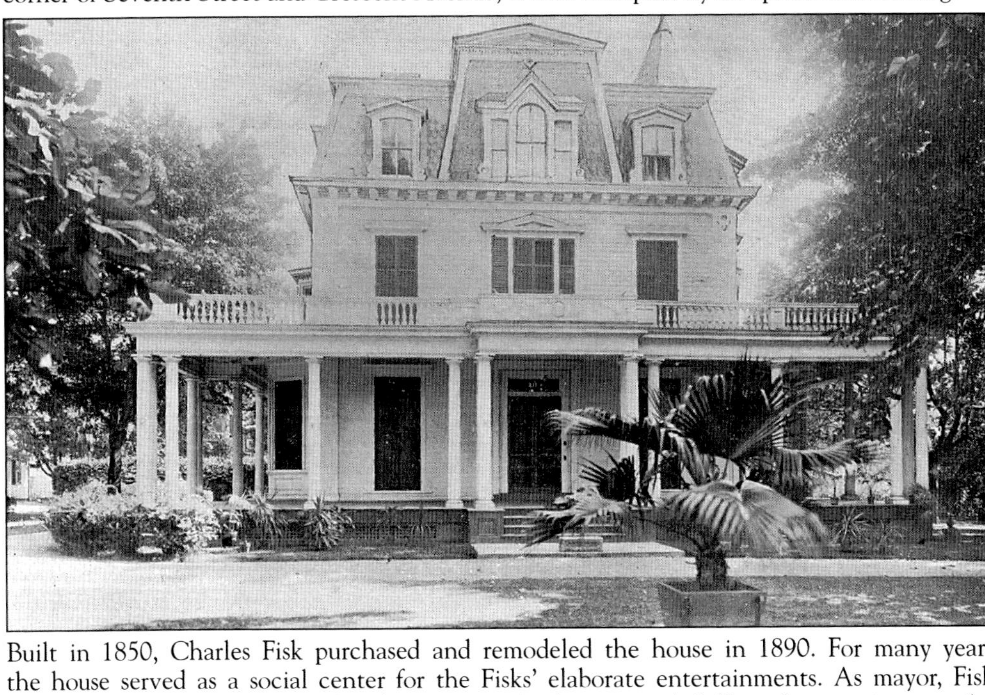

Built in 1850, Charles Fisk purchased and remodeled the house in 1890. For many years the house served as a social center for the Fisks' elaborate entertainments. As mayor, Fisk frequently had the police and fire departments do their annual drills and inspections on the front lawn of his Seventh Street mansion, which straddled the block between Arlington and Madison Avenues.

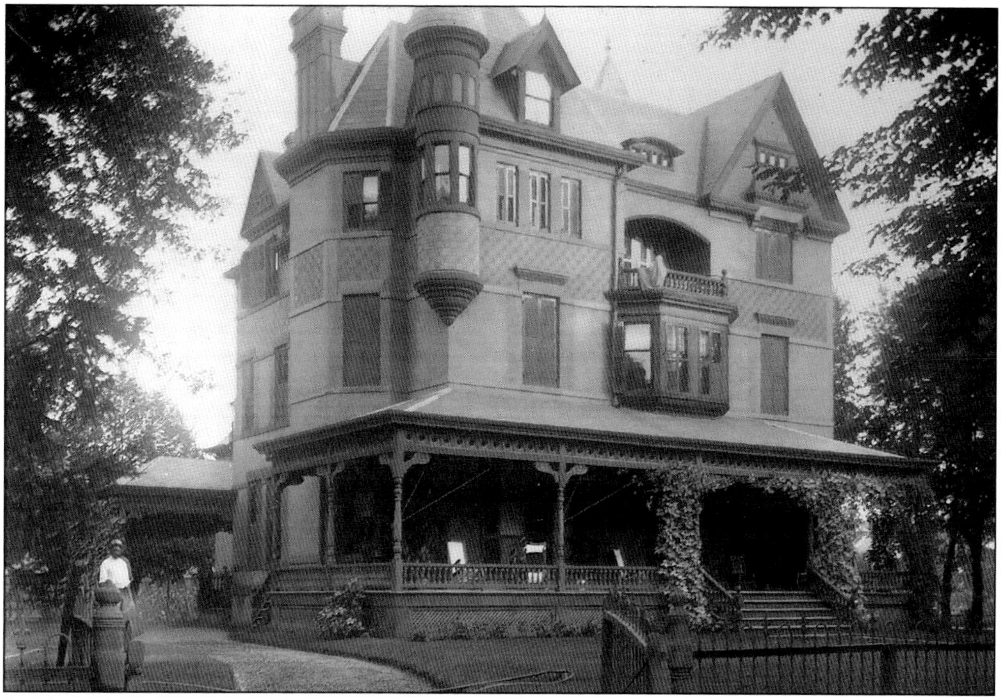

Jacob Kirkner, a New York stock exchange broker, the president of the Plainfield Board of Education, and an ardent mason, built this fanciful Queen Anne confection on West Eighth Street. It was said to be one of the first fireproof houses in the city. Unfortunately, it was not bulldozer proof. Two newer homes occupy the site.

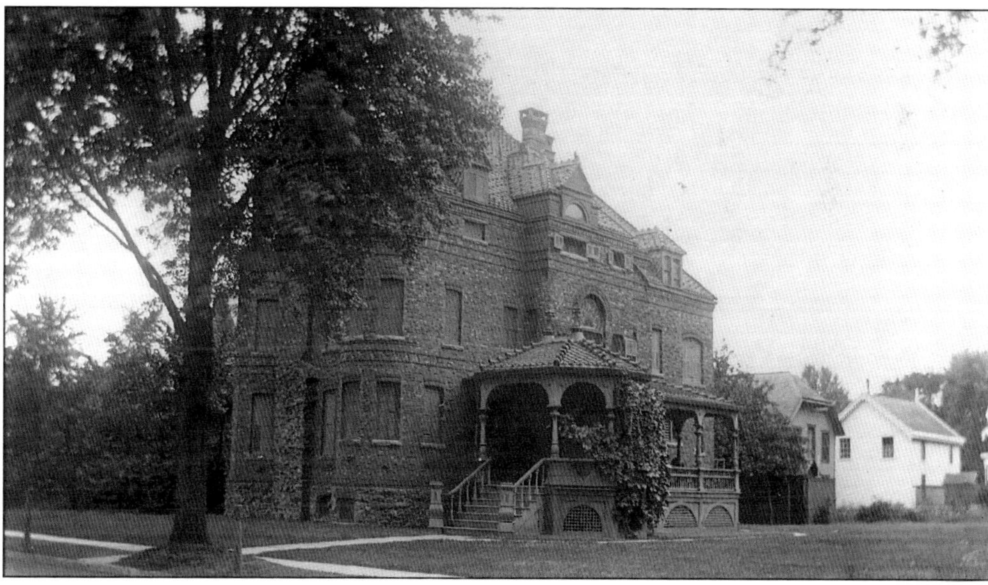

Best classified as Ruskinian Gothic, this unusual house is surely one of a kind. This description from the 1890s says it best: "The design is treated in a very odd and picturesque manner. The exterior walls are constructed of selected burned brick, with accidents of terra cotta and Philadelphia pressed brick, laid up at random without regard to uniformity." The architect was E.L. Hyde of New York.

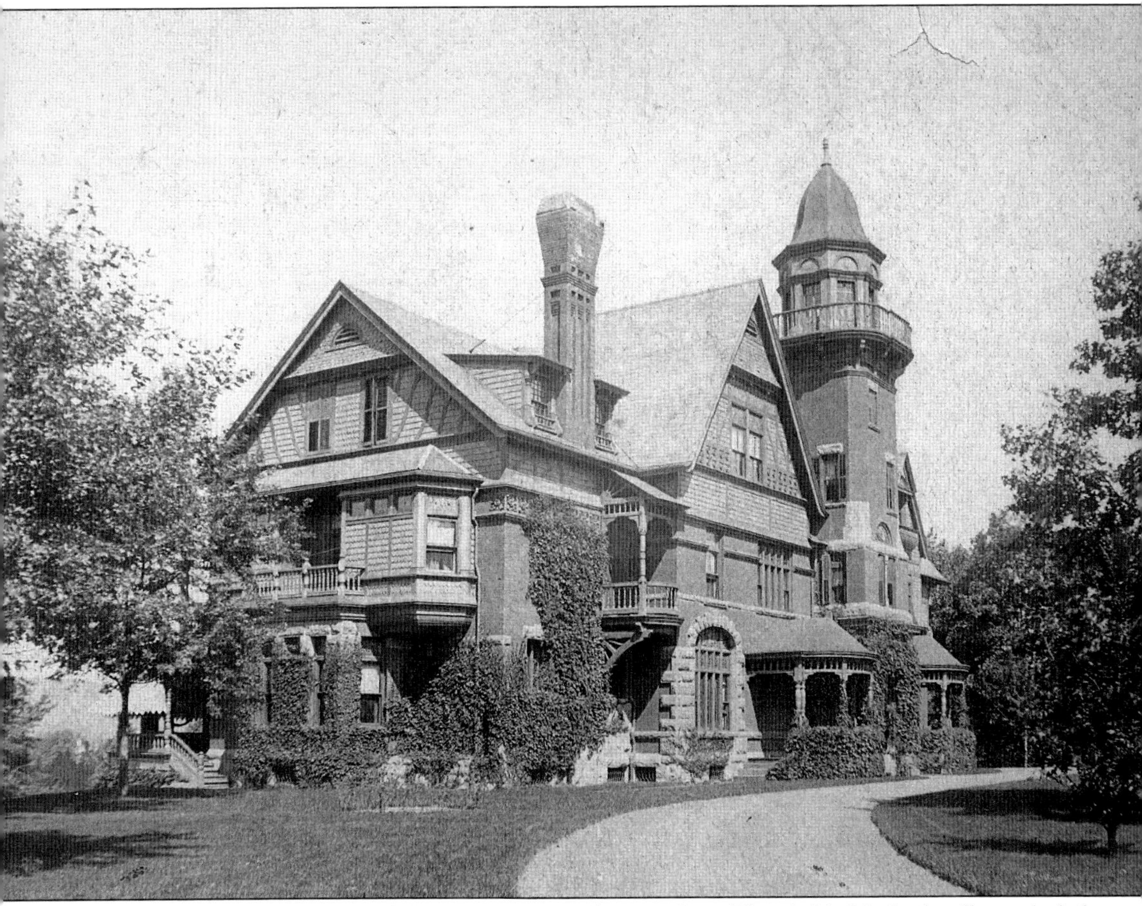

Van Wyck Brooks wrote of the "quiet men of money" in Plainfield. Undoubtedly included would have been the conservative New York banker Henry Pearl Talmadge, head of Henry Talmadge and Company, who constructed a Queen Anne house diametrically opposed to his sober nature. The design of the house is not expressed apologetically. The home was 92 feet long and 62 feet wide, and it rose 48 feet to the tower balcony. It was constructed of wood shingle, Belleville stone, and brick.

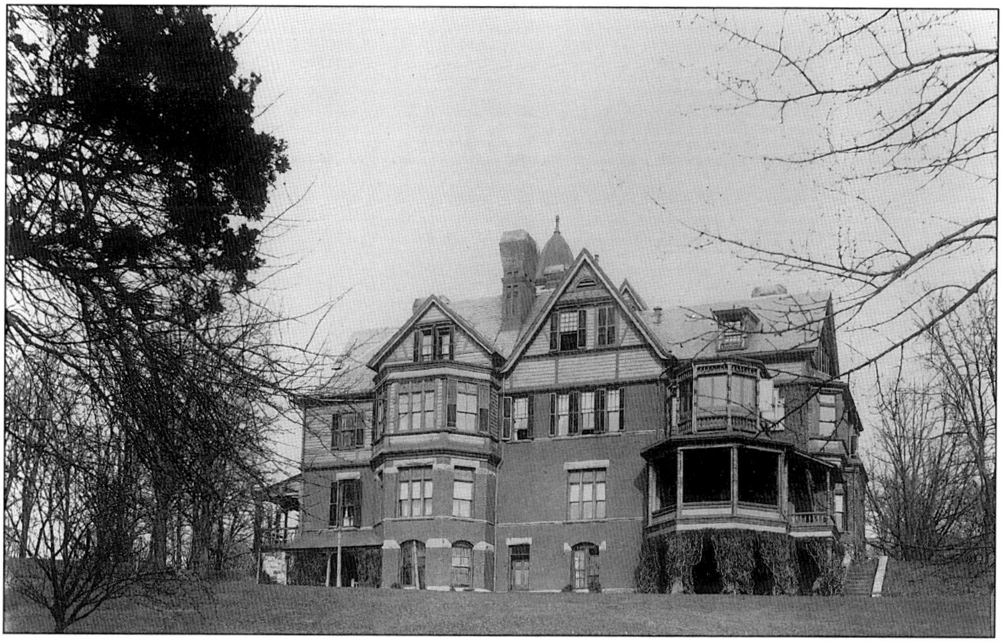

Designed by New York architect Douglas Smythe, the Talmadge house appears even more expansive from the rear. Built on the slope of the hill, the house had a walk-out basement with a kitchen, laundry room, furnace room, and wine cellar, plus storage rooms.

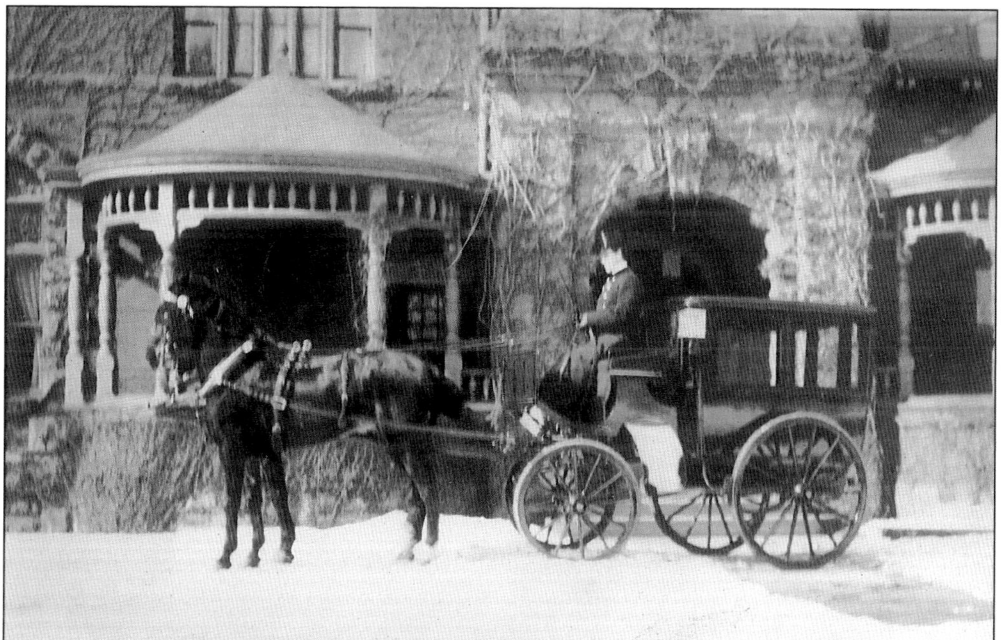

Many summer homes provided living quarters for coachmen and grooms above the carriage house. However, men with families might opt to live in the numerous row houses in town, which were constructed especially for that purpose.

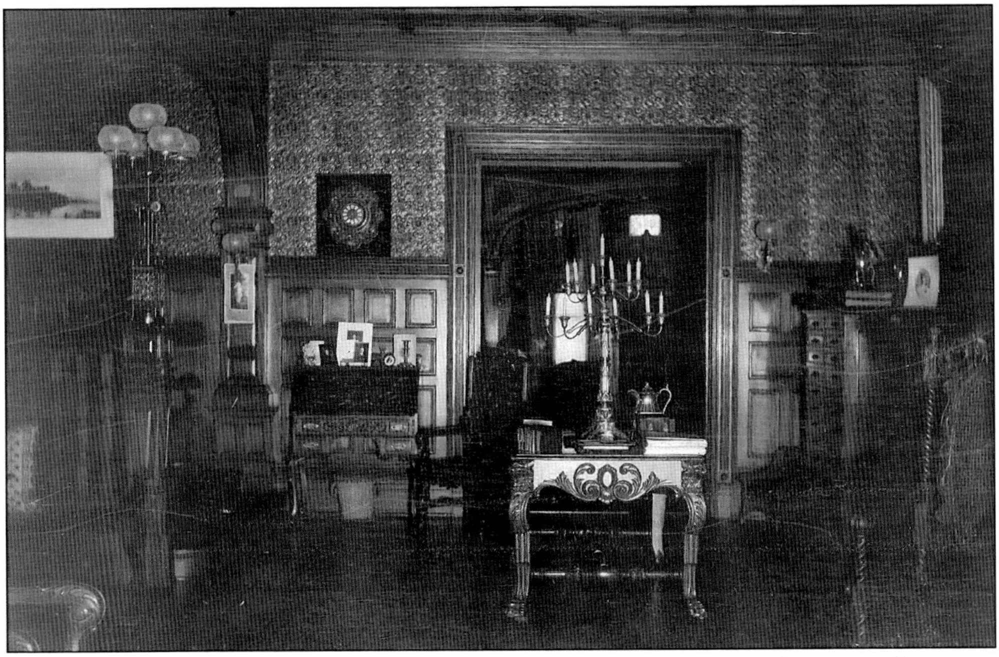

A view of the hall (above) and the library (below) gives an idea of the well-appointed interiors in the Talmadge house. The hall was 25 feet by 38 feet, with antique oak wainscoting and a paneled wood ceiling. The walls were covered with an elaborately embossed and patterned paper covering called lincrusta-walton. The library, which was 18 feet by 32 feet, was paneled in cherry and featured red patterned paper with multitoned red stained glass windows.

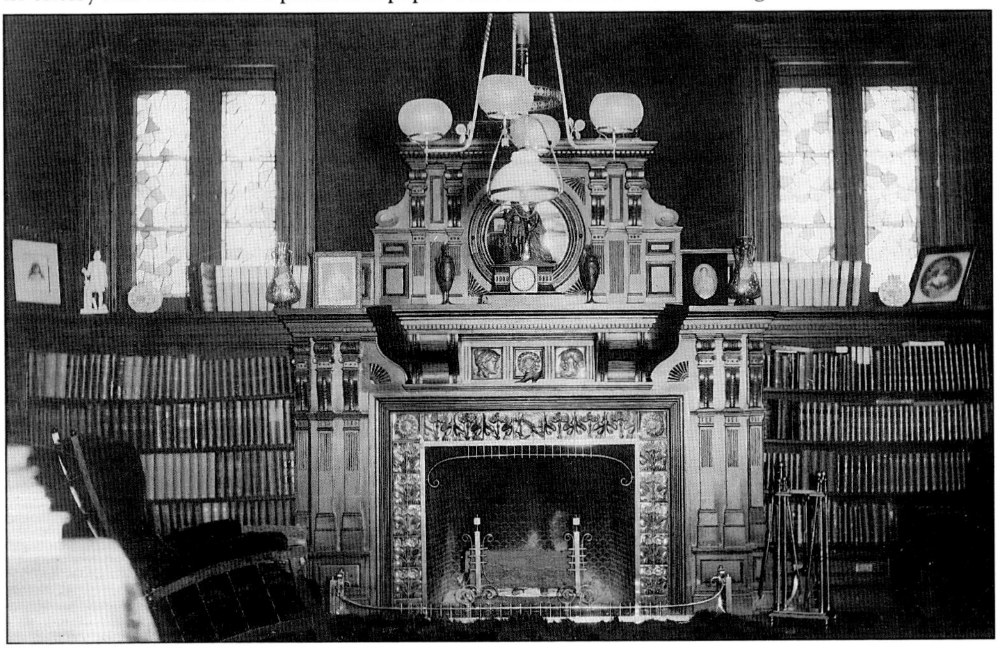

Homes of the Gilded Age-era were as distinctive as the individuals who built them, reflecting their tastes and aspirations. It was a time of the rugged individualist. Several architectural styles were being built simultaneously, as shown by these two homes. The Queen Anne house (right) is on Franklin Place, and the Italianate Villa home stands today on Woodland Avenue.

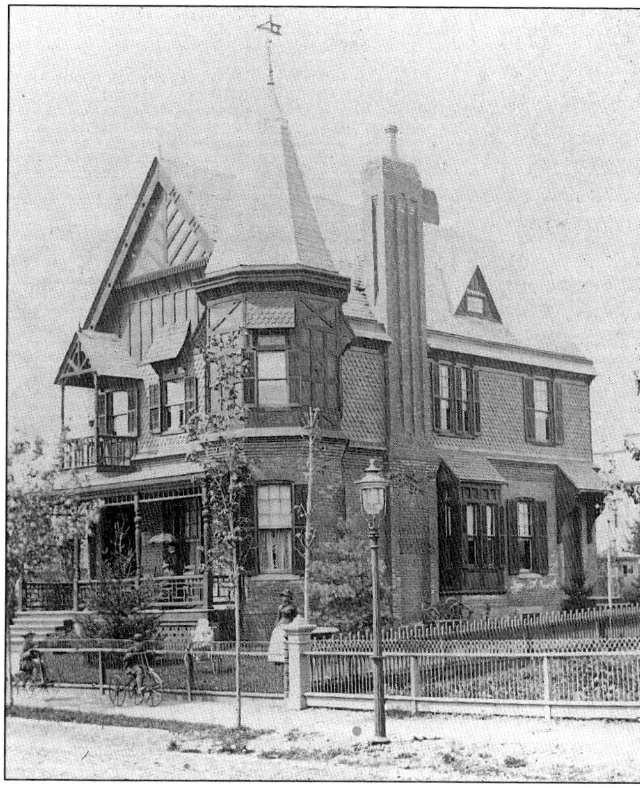

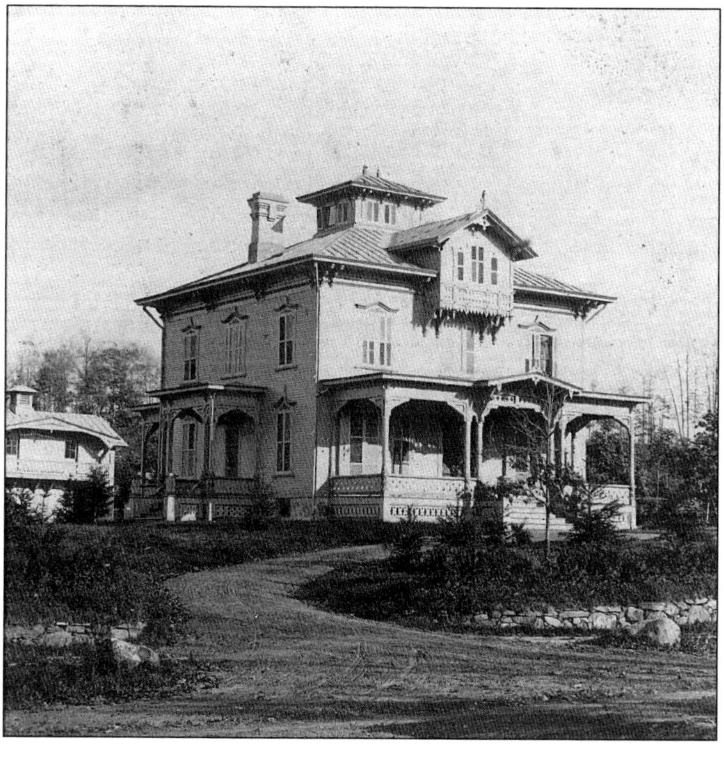

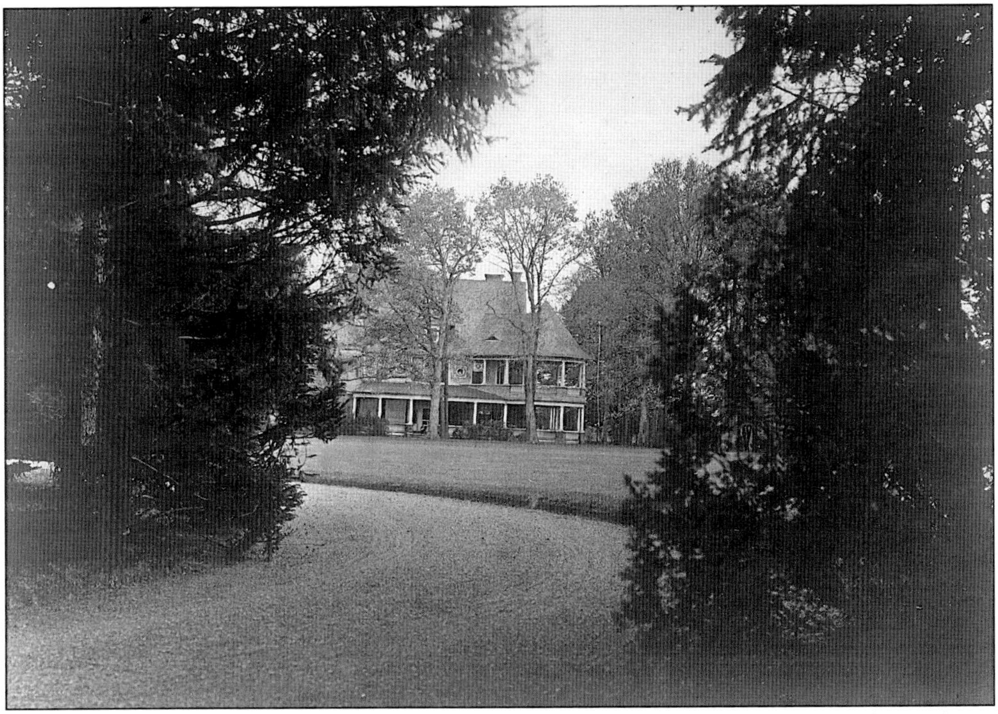

The handsome Queen Anne mansion "Oakwood" (above) and its companion gatehouse (page 111) stand as a reminder of the early resort days of Plainfield, a time when people came to Plainfield for the summer. These days inspired a writer to say "Plainfield is a city of handsome residences, of salubrious climate, and the best of everything a city wants."

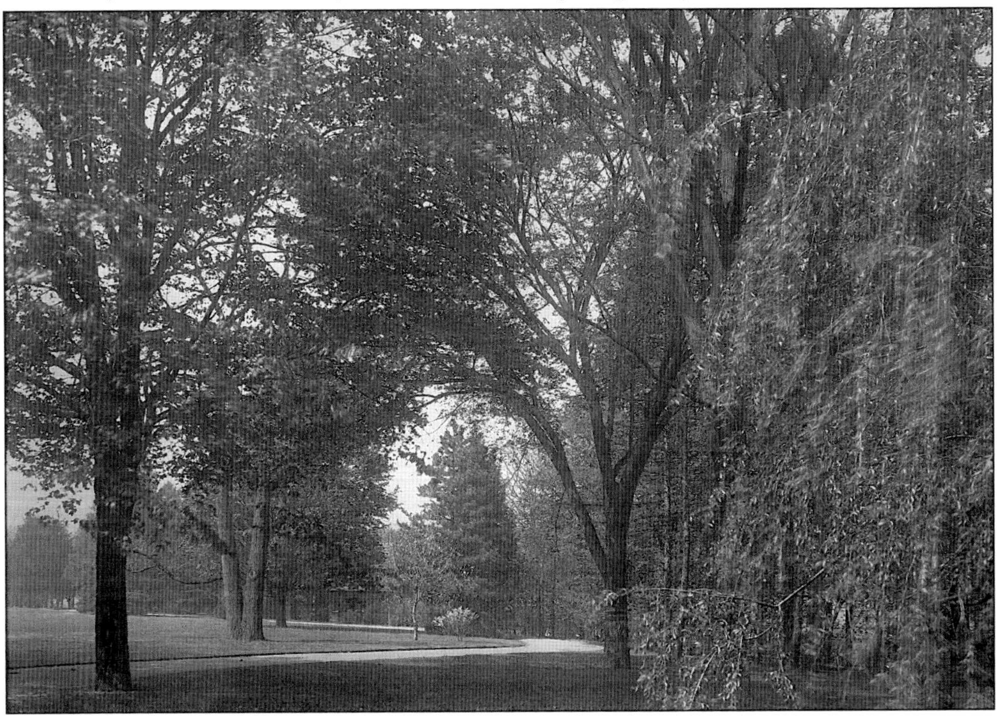

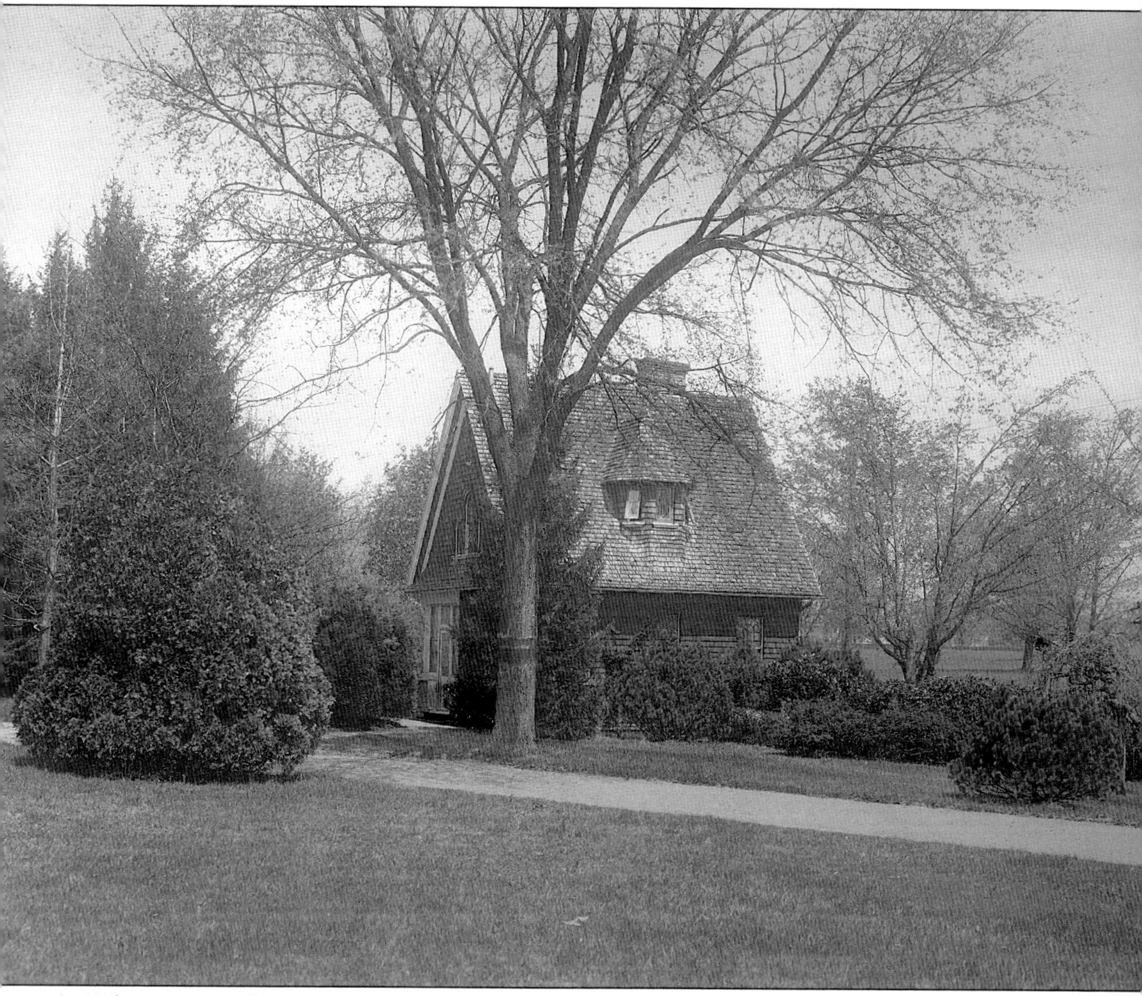

A 19th-century reflection states "The town (Plainfield) is laid out with an idea to landscape beauties, and to the ornamentation by beautiful shade trees, many of them majestic with age, and all of such age that there is none of the 'boom' appearance that characterizes towns of forced growth."

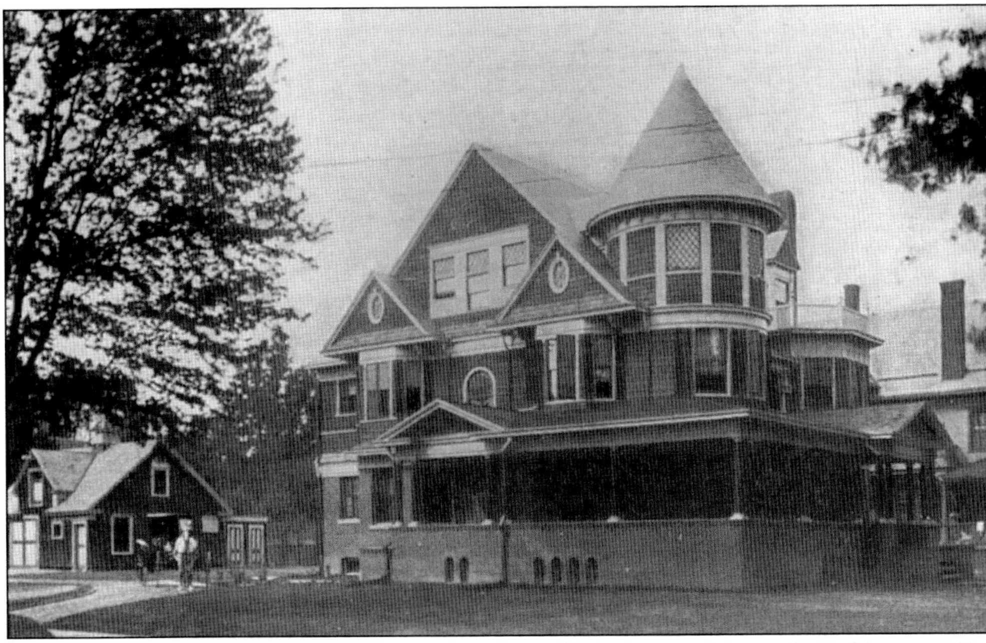

J.V. Beekman, a mechanical engineer and maker of hoisting machinery, built his new West Eighth Street home in 1892. New York architects Rossiter and Wright designed the 14-room house, which boasted a third-floor conservatory. Oak, cherry, poplar, and ash were used in various first-floor rooms. The 1892 cost of the home was $9,185, complete.

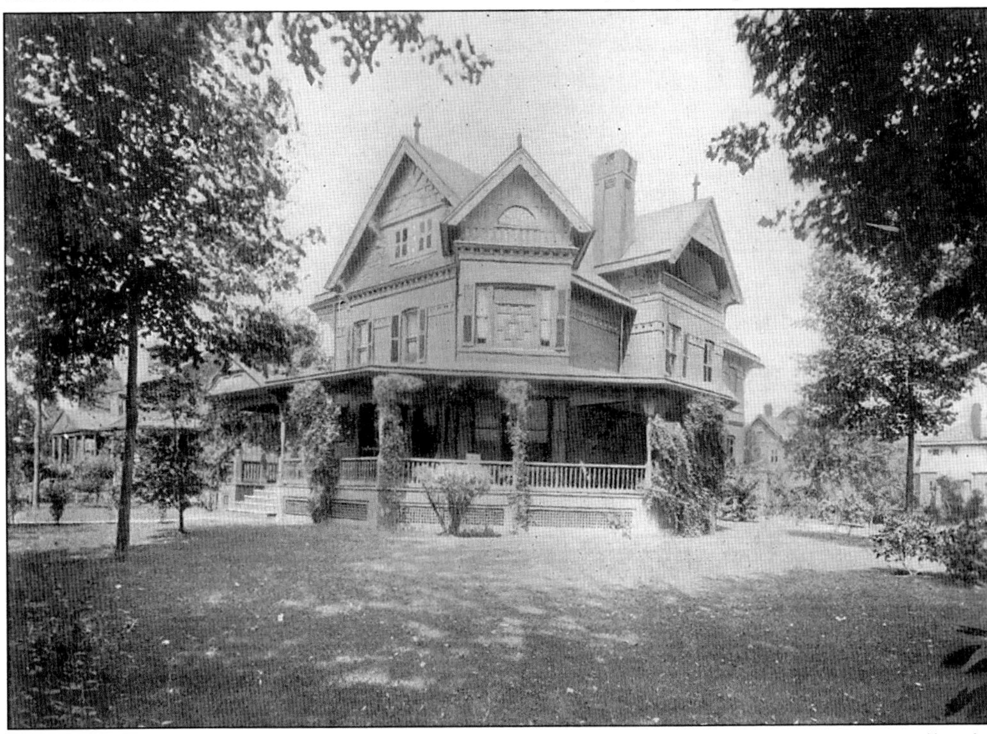

This Central Avenue Queen Anne-style home was built for John Bushnell, a comptroller for Standard Oil in New York. The house was razed in the 1960s.

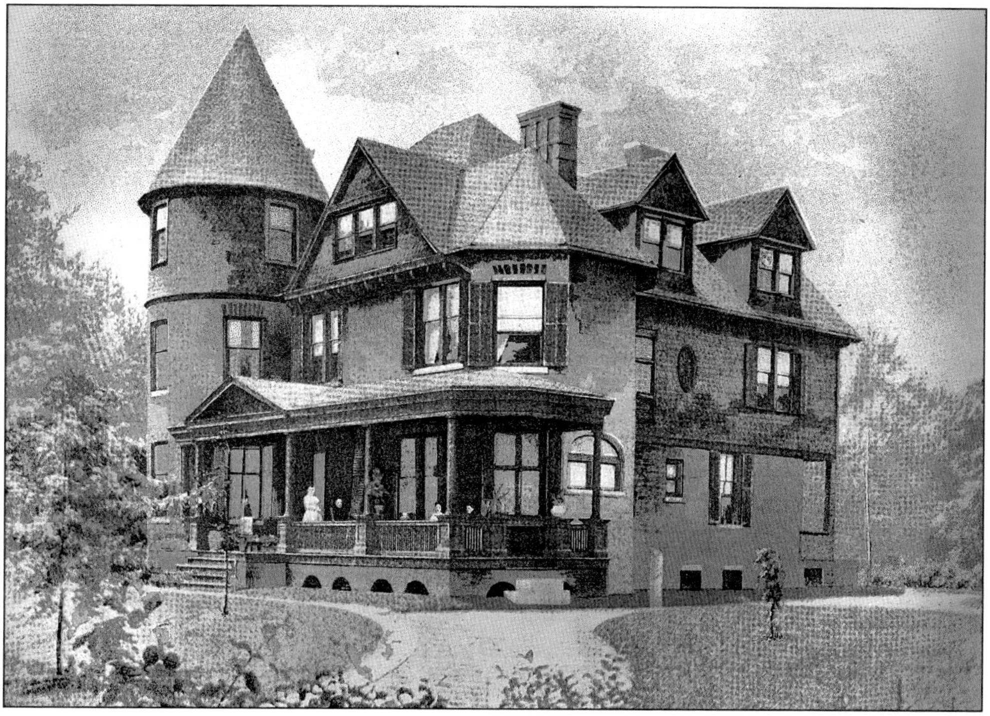

Alexander Gilbert (right), president of the New York Market and Fulton Bank, built this turreted residence on West Eighth Street, then one of Plainfield's finest thoroughfares. Gilbert served on the Common Council, helping revise the city charter. He served three terms as mayor, running unopposed twice. He helped establish the Plainfield YMCA and served as its first president.

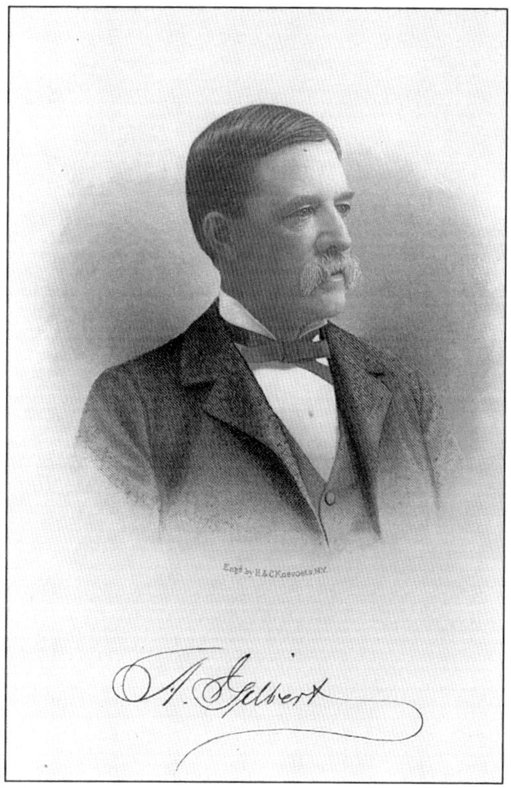

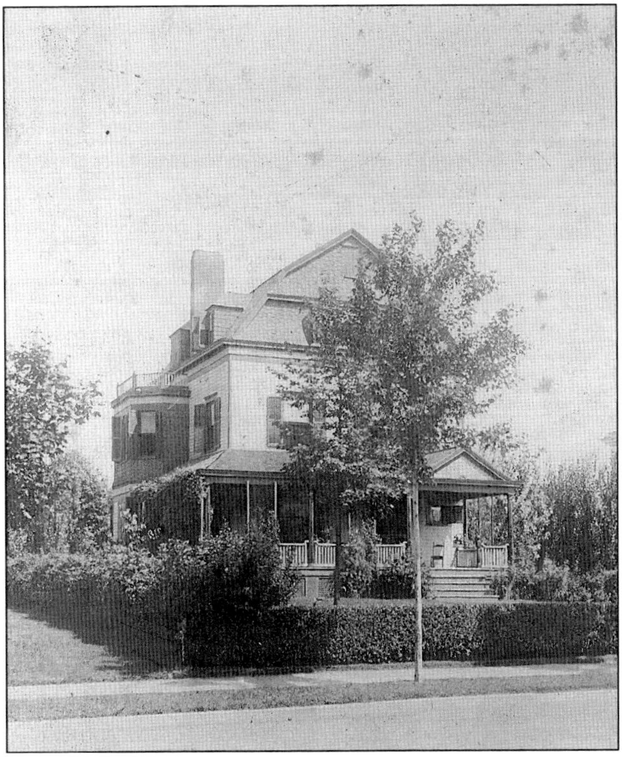

The Katherine Dix Lawrence house, on Stelle Avenue, was built c. 1882 and remained in the same family until 1979. Today, restored and done in period colors, it looks like its old self.

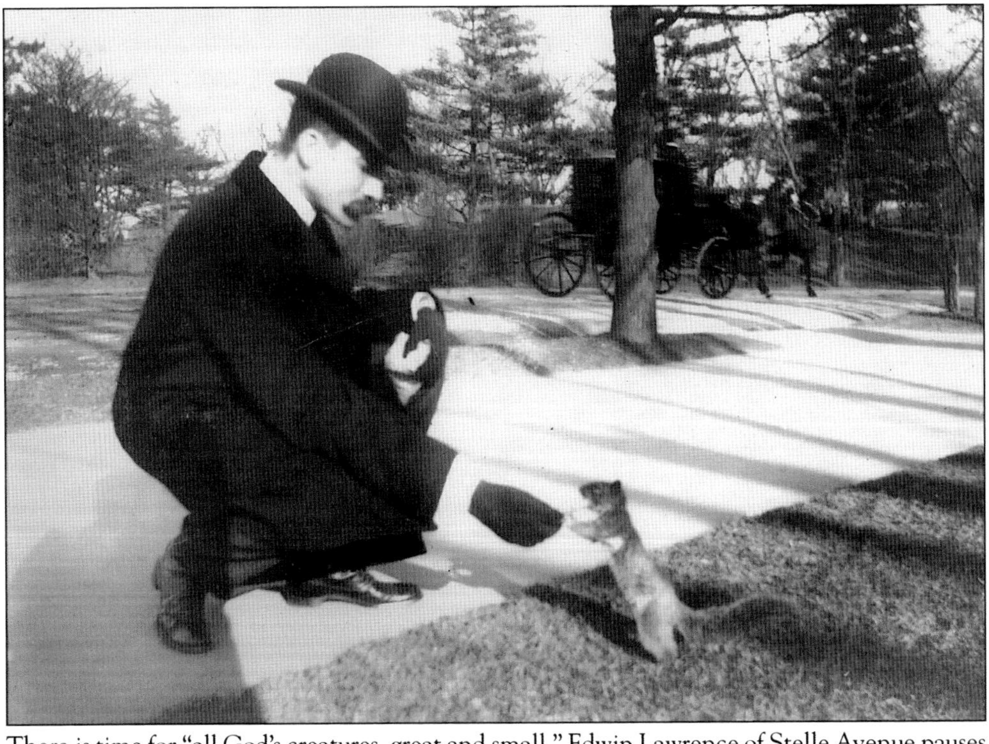

There is time for "all God's creatures, great and small." Edwin Lawrence of Stelle Avenue pauses in his routine to greet a very friendly, furry friend.

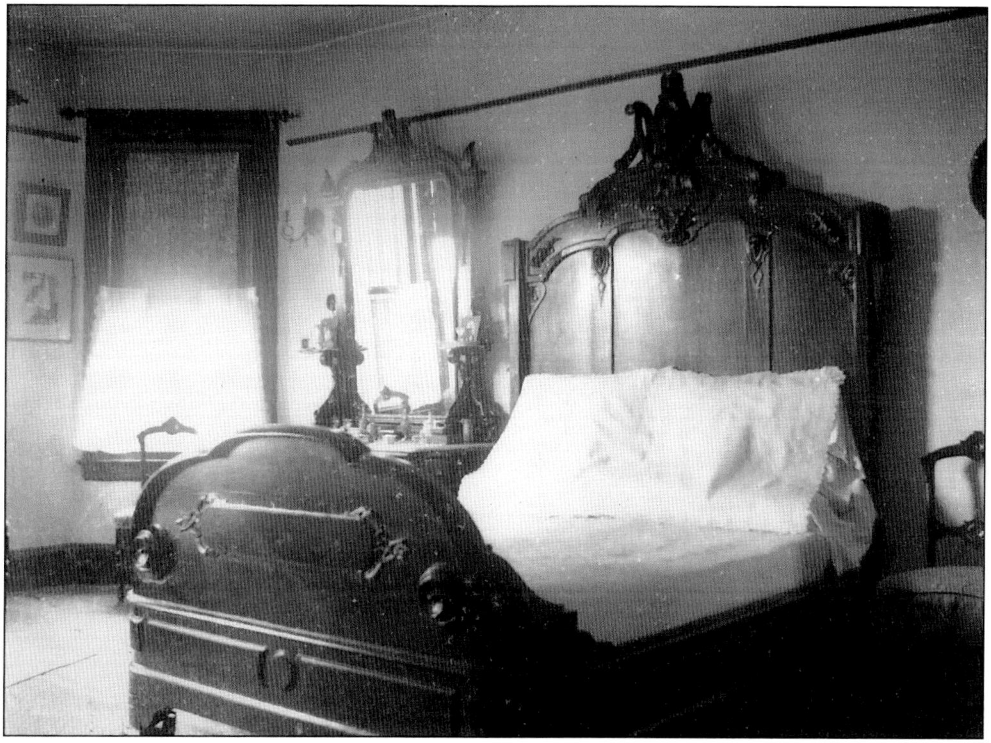

These two interior images of the Lawrence home remind us of a fussy and more formal lifestyle. A ponderous sideboard echoing the architecture of the era predominates in the dining room.

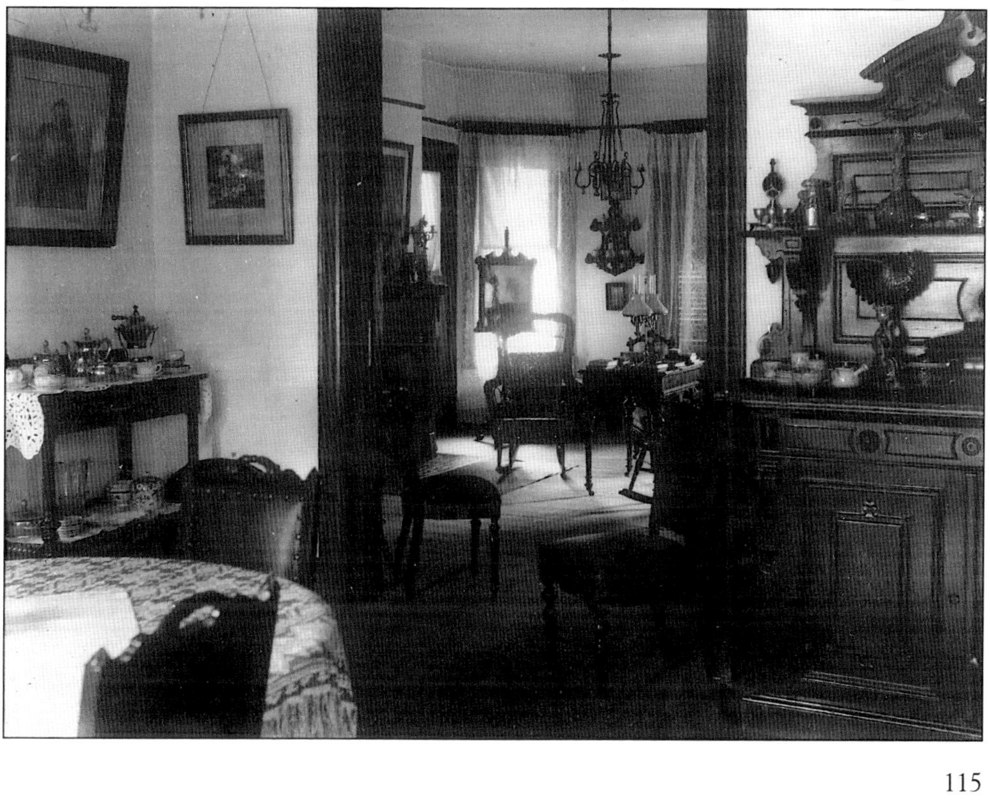

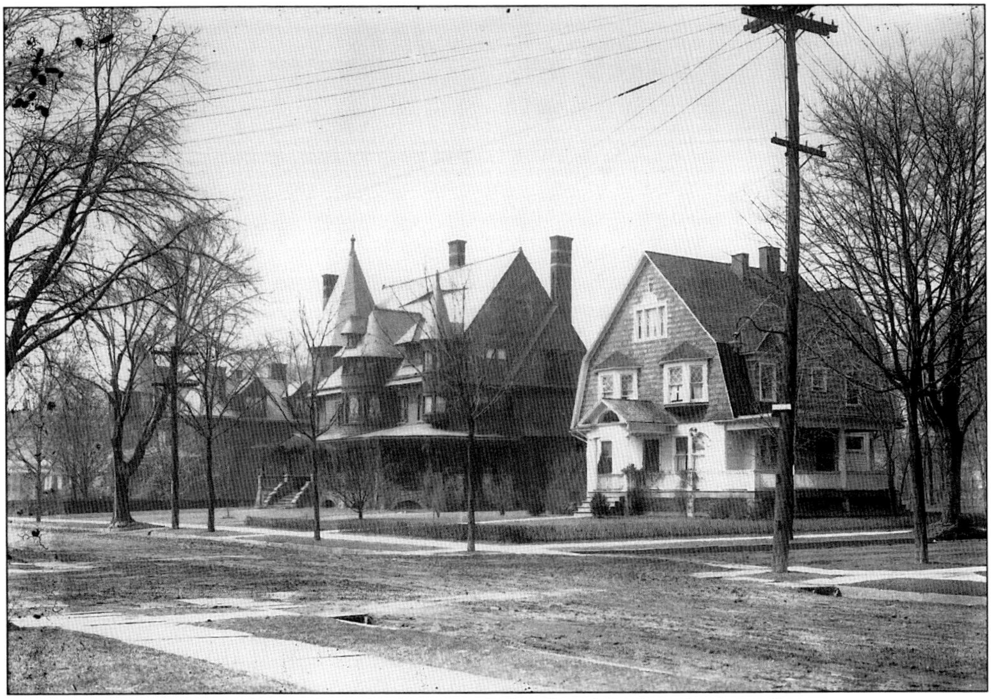

"Here are streets as we have described . . . each bordered by handsome villas or cottages set in the midst of fine lawns and beautiful gardens."

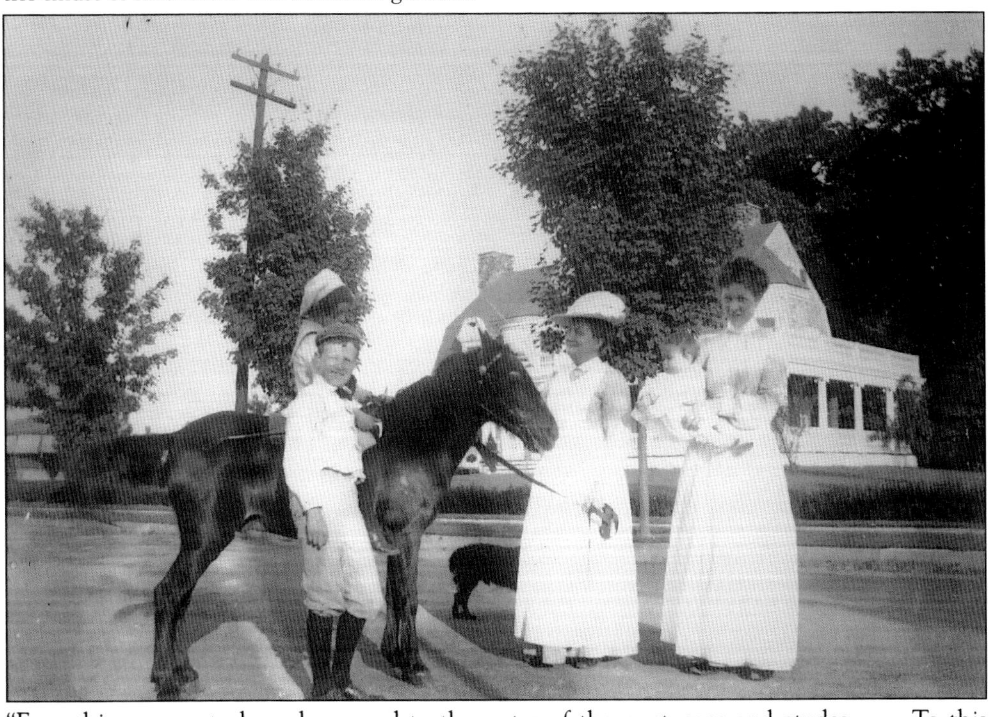

"Everything seems to have happened to the notes of the nocturnes and etudes. . . . To this day, I always associate Chopin with ladies in white organdie dresses and the gentle flapping of curtains in a languid summer breeze."

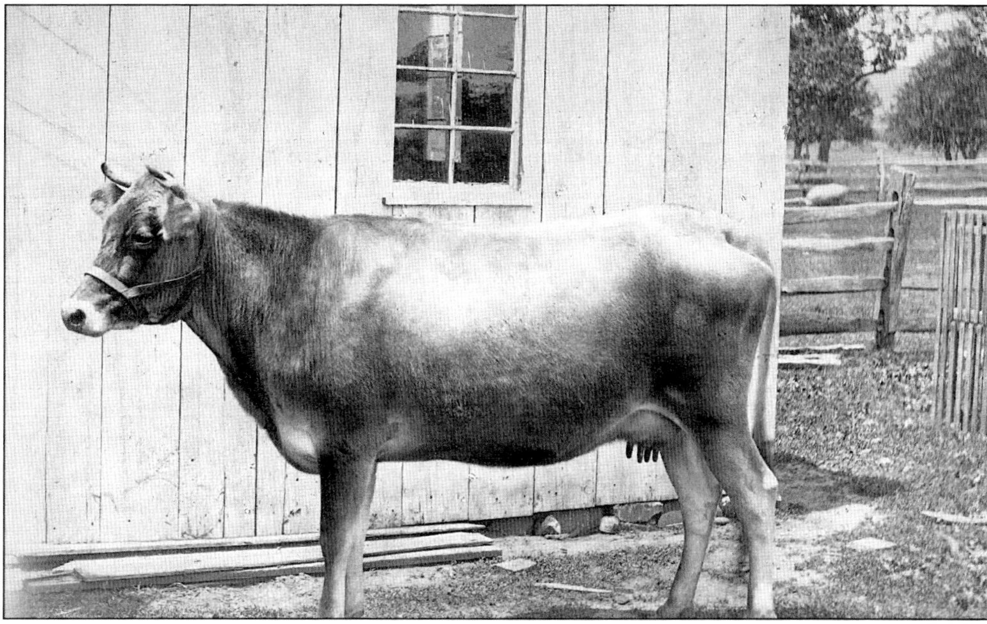

In the midst of mansion building, Plainfield still had its rural roots. In May 1900, Mrs. Brown, who lived on a farm near Watchung Avenue and Ninth Street, reported her cow stolen from the barn. It was determined that tramps had slept in the barn, leaving the door open. "Finding the world before her, the cow strolled out to view the beauties of nature." She was found later wandering around Netherwood and was returned to her owner.

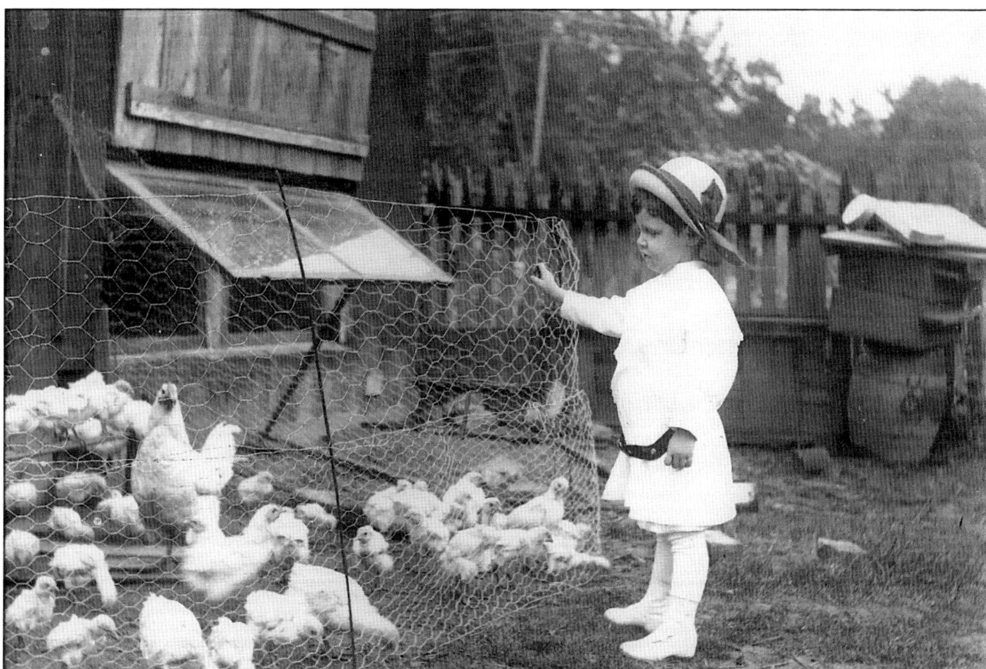

Why move to the suburbs? Three reasons given were safety, sanitation, and savings. The savings came about by having your own vegetable garden and chicken coop. On West Front Street, a properly dressed little girl cannot resist greeting her feathered friends.

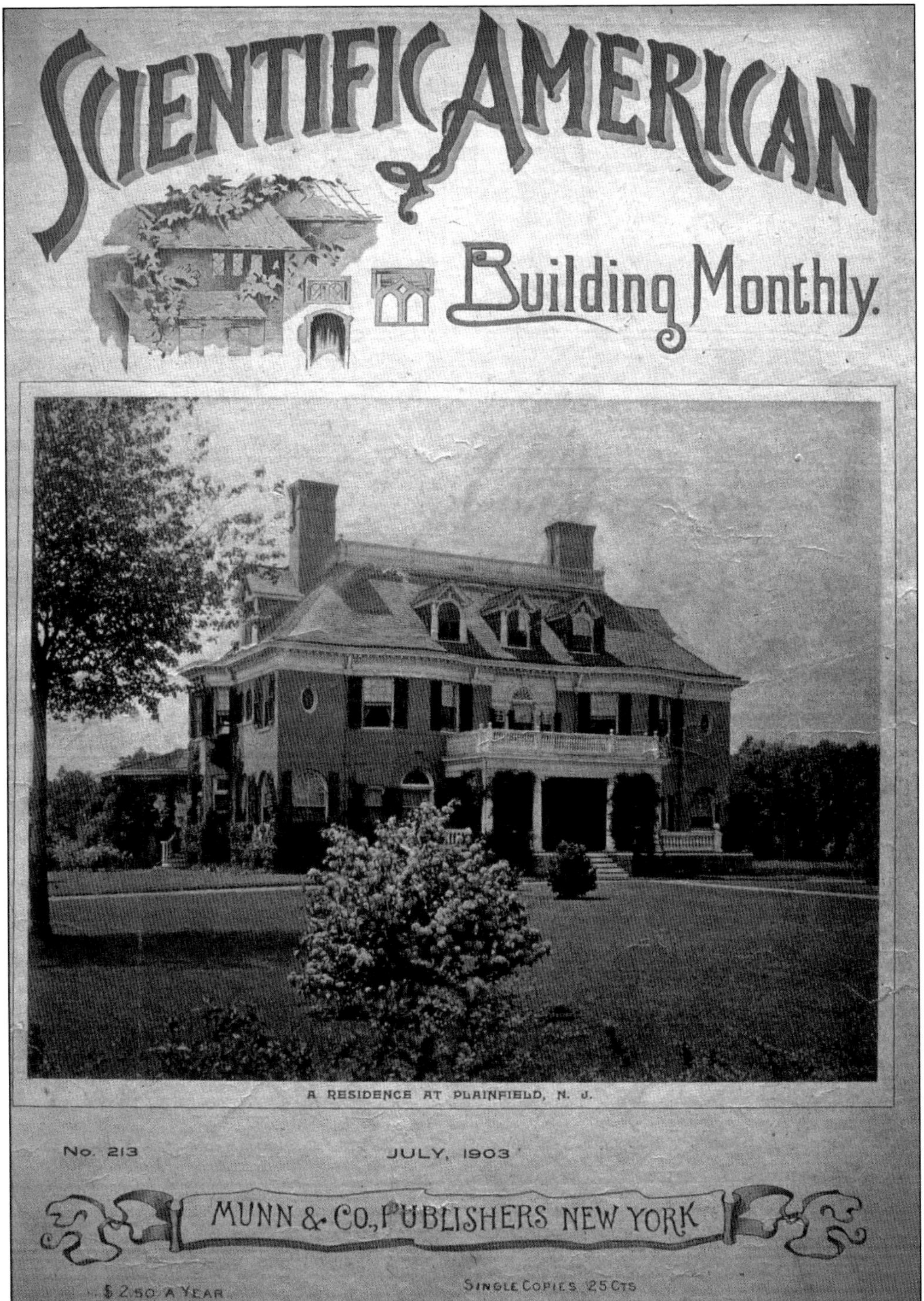

The cover picture on this magazine is the Colonial Revival mansion built for George A. Strong, Esq. The house was constructed of buff brick with buff mortar and white trimmings. The wood roof was stained a dull shade of green. New York architects Rossiter and Wright designed the home.

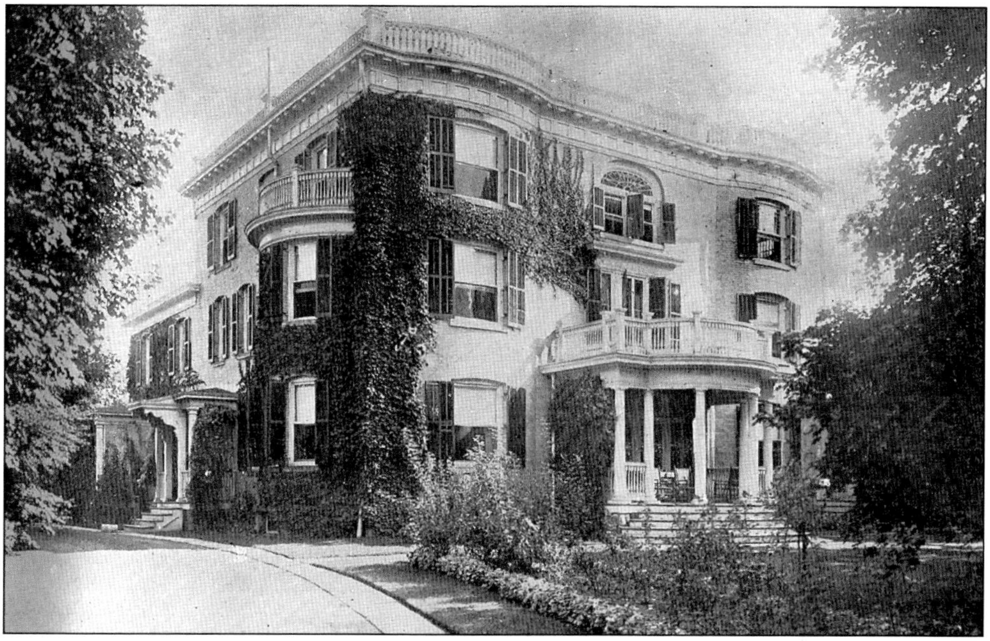

Originally occupied by the Ames-Brooks family, this West Eighth Street house was acquired in 1900 by Rep. Percy Hamilton Stewart and his wife, Elinor Cochran. In the decade that followed, the home was doubled in size and was outfitted with the walls, panels, and doors from an ancient Scottish castle.

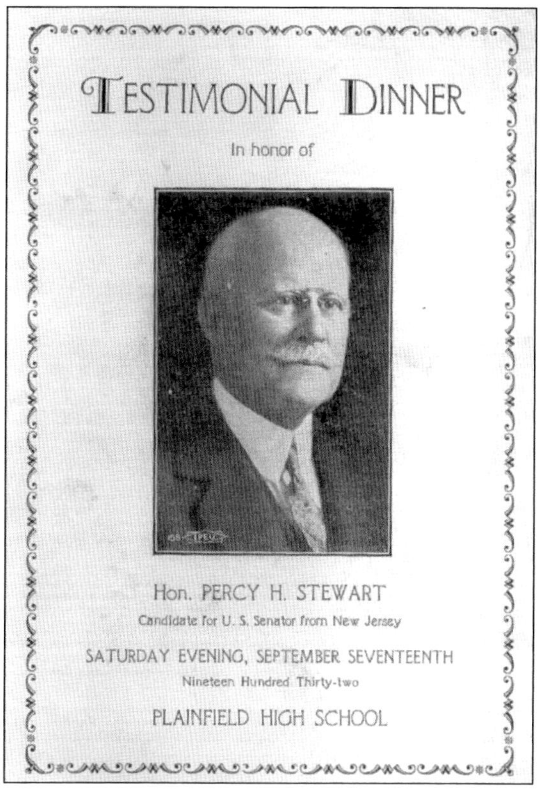

In Republican Plainfield, Democrat Percy Stewart was elected mayor. He also served in the U.S. House of Representatives but was unsuccessful in his Senate bid. His popularity was attested to, however, when over 400 Plainfielders of both parties turned out to pay respect to their fellow townsman.

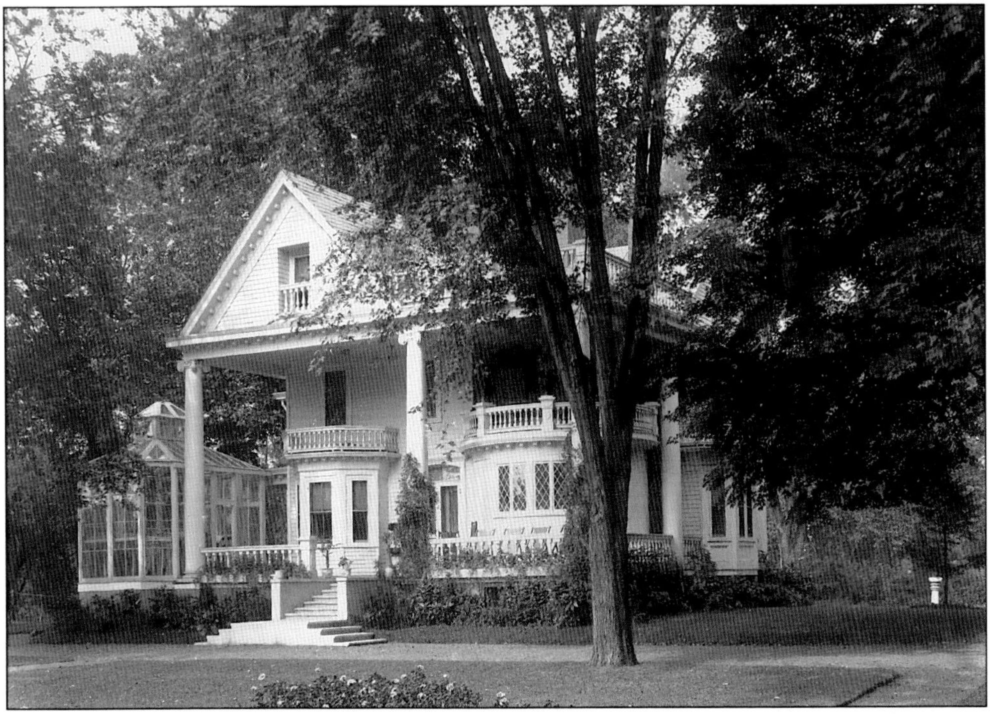

The Stillman estate was a remodeling of an old farmhouse. Apparently, there is nothing new about wanting the latest fashion. As early as the 1860s, a local newspaper noted the home-remodeling craze and praised it, saying "the plain roofs of the homes had been 'metamorphosed' by pediments, fancy gables and cornices, and their primitive simplicity had been converted to modern beauty by wings, bay windows, recesses, projections and every variety of architectural device." The home is shown below with Australian singer Marjorie Lawrence on the verandah.

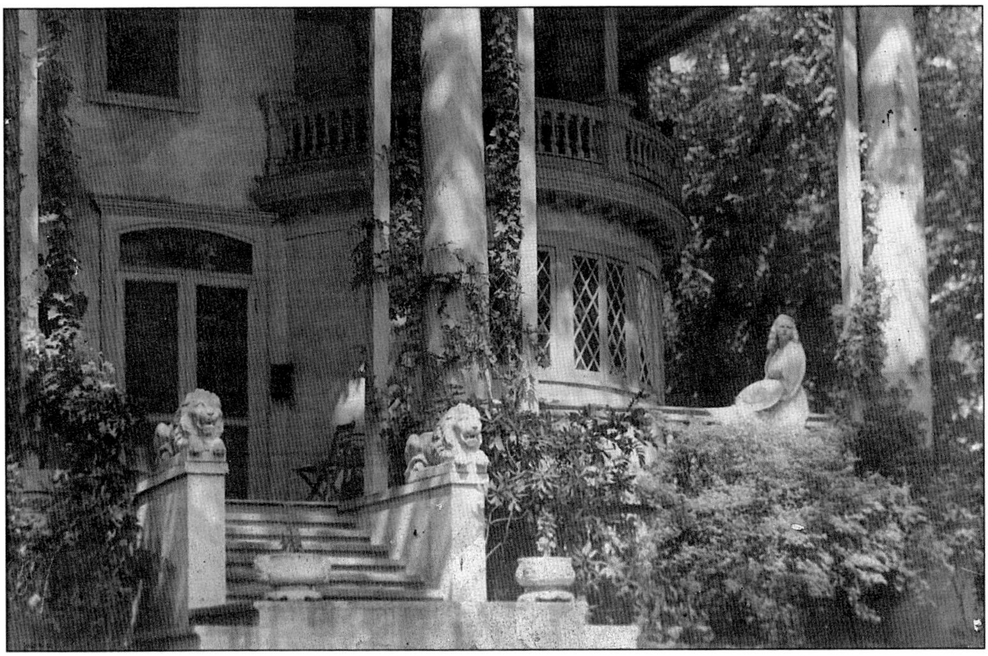

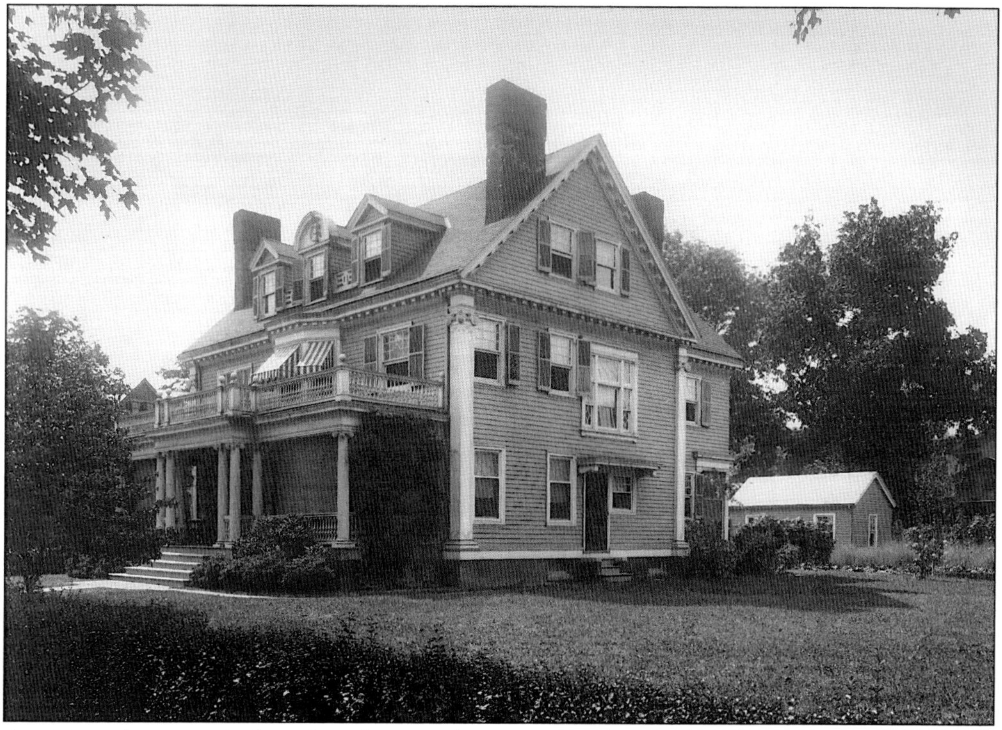

As citizens began to look to their historical roots, many fine, Colonial-style homes were built. The Sixth Street house above, another of A.L.C. Marsh's designs, appeared in the *Scientific American* building edition as a "New England Colonial." The home was painted light green with trimmings of old ivory. The roof was stained green. Both homes attest to Plainfield's image as a City of Homes. The Colonial-style home below is located on Cedar Brook Road.

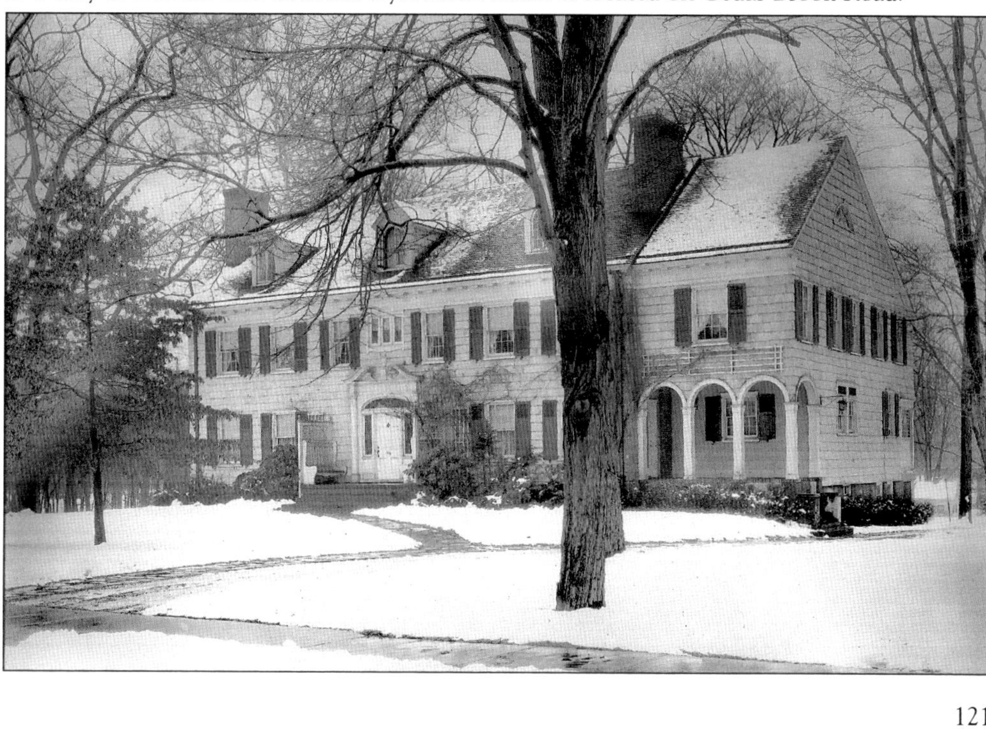

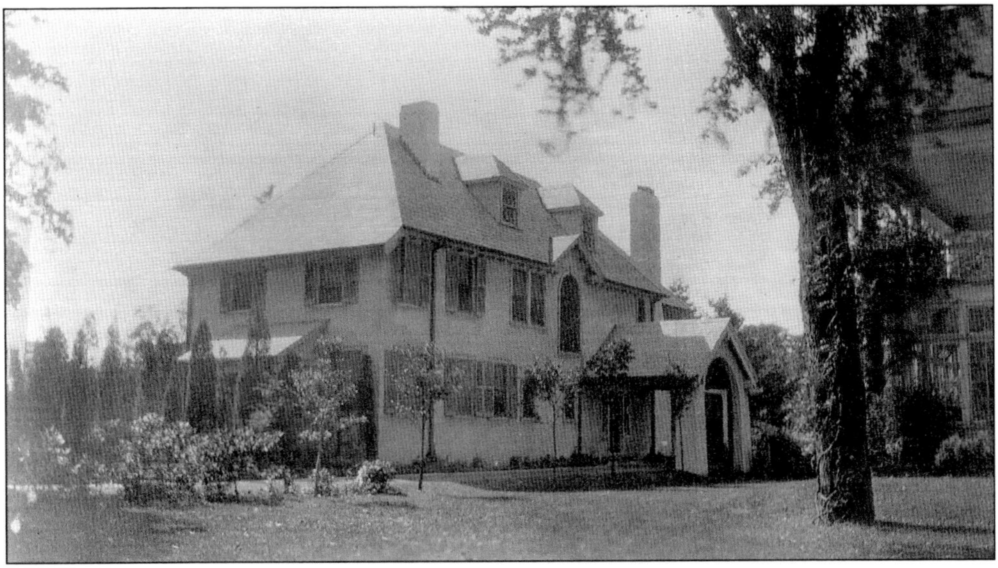

In the 1920s, attorney Albert Atterbury and his wife, Emma, moved from their West Seventh Street mansion to a more comfortable home on Hillside Avenue. The Atterburys were active for many years in the cultural and civic life of Plainfield.

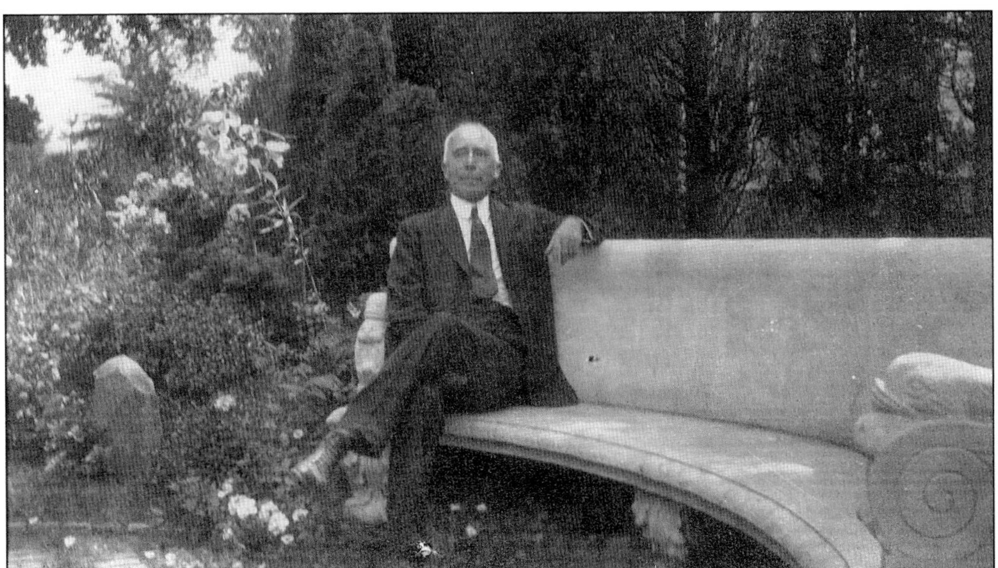

Seen here is Albert Hoffman Atterbury in his Hillside Avenue garden. Atterbury was a world traveler and a collector of first editions, which he presented to his alma mater, Yale. Atterbury lived in his home until his death in 1955 at age 95.

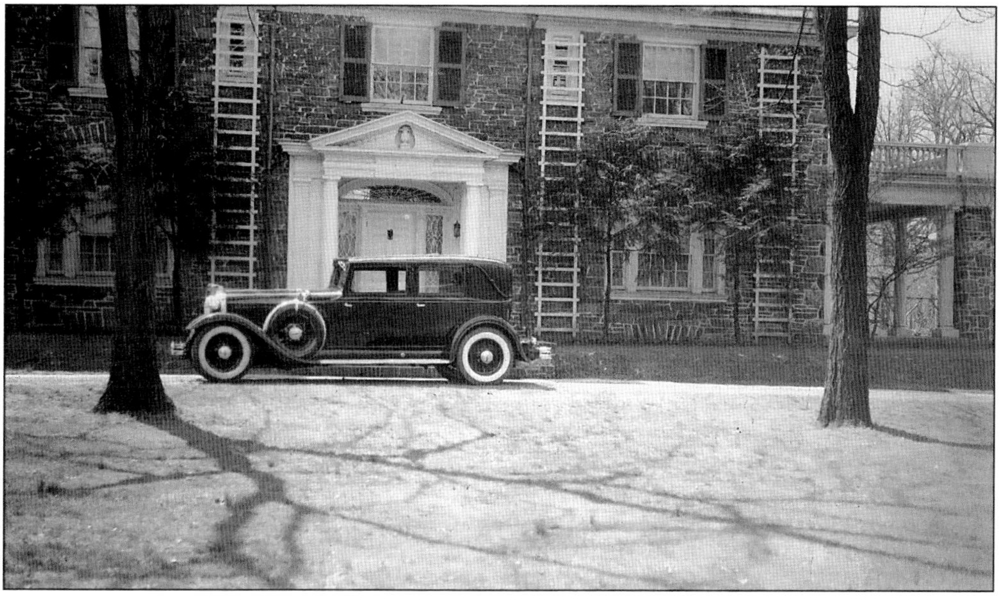

Evidently, this shiny new car thrilled its owner. Today, it is the house that catches the eye of the passerby. Built of Pennsylvania mica stone, this impressive Colonial-style home was built for a prominent New York attorney and his wife, Frederick and Bertha Yates.

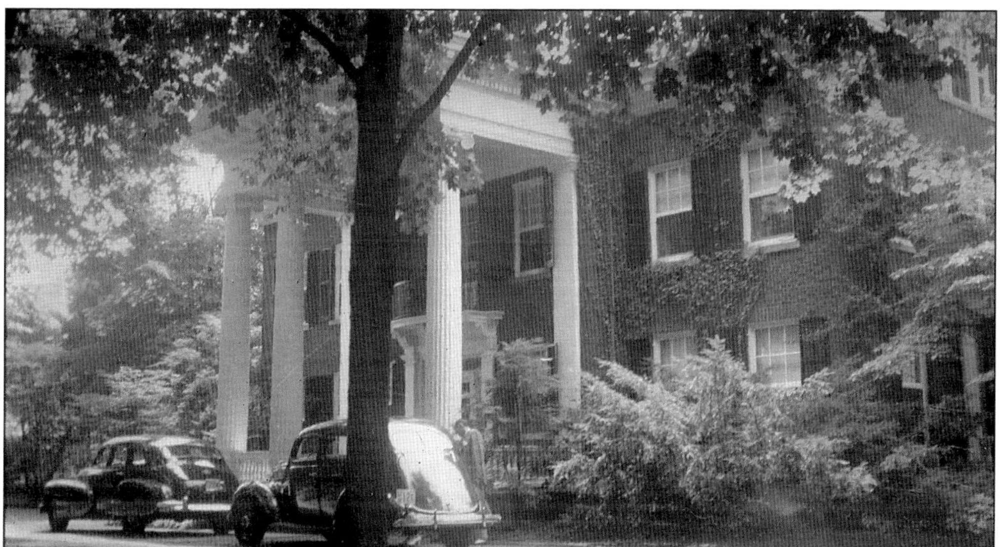

Steel magnate William Garrigues built his fine brick mansion on Hillside Avenue in 1917 for a cost of $25,000. It stands today as a landmark in the Hillside Avenue Historic District.

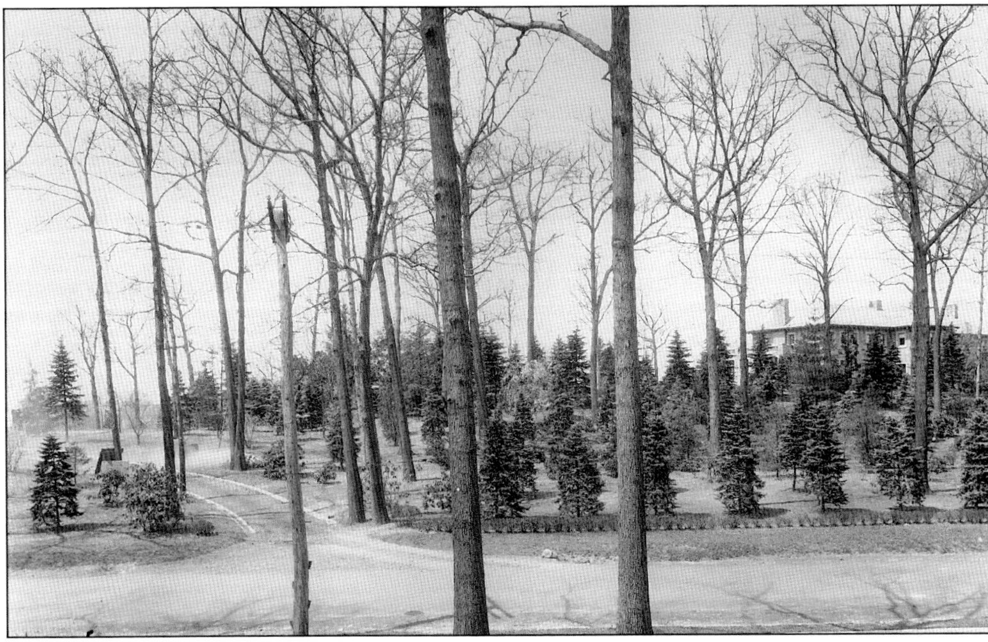

Samuel Rushmore, a gifted inventor, made a fortune perfecting the automobile headlight. Rushmore began construction on his unique Netherwood home *c.* 1915.

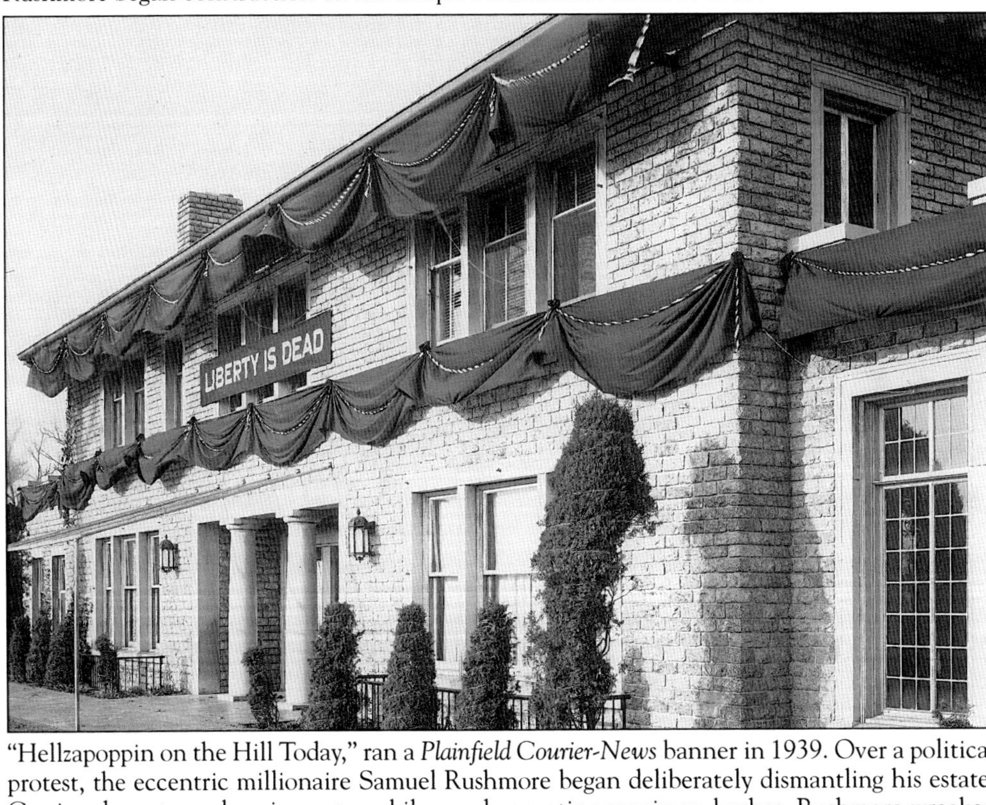

"Hellzapoppin on the Hill Today," ran a *Plainfield Courier-News* banner in 1939. Over a political protest, the eccentric millionaire Samuel Rushmore began deliberately dismantling his estate. Cutting down trees, burning automobiles, and uprooting specimen bushes, Rushmore wreaked considerable damage to his property. Fortunately, the house was ultimately spared.

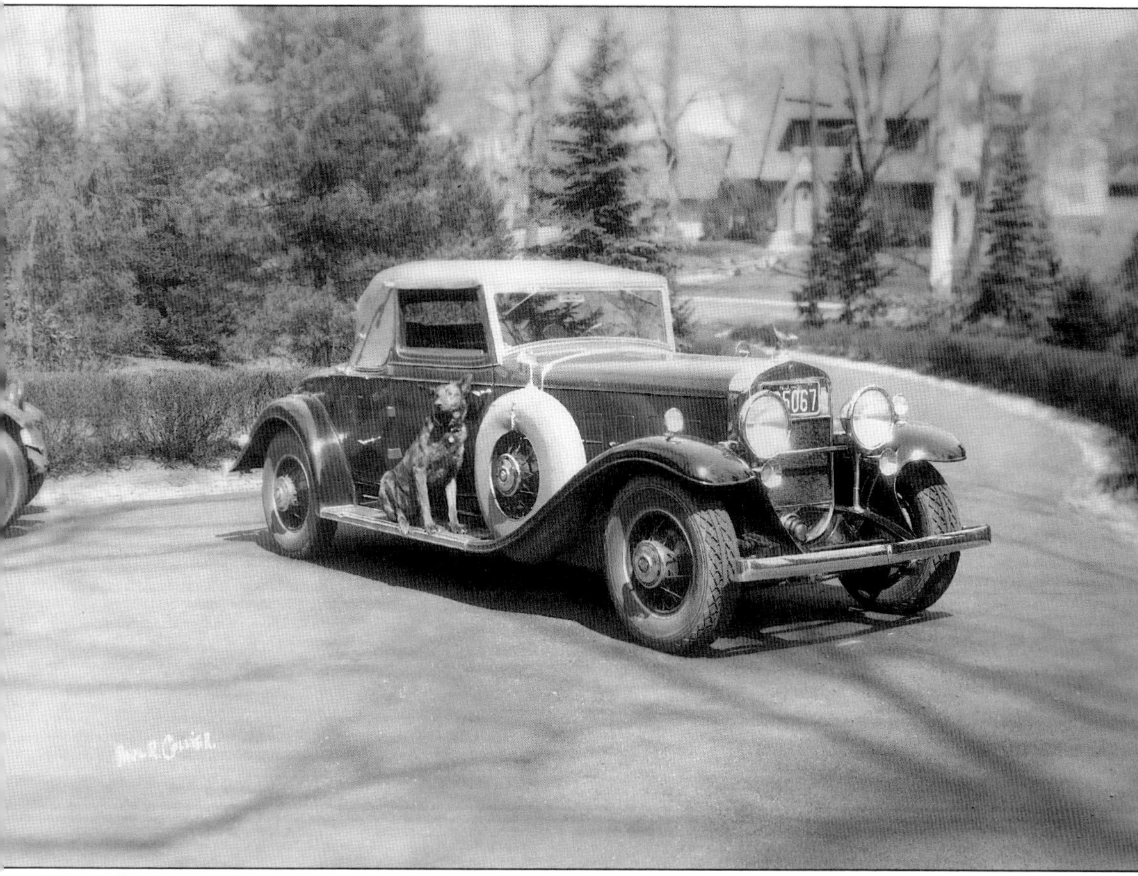

They also serve who only sit and wait. A Rushmore family pet begs chauffeured transportation to a neighborhood with more trees and less political controversy.

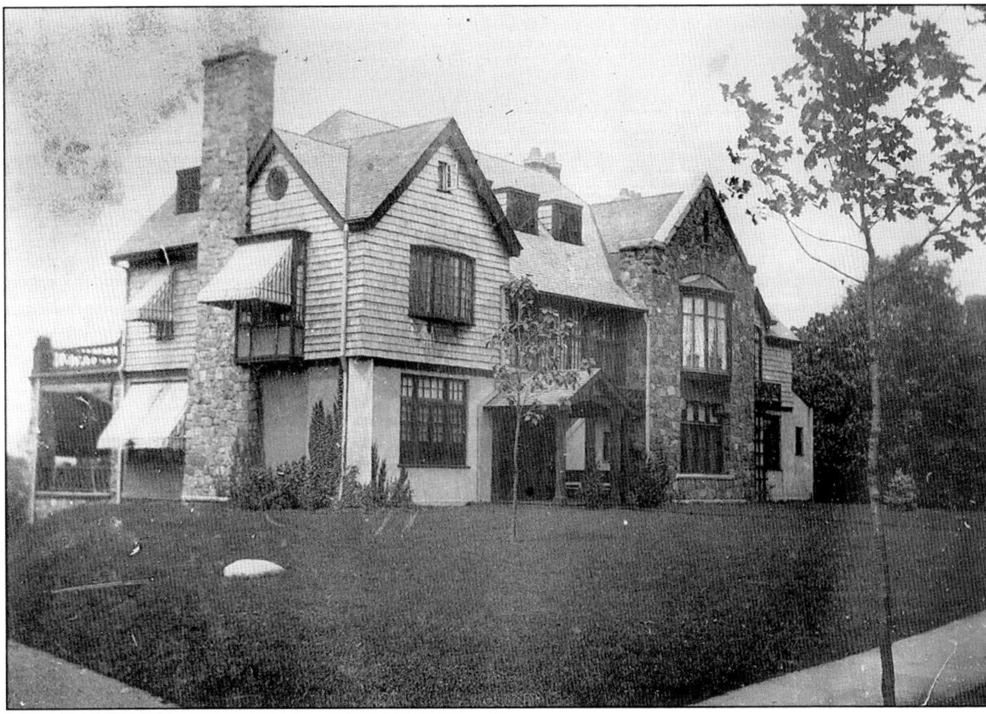

The first decades of the 20th century still saw large and commodious homes being constructed in an array of revival styles. Among them was this avant-garde, 1904 Jacobethan mansion on Belvidere Avenue.

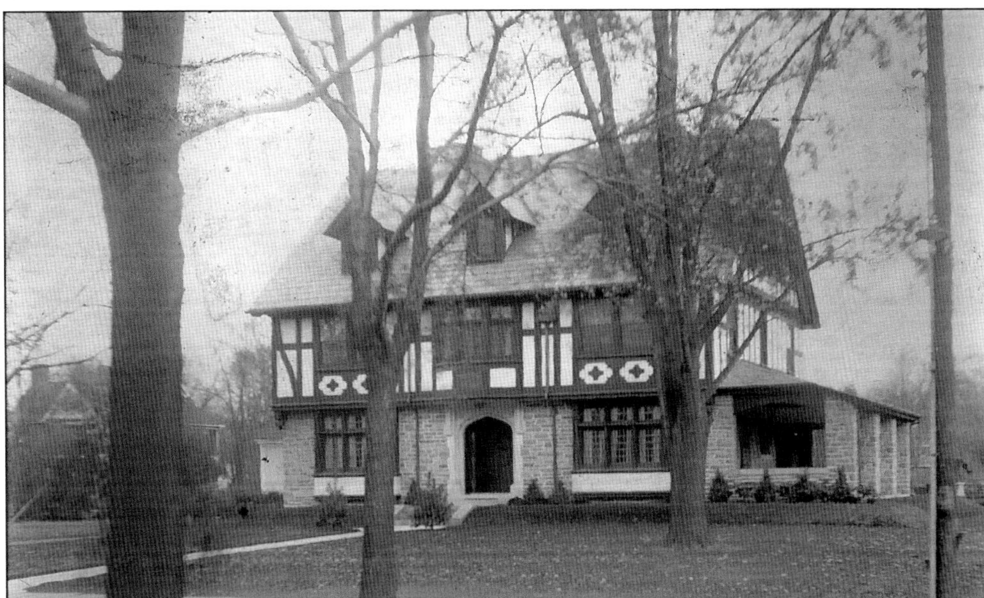

When Clara McKinley Mumford died in 1912, her husband, Thomas Jefferson Mumford, built this Tudor-style home in her memory as a gift to Grace Episcopal Church. The cost was $55,000. A bronze plaque over the front door memorializes his gift. Still a showpiece, the house continues to be used today as the rector's home.

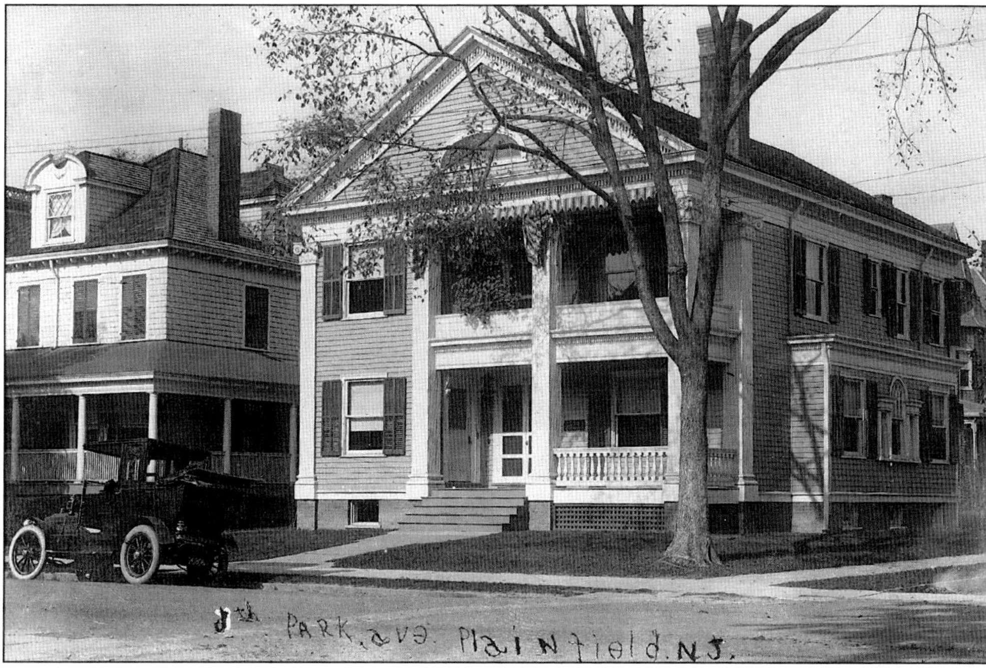

A sign of the changing times is this Park Avenue home, constructed for both professional and residential use. As neighborhoods evolved so did use and residential design. Although many changes have come with the years, Plainfield remains a unique and inviting place.

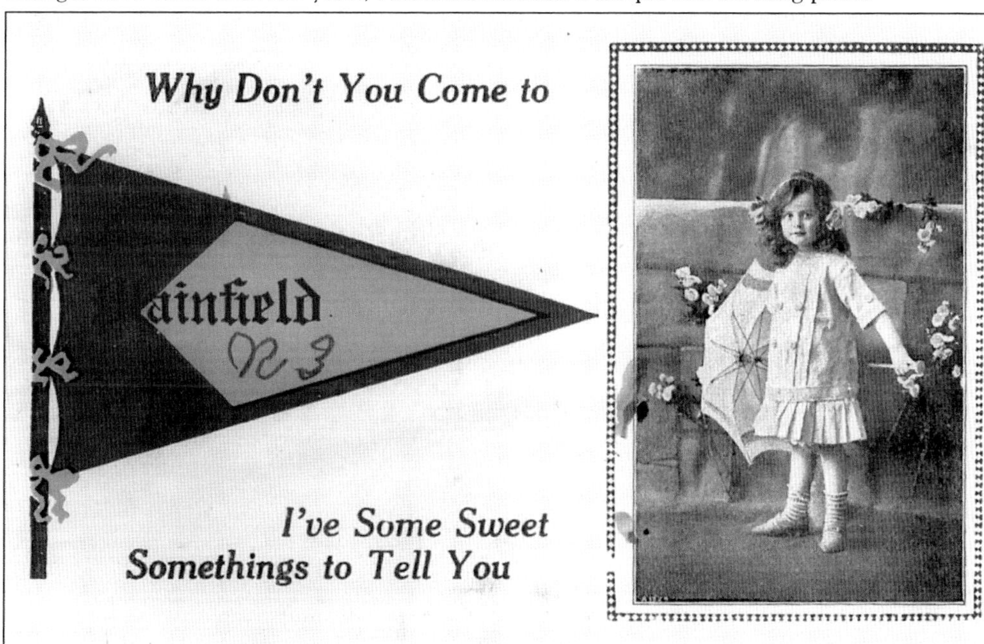

BIBLIOGRAPHY

Bailey, Judith A., and Robert I.Cottom; *After Chancellorsville, Letters from the Heart*; Maryland Historical Society, Baltimore; 1998.

Brooks, Van Wyck; *Scenes and Portraits, Memories of Childhood and Youth*; E.P. Dutton and Company, New York; 1954.

City National Bank; *Plainfield, N.J., the City Beautiful*; Courier-News Publishing Company, Plainfield, N.J.; 1897.

Coates, Alice Canoune; *The Kenyon Gardens Association, 1915–1927*; Courtesy Wardlaw Country Day School; 1958.

Coates, Alice Canoune, and Edward W. Taylor; *Excerpts from Eliza Elvira Kenyon's Journal*; Plainfield, N.J.; 1973

Commemorative Book Committee; Plainfield 300 Years, 1684–1984; Josten's Incorporated; 1987.

Green Brook Bicentennial Celebration Committee; *A History of Green Brook*; Green Brook, N.J.; 1976.

Honeyman, A. Van Doren; *History of Union County, N.J.,1664–1923*; Lewis Historical Publishing Company, New York; 1923.

Hooker, Ralph Moreton, and Rev. A.H. Lewis; *Plainfield, New Jersey*; the Plainfield Daily Press, Plainfield, N.J.; 1895.

Lewis, Arnold; *American Country Houses of the Gilded Ages*; Dover Publications, New York; 1982.

Proceedings of the New Jersey Historical Society; *A Magazine of New Jersey History*; April 1, 1965.

Rawson, Marion Nicholl; *Under the Blue Hills*; Interstate Printing, Plainfield, N.J.; 1974.

Smiley, F.T.; *History of Plainfield and North Plainfield*; the Plainfield Courier-News, Plainfield, N.J.; 1901.

Taylor, Edward W.; *Reflections of Old Plainfield*; Plainfield, N.J.; 1976.